C000181280

# The So

## CONTENTS

**Contents**                                                          3

**The Author**                                                        7

**Acknowledgements, and Dedication**                                  7

**Introduction**
    In The Beginning                              8
    Where's That?                                  9
    A Brief History                                10
    Come the Revolution                            11
    The South Pennines Today                       11
    The People: A Sense of Place                   12
    Transport Links; Getting Around                13
    Refreshments                                   14
    Safety, etc.                                   15
    Walking Equipment                              15
    Notes on GPS Reception                         16

**Map & Walking Information**
    Symbols Rating Guide                           17
    Ordnance Survey Mapping Notes                  17
    Location Map                                   18
    Travel Notes                                   19
    Using GPS in the South Pennines                20

### THE WALKS

1    **Broadbottom to Stalybridge**                 21
    5 walker, 4½ hours, 10.6 miles/17km, ascents 429
    metres, descents 466 metres, 5 refreshments (linear)

2    **Smithy Bridge to Littleborough**             25
    2 walker, 2 hours, 5.3 miles/8½km, ascents & descents
    negligible, 4 refreshments (linear/circular)

3    **Rake Inn Circular**                          28
    3 walker, 2 hours, 4.7 miles/7½km, ascents & descents
    156 metres, 4 refreshments (circular)

4    **White House Circular**                       31
    4 walker, 4¼ hours, 10.6 miles/17km, ascents &
    descents 515 metres, 4 refreshments (circular)

5    Rose Hill to Romiley                                    35
     3 walker, 2 hours, 4.7 miles/7½ kilometres, ascents 137
     metres, descents 146 metres, 3 refreshments (linear)

6    Middlewood Lyme Park Circular                           38
     3 walker, 2 hours 25 mins, 5.6 miles/9km, ascents &
     descents 167 metres, 2 refreshments (circular)

7    Middlewood to Marple via Marple Ridge                   41
     3 walker, 1½ hours, 4.4 miles/7km, ascents 105 metres,
     descents 142 metres, 3 refreshments (linear)

8    Piethorne Valley & Crompton Moor                        44
     4 walker, 2½ hours, 6¼ miles/10km, ascents &
     descents 344 metres, 3 refreshments (circular)

9    Strines Circular                                        48
     3 walker, 2½ hours, 6¼ miles/10km, ascents &
     descents 250 metres, vertigo risk, 3 refreshments
     (circular)

10   Romiley to Hyde                                         51
     2 walker, 1½ hours, 4.4 miles/7km, ascents & descents
     negligible, 2 refreshments (linear)

11   Hyde to Stalybridge via Portland Basin                  53
     2 walker, 1¾ hours, 5 miles/8km, ascents & descents
     negligible, 5 refreshments (linear)

12   Stalybridge to Greenfield                               55
     2 walker, 2 hours, 5.6 miles/9km, ascents 139 metres,
     descents 81 metres, 3 refreshments (linear)

13   Greenfield Circular via Diggle                          58
     3 walker, 2½ hours, 6¼ miles/10km, ascents &
     descents 213 metres, 3 refreshments (circular)

14   Marple to Strines via Roman Lakes                       61
      2 walker, 1 hour, 2.8 miles/4½km, ascents 106 metres,
     descents 90 metres, 2 refreshments (linear)

15   Strines to Marple via Mellor                            63
     3 walker, 2¾ hours, 5.6 miles/9km, ascents 287 metres,
     descents 304 metres, 3 refreshments (linear)

16   Marple to Broadbottom via Etherow                       66
     4 walker, 2½ hours, 6 miles/9.5km, 292 metres ascents,
     261 metres descents, 1 refreshments  (linear)

17   Mills Hill to Newhey via Tandle Hill                    69
     3 walker, 2¾ hours, 6.9 miles/11km, 299 metres
     ascents, 167 metres descents, 3 refreshments (linear)

18    Woodley to Broadbottom via Werneth                    **73**
      3 walker, 2¼ hours, 5.6 miles/9km, 268 metres ascents,
      242 metres descents, 1 refreshments (linear)

19    Marple to Broadbottom via Cown Edge                   **77**
      3 walker, 4 hours, 9.4 miles/15km, 441 metres ascents,
      410 metres descents, 0 refreshments (linear)

20    Broadbottom to Stalybridge via Mottram                **82**
      3 walker, 2½ hours, 5.6 miles/9km, 209 metres ascents,
      244 descents, 5 refreshments (linear)

21    Another View of Stalybridge to Greenfield             **86**
      4 walker, 4 hours, 8¾ miles/14km, 515 metres ascents,
      454 metres descents, 3 refreshments (linear)

22    Greenfield Circular via Pots & Pans                   **90**
      3 walker, 4 hours, 9.4 miles/15km, 505 metres
      ascents & descents, 3 refreshments (circular)

23    Hadfield Circular                                     **94**
      2 walker, 3½ hours, 10 miles/16km, 286 metres
      ascents & descents, 2 refreshments (circular)

24    Mossley to Greenfield via Hartshead Pike              **98**
      4 walker, 3 hours, 6 miles/9½km, 344 metres ascents,
      326 metres descents, 3 refreshments (linear)

25    Greenfield to Newhey via The Tame Valley              **102**
      3 walker, 3½ hours, 8.1 miles/13km, 373 metres
      ascents, 384 metres descents, 3 refreshments (linear)

26    Newhey to Littleborough via Blackstone Edge           **107**
      4/5 walker, 4 hours, 10 miles/16km, 437 metres
      ascents, 456 metres descents, 4 refreshments (linear)

27    Hadfield to Greenfield via Chew Reservoir             **111**
      5 walker, 3¾ hours, 9.4 miles/15km, 488 metres
      ascents, 493 metres descents, 3 refreshments (linear)

28    Greenfield to Shaw                                    **115**
      3 walker, 2¾ hours, 5.6 miles/9km,  ascents &
      descents 276 metres, 2 refreshments (linear)

29    Shaw to Newhey                                        **119**
      3 walker, 3 hours, 7½ miles/12km, 349 metres
      ascents, 360 metres descents, 3 refreshments (linear)

30    Greenfield to Marsden                                 **123**
      3 walker, 3¼ hours, 7.8 miles/12½km, ascents &
      descents 442 metres, 4 refreshments (circular)

31    Marsden to Littleborough                                127
      4 walker, 4 hours, 10.9 miles/17½km, 489 metres
      ascents, 547 metres descents, 4 refreshments (linear,
      with circular option)

      The Wayfarer Walks: an Introduction                     132

32    Wisley to Whaley Bridge                                 132
      4 walker, 2 hours 5.3 miles/8½km, 210 metres
      ascents, 228 metres descents, 4 refreshments (linear)
32A   Bowstones Extension                                     135
      4 walker, 1 hour, 3¾ miles/6km, 173 metres ascents
      & descents, 3 refreshments (linear/circular)

33    Whaley Bridge Circular via Bugsworth Basin              138
      3 walker, 1¼ hours, 3 miles/5km, 143 metres ascents
      & descents, 4 refreshments (circular)

34    Whaley Bridge Circular via The Dipping Stone            140
      3 walker, 1¾ hours, 4.7 miles/7½km, 221 metres
      ascents & descents, 4 refreshments (circular)

35    Bromley Cross - A Taste of the West                     143
      3 walker, 4½ hours, 11.9 miles/19km, 412 metres
      ascents & descents, 4 refreshments (circular)

      An Historical Stroll: Flixton                           148

GPS Waypoints Lists                                           150

      Glossary                                                154

      Appendices
          Useful Telephone Numbers                            155
          Web Links                                           155
          Bibliography                                        156
          Peak & Northern Footpath Society                    156
          Pubs & Inns found on the routes                     157

Place Names Index                                             158

Born in Lancashire, Clarke Rogerson has lived within a few miles of the South Pennines throughout his life. He has travelled extensively throughout the UK and Europe both for work and pleasure. A former Scout Leader and British Canoe Union Coach, he chose to retire early after 34 years in the Communications Industry, to indulge his passion for travel and walking.

With a keen interest in the environment, history and archaeology, he combines traditional map and compass skills with GPS and other digital technologies in his research and exploration at home and abroad.

---

# ACKNOWLEDGEMENTS

This book has been made possible only with the help of many people. My thanks go to Liz for the Magellan, food testing and IT support. Thanks to Barry, Peter and Tommy for 'the idea' and beer tasting beyond the call of duty. Thanks also to the many friends who lent books and suggested walks. Thanks must also go to the walkers I met on route for the invaluable snippets; 'Uncle Bob' (Stansfield) for encouraging me to write up the walks and finally to David & Ros Brawn for having faith in 'the idea'; their support and advice have been invaluable.

---

# DEDICATION

I dedicate this book to my grandchildren Tegan and Morgan.

---

### THE COUNTRYSIDE CODE

- Be Safe – plan ahead and follow signs
- Protect plants and animals, and take your litter home
- Keep dogs under close control
- Leave gates and property as you find them
- Consider other people

## IN THE BEGINNING

The concept for this series of walks was conceived, as these things often are, over a few pints with a group of like-minded friends. Fuelled with bonhomie and wanting to get out into the hills on a regular basis, unencumbered by the car, or restricted to a quick half before driving home, the idea, "let's see how many walks we can do using that cheap rail ticket" was born.

I don't remember volunteering, but the task of planning the routes was left to me. Like all walking groups, this bunch can be a bit choosy and just because we could get there on a cheap rail ticket didn't mean any old walk would do. Minor requirements such as variety, plenty to see and discuss, and a pub, preferably at the end of the walk, were never stated; but high quality routes were definitely expected.

Open moors ...

When David & Ros first read the outline for the book they were impressed that all the walks could be accessed by rail, and the cheap ticket didn't go unnoticed either. My description of the area, varied landscape, open moors, wooded *cloughs*, canal side strolls had them intrigued.

I'd explained that the walks would cover four counties, taking in ancient tracks, packhorse routes, six rivers and four canals. There was a list of thing of interest along the way, something for everyone whether art, archaeology, bird watching, botany, industrial and landscape history.

... gentle hills ...

I included the record breakers, deepest, highest, longest and shortest. The mention of real ale served in more than a few pubs, locally produced food cooked on the premises had them asking where this South Pennine walking utopia was.

... canal art ...

Geographically, the South Pennines are made up of the central part of the main Pennine Anticline, the smaller Clitheroe and Lothersdale Anticlines and the Rossendale Dome; which is a bit confusing as they all sit near the centre rather than the south of the Pennine Chain. The term was first used to describe the area in the Hobhouse Committee Report, 1947, in which the area was considered for National Park designation. The area was never clearly defined and the OS Map Sheet OL21 doesn't help much either.

A search of the internet using Google returns more than 74,000 references to the South Pennines; from SCOSPA the Standing Committee of South Pennine Authorities to SPITS the South Pennine Integrated Transport Strategy each of which has a different idea as to the location and scope of the area. The South Pennine Moors Special Protection Area (SPA) defines the area as, "the major blocks of the South Pennines from Ilkley in the north to Leek and Matlock in the south", an area covered by 13 Unitary Authorities.

Looking elsewhere for a definition, the late Gladys Sellers described the area as "a vast amount of varied and interesting walking for the modest walker". Stephen Gough the "Naked Rambler"had not hit the headlines when Gladys wrote the words "modest walker"; so it's fair to assume the reference has more to do with the fact that there are no great peaks to be conquered in the South Pennines.

Whichever definition we use, the South Pennines covers a huge land mass and it has to be said that the majority of it is not accessible by train; especially not with the cheap rail ticket my friends wanted to use. Set to the east of Manchester our walking area extends just 20km east to west, 40km north to south, which may sound an impossibly small area in which to set so many walks each with plenty to offer.

The hills that surround Greater Manchester form the western watershed, with eight rivers flowing into the River Mersey. Water power together with coal, found in the same hills, plus two of the shortest 'Cross Pennine' trade routes contributed to industrial growth.

**A canal-side stroll**

Even before the industrial revolution packhorse trails crossed these hills, carrying raw materials and finished goods from east to west. During the 18th century legislation allowed Turnpike Trusts to be formed to improve the most important routes; **Saddleworth** became congested with more turnpike roads than any other valley in England. As trade grew two canals, later replaced by railways, were forged through the hills improving trade links considerably.

Our legacy from this era is a rich tapestry of paths and tracks; **Rochdale** boasts 1,485 paths which together with its 223 bridleways cover over 500kms. **Oldham**, which encompasses **Saddleworth**, has over 400kms of paths and tracks. With new legislation giving us the freedom to roam away from these paths, there is plenty to explore in this compact area.

If the facts and figures haven't surprised you already, the peace and quiet will; apart from a few 'honey pots' the area does not draw crowds of tourists. It's an area often overlooked by walkers as they head off for the classic walking areas in the Lakes or the Peak District. And as those who know the area will tell you, you're more likely to meet a sheep or a camelid than another person as you roam the South Pennine moors and valleys in relative solitude.

**South Pennine Alpacas**

A BRIEF HISTORY

With limited space and even more limited knowledge of the geological formation of the area, it must suffice to say that the formation of the Millstone Grit and Coal Measures, which characterise the South Pennines, started 350 million years ago in a warm shallow sea. Seventy million years later the sea bed was raised to a height of 4000 metres, forming the land. Several million years of weathering and the odd ice age along the way have reduced these alpine monsters to the hills we know today; **Blackstone Edge** the highest point on our walks is a mere 472 metres above sea level.

**Ancient tree stump remains**

Evidence, in the form of arrow heads and stone tools, proves that humans inhabited the South Pennines from 7500BC; the landscape they would have seen was mainly covered by forest; it's still possible to find the twisted remains of old tree stumps on the peat moors.

The Roman occupation left scant evidence with forts at **Castlefields**, **Melandra** and **Castleshaw** and the odd stretch of road; as the historians can't agree, you'll have to make your own mind up about the 'Roman Road' into **Littleborough**. However the track we follow below **Buckton Castle** was certainly used to link **Melandra** and **Castleshaw** and continued in military use into Norman times.

The names of towns, villages and hamlets are largely the legacy of the Anglo-Saxon colonisation from the 5th century and the Danes who followed; few names have French origins from the Norman Conquest. Throughout time man has been shaping the landscape; the clearance of trees for fuel and building making land available for settlement and the farming needed to support a growing population. A harsh terrain, poor soils and inclement climate make the Pennines more suited to grazing than crops. Animal husbandry alone was not sufficient to support a family and textile production brought in the extra cash. Small scale at first in what is known as the 'Domestic System', textile production relied upon the women and children cleaning, carding and spinning the wool while the men worked the looms. Needing five or six women to spin enough wool for one man to produce eight yards of cloth a day the system had its limitations.

## COME THE REVOLUTION

It started with the invention of the flying shuttle, by John Kay of Bury, in 1733 which speeded up the weaving process, exacerbating the problem of spinning. Several inventions followed; James Hargreaves' Spinning Jenny, Richard Arkwright's Water Frame and finally Samuel Compton's Mule in 1779. The original Mule had 48 spindles and by 1810 it had been improved to 400 spindles. Cotton, silk and calico had been added to the list of textiles that were produced in the area; these new inventions paved the way for the move from farming and domestic spinning and weaving to a more industrialised way of life. It was boom time in the South Pennines; nearly a hundred mills were built along the **River Tame** and its tributaries and many more on the other rivers across the region. Coal had been mined, if only on a small scale, since the 13th century; the invention of steam power led to the next round of mill building; the industrial revolution gathered pace. Packhorse routes and turnpike roads could no longer cope with the need to move raw materials and finished goods, so canals and then railways were built. From small scale mining near the surface, deep level pits were needed to provide the fuel to power the revolution; 72 pits in the **Poynton** area alone.

During the boom a few people were getting rich but not so the worker. From the start of the 19th century workers wages were being cut and hours increased and inflation in the form of increased wheat prices which had risen by nearly 50%, all of which meant that children as young as six were sent to the mills to supplement family income. Luddite campaigns were to follow; demonstrations were planned in such public houses as **The Rose of Lancaster**, and though peaceful in intent, they ended in the Peterloo Massacre. Boom and bust became a pattern of life; the American Civil War in the 1860s brought a cotton famine, by the middle of the 20th century man made fibres and cheap imports sounded the death knell for King Cotton.

## THE SOUTH PENNINES TODAY

The visitor with a perception of dark satanic mills, pit winding gear, chimneys belching smoke that cast a shadow over the landscape is in for a surprise. Industry has moved on; city centre offices have replaced mills as the economic powerhouse. With a few exceptions the mills have been converted to modern day living accommodation, or craft and heritage centres. The long abandoned canals, once filled with rubbish, have been reopened to provide a major recreational resource. Old railway lines, closed as result of the Beeching report of 1963, provide traffic-free routes for walkers and other recreational users.

Cows and sheep still graze the hills, horses are once again commonplace, while llamas and alpacas have been added to the countryside economy. The South Pennine Special Protection Area was created to protect the semi-natural moorland habitats which are important for upland breeding birds, in particular the Merlin Falco columbarius, Golden Plover Pluvialis apricaria and during the breeding season, Dunlin Calidris alpina schinzii.

**Compstall Nature Reserve**, the **Huddersfield Narrow** and the **Rochdale Canal** are all designated Sites of Special Scientific Interest. Nine species of pondweed, including extensive colonies of the nationally scarce floating water-plantain Luronium natans, can to be found on the **Rochdale Canal**. **Jackson's Brickworks** is a Grade A Site of Biological Interest listing the Great crested newt Triurus cristatu several Dragonflies, birds and wild flowers. **Longdendale** has the sole English population of Mountain Hares.

The South Pennine dialect includes plant names you may not be familiar with: When people go Wimberry picking they are looking for Vaccinium myrtilli which you may know as Bilberry; common Sorrel Rubex acetosa is known as Greensauce; Bird's-foot trefoil Lotus corniculatus is Lady's finger or Bacon and Eggs; poisonous to cattle and horses Ragwort Senecio jaobea is know as Cattle Dock; whilst not as exotic sounding as "Belle de jour" Bindweed Calystegia sepium has the descriptive name Robin Run I'th Hedge.

I'll leave comprehensive lists of flora and fauna to specialist books; but look out for Adder's- tongue fern Ophioglossum vulgatum on the walk from **Mills Hill**. The bright red fruit of the lichen Cladonia macilenta, though not easy to spot, can be found on the walks near **Compton Moor**. You'll find Harebell Campanula rotundifolia nodding in the breeze near the **Dipping Stone**.

Cotton-Grass

Drifts of Hare's-Tail Cotton-Grass Eriophorum vaginatum, are a sure sign of summer and more often than not boggy ground on the moors. Red Campion Silene dioica is to be found along the **Delph Donkey**. The English population of Twite Carduelis flavirostris is almost entirely confined to the South Pennines. Curlew, Snipe, Lapwing, Reed Bunting, Yellow wagtail and Meadow pipit are just some of the notable species of birds to be found.

## THE PEOPLE; A SENSE OF PLACE

When travelling in foreign lands, it's as well to be aware of the cultural differences and politics of the region; failure to observe these niceties can provoke strong reactions from the locals. Not that the locals are unfriendly, quite the opposite is true; you will generally find them helpful when asking for directions. As an expedient in describing the walking area, I've mentioned Greater Manchester; but what is important to remember is that none of the walks are in Manchester and that as a County Council, Greater Manchester no longer exists.

If I explain that as far back as the early 12th century **Saddleworth** was an administrative authority within The West Riding of Yorkshire; then in 1974 the government of the day moved administration, of the area, to the short lived Greater Manchester County Council. With the abolition of GMCC in 1985 administration again moved, this time to the Metropolitan Borough of Oldham. Now traditionally, if not administratively, Oldham sits in Lancashire and witty comments about Saddleworth having moved from the White to the Red Rose County do not go down well. This depth of feeling is best expressed by the Saddleworth White Rose Society; when a local dignitary described Saddleworth as "the Jewel in Oldham's Crown", their response was "Saddleworth is not Oldham's anything, jewel or otherwise". So as far as possible I'll use the old county names, town, village and hamlet names; I'll apologise now for any cases of mistaken identity and hope to be let back into Cheshire, Derbyshire and Yorkshire, for they all have some fine walking.

## TRANSPORT LINKS, GETTING AROUND

You won't get lost trying to find the start of any of the walks if you are travelling by train; I've included details for parking for those going by car; the walks from **Middlewood** would need a long walk in, so travel by train is recommended. Since deregulation of the bus services the number of service providers makes advice impractical; the contact number and web site detailed in the appendices will provide the necessary information for anyone wishing to travel by bus.

Most of the walks can be accessed using the modestly priced Rail Ranger Ticket, £2.70 for adults £1.35 for under 16's at the time of writing. The ticket gives unlimited travel after 9.30am on weekdays and all day at weekends and Bank Holidays; from over 100 stations and includes free travel on the Metrolink in Manchester City Centre. With the exception of the walk into and out of **Marsden**, the other walks use the Wayfarer ticket; more information is provided as an introduction to the walks.

All of the walk descriptions assume travel from one of the Manchester Main line stations, travellers from stations outside Manchester need to take this into account when leaving the station. Timings, rounded to the nearest minute, record moving time only; extra time should be allowed for taking in the view, studying the detail, sitting watching the clouds drift by, eating a snack or simply catching your breath on the more demanding routes. Try an easy walk, then adjust my timings accordingly to match your own pace..

Walk descriptions are kept brief, but provide the detail to ensure you stay on the right path; however it has to be remembered that this is a living, working landscape things on the ground change. Wear and tear, erosion and the ravages of time mean that paths, stiles, gates and fences need repair or replacement.

Whilst researching this book I've encountered Local Authority Rangers and walking group members clearing and upgrading routes; all the broken signs etc. mentioned in the walks have been reported and may well be repaired by the time you pass that way. If you encounter a problem you can report it to the relevant Local Authority Rights of Way Officer; my preference is to report faults to the Peak and Northern Footpath Society who will check and process your complaint with the relevant authority. When reporting a problem, supply as much information as possible; photographs and a grid reference, ideally from a GPS unit, are a real bonus to the people who will deal with the report.

Though not used exclusively, the adjectives gentle, steady and steep describe the gradient of the path you should be following. Route marches on tarmac are not my idea of fun and have been avoided unless there's no possible alternative. Path surfaces vary and I've tried to indicate the surface of the track or path to follow. During the research period the weather was unusually dry; paths noted as muddy are sure to be joined by others in wet weather. The word *clough*, when not part of a place name, is a northern term describing a cleft in a hill ranging from a steep sided ravine to a gently sloping gully; other local terms are included in the glossary.

It is usual, in guide books, to group walks by the area visited or the severity of the walk. However in this book, it's not the case; rather I've chosen to present them chronologically with the aim of showing each area in different seasons. From the overview map you will see that it's possible to set off from **Middlewood Station** and walk all the way to **Littleborough**, choosing either a low level or a more strenuous high level route; if you want such a challenge, I leave you to choose the route. Perhaps more importantly it's possible, having arrived at a station to find the weather conditions unsuitable for a high level walk, to choose another low level walk from the same place, thus avoiding total disappointment.

## REFRESHMENT

The author, researching at the Cross Keys, Uppermill

Whilst not compulsory, it's traditional for walkers to round off a route with a pint and maybe some food. The connoisseur of real ale will find that the area covered by the walks is well served by four independently owned regional breweries and more than a dozen small craft brewers. You'll have the opportunity to sample Hydes', J. W. Lees & Robinson's in their estate owned pubs on route; Holt's is a regular guest at **The Church, Uppermill**, home of the Saddleworth Brewery. In **Marsden**, **The River Head Brewery Tap** is on **Peel Street**. **The Buffet Bar**, at **Stalybridge Station**, has a continuously changing range of ales and it's worth looking out for beers from the craft brewers Marble, Phoenix and Pictish.

One of the first thing visitors to the area will notice is that it is normal to serve a pint with a thick creamy head, do ask for a top up if the head is too large; the second thing to be noticed is the price, which is often considerably cheaper than in other parts of the country.

Many pubs serve food, and though standards vary considerably, the trend towards serving locally sourced produce prepared on the premises is good news for the hungry walker, and I also mention some non-licensed premises serving refreshments. Refreshment rating and comments are based on the quality and service experienced on the day I visited; however management, ownership and staff can change and the opinions expressed or the experience you have may not match my own.

Note: not all pubs were visited (Doctor's orders) which may be reflected in the refreshment rating where no specific mention is made in the description.

Changeable weather on the hills and moors and curious cows are the two main hazards you are likely to come across on these walks.

Before setting of on the hills check the weather, and let someone know where you are going and what time you expect to return. If your plans change let the same person know; the mountain rescue teams will not be pleased to hear that you have been enjoying an extra pint or two whilst they have been searching for you. I've included decision points on all high level walks if the weather looks

**Changeable weather**

**Curious cows**

doubtful it's better to leave the walk for another day.

Calves in particular can be quite curious; a charging herd is no time to find out how fast you can sprint and leap over a stile. Where possible I will divert through neighbouring fields taking care not to damage property or crops.

## WALKING KIT - BE PREPARED

When it comes to kit the Scout Motto, 'Be Prepared' is as relevant today as it was in 1908 when it was first published in 'Scouting for Boys'. I can be tempted as much as the next man when it comes to kit; but northern thrift rules my wallet when it comes to handing over plastic or hard-earned cash. Sales, factory outlets and Ebay are all a good sources for last seasons 'must have kit' at knock-down prices.

### FOOTWEAR
Boots are an exception; fit, comfort and ankle support come first. I prefer leather upper with a good tread; my Meindl 'Burmas', the ones without Gore-tex, have served me well over many thousands of kilometres. Wicking inner and thick outer socks help keep my feet happy.

### WATERPROOF CLOTHING
Waterproofs are the next priority. A good jacket will keep the wind and the rain out; both essential qualities on the moors. I have a lightweight summer and a Gore-tex winter jacket. Overtrousers for wet weather and gaiters for bog

trotting make up my outerwear. Lightweight Rohan Bags protect my legs from nettles and are near indestructible; Winter Bags keep the wind chill factor down and dry quickly. I find a wicking base layer, under whatever shirt I'm wearing, stops that sticky feeling especially on the steady climbs.

**HATS**

I'm a sucker for hats; wide brimmed Tilley's keep the sun from my eyes and the rain off my glasses. On high level winter walks a fleece-lined hat with a waterproof outer that covers my ears may not be pretty, but it stops the huge heat loss from the head.

**RUCKSACK**

Keeping your kit dry is as important as keeping yourself dry; I use a Deuter 32 litre rucksack which has an air-flow frame and built-in waterproof cover which helps keep us both dry.

**OTHER EQUIPMENT**

Apart from extra clothing and gloves I carry compass, whistle, small torch, maps, first aid kit, survival bag, a piece of closed cell foam to keep the cold and damp from my nether regions during lunch breaks, mobile phone (turned off) sunglasses, sun block, camera, and spare batteries for the GPS which is attached high on the shoulder straps for best reception.

A Sigg sandwich box, free with a magazine subscription, helps keep the sandwiches, bananas and cereal bars from being squashed; any Tupperware type container or an old ice cream tub will do a similar job. In winter an unbreakable flask for a warm drink, in summer, plenty of water. Depending on the route I'm walking, I add walking sticks which have saved many a slip and are useful for dealing with overgrown paths as are secateurs; binoculars for bird watching and spotting the next stile.

For the shorter canal side strolls, if in fine weather, I take the bare essentials: food, drink and a 'pack in a pocket' waterproof top carried in a 15 litre day sac. In prolonged dry spells shorts and sandals replace 'bags' and boots.

OS Maps are probably the best maps you will ever use for walking in the UK; however minor errors do occur and these are noted in the walk descriptions. You need OS Explorer Map sheets OL1, OL21 & 277 (Walks 1 to 34 & Walk 36). Sheet 287 is needed for Walk 35, in the West Pennines.

**NOTES ON GPS RECEPTION IN THE SOUTH PENNINES**

Though generally good satellite acquisition can be slow near some stations due to buildings, footbridges etc. At **Broadbottom** in particular, it's best to move out into the car park to acquire a good signal. All tracks were recorded on a Magellan Map 330 receiver. The few areas of poor reception listed below are unlikely to cause navigational problems.

**10** Romiley to Hyde GPS Reception good except through tunnel; includes track to **Woodley Station**

**12** Stalybridge to Greenfield GPS Reception good except through tunnel; includes track to **Mossley Station.**

**17** Mills Hill to Newhey via Tandle Hill GPS Reception good; includes extension to trig point.

**20** Broadbottom to Stalybridge via Mottram GPS Reception good; includes extension to L S Lowry's house.

**21** Another View of Stalybridge to Greenfield GPS Reception generally good with the exception of track to **Sidebottom Fold**; follow the instructions and stay on the track.

**32A** Bowstones Extension GPS Reception good; track only shows circular extension and should be loaded in conjunction with the track for Walk 32.

3 our rating for effort/exertion:-
**1** very easy **2** easy **3** average
**4** energetic **5** strenuous

2½ H — approximate **time** to complete a walk (compare your times against ours early in a walk) - does not include stopping time

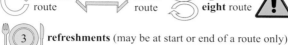

5 miles/8km — approximate walking **distance** in miles/kilometres

250m approximate **ascents/descents** in 850m metres (N=negligible)

**circular** route      **linear** route      **figure of eight** route      risk of **vertigo**

3 — **refreshments** (may be at start or end of a route only)

- Walk descriptions include:
- timing in minutes, shown as (40M)
- compass directions, shown as (NW)
- heights in metres, shown as (1355m)
- GPS waypoints, shown as (Wp.3)

**Notes on the text**
Place names are shown in **bold text**, except where we refer to a written sign, when they are enclosed in single quotation marks. Local or unusual words are shown in *italics*, and are explained in the accompanying text.

All the map sections which accompany the detailed walk descriptions in Walk! The South Pennines are reproduced under Ordnance Survey licence from the digital versions of the latest Explorer 1:25,000 scale maps. Each map section is then re-scaled to the 40,000 scale used in DWG's Walk!/Walks series of guide books. Walking Route and GPS Waypoints are then drawn onto the map section to produce the map illustrating the detailed walk description.

Walk! The South Pennines map sections are sufficient for following alongside the detailed walk descriptions, but for planning your adventures in this region, and if you want to divert from the walking routes, we strongly recommend that you purchase the latest OS Explorer maps.

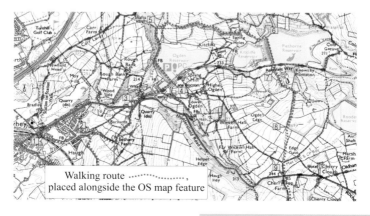

Walking route ·············,
placed alongside the OS map feature

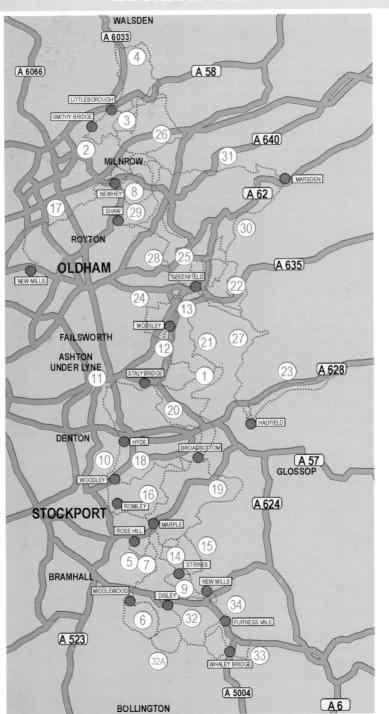

The map opposite shows the major road routes, railway stations and location of the walks described in the book. The following notes are aimed at assisting the visitor travelling by public transport. The Greater Manchester Public Transport Authority provides an excellent integrated public transport system with direct rail links to most parts of

Piccadilly Station

Metrolink Tram 4

the country. There's an International Airport linked by rail to the city and Metrolink, the UK's first modern tram system, connecting **Altrincham**, **Eccles** and **Bury** to the city centre.

The majority of rail links from outside the **Greater Manchester** area terminate at **Piccadilly Station**, from where more than half the walks can be accessed and the average journey time to the outlying stations is 20 minutes. The remaining walks are accessed from **Manchester Victoria Station**; again, expect an average journey of around 20 minutes.

Metroshuttle Bus

Rail Ranger and Wayfarer tickets offer exceptional value and include free travel within the city centre on the Metrolink, as do many tickets involving a cross city connection, but check before travelling. A free Metroshuttle bus service also links the city centre stations; experience has shown the tram to be faster, especially between **Piccadilly** and **Victoria**.

For travellers whose rail journey terminates at **Manchester Oxford Road Station**, I offer the following tips based on current time tables. If you need to get to **Piccadilly**, most through trains stop there, check the destination boards; don't be put off by the final destination, even a train to **Scarborough** will take you from **Oxford Road** to **Piccadilly** faster than you can walk. For transfer to **Victoria**, I recommend ending your journey at **Deansgate Station**, taking the footbridge to **G-MEX Metrolink Station** and then the tram to **Victoria**.

For a pint in the city centre, **The Grey Horse Inn** (Hydes Ales) on **Portland Street** is a short walk from either **Piccadilly Gardens Metrolink Station** or **Oxford Road Rail Station**. I've often called in, once with 20 walkers in full gear; the landlady happily served us several rounds of excellent ale.

# USING GPS IN THE SOUTH PENNINES

The GPS Waypoint lists provided in this book are as recorded by Clarke Rogerson while researching the detailed walk descriptions. Waypoint symbols are numbered so that they can be directly identified with the walk description and waypoint list. All GPS Waypoints are subject to the accuracy of GPS units in the particular location of each waypoint.

In the landscapes of the South Pennines, GPS reception is surprisingly good for the majority of Clarke's walking routes. (See Clarke's notes on page 17.)

### Satellite Reception
Accurate location fixes for your GPS unit depend upon you receiving signals from four or more satellites. Providing you have good batteries, and that you wait until your GPS has full 'satellite acquisition' before starting out, your GPS will perform well in the South Pennines. Where Clarke has encountered poor satellite reception, it is mentioned in the walk description.

### Manually Inputting Waypoints
GPS Waypoints are quoted for the OSGB (Ordnance Survey Great Britain) datum and BNG (British National Grid) coordinates, making them identical with the OS grid coordinates of the position they refer to. To manually input the Waypoints into your GPS we suggest that you:

- switch on your GPS and select 'simulator/standby' mode.
- check that your GPS is set to the OSGB datum and BNG 'location/position format'.
- input the GPS Waypoints into a 'route' with the same number as the walking route; then when you call up the 'route' in the South Pennines there will be no confusion as to which walking route it refers
- repeat the inputting of waypoints into routes until you have covered all the routes you plan to walk, or until you have used up the memory capacity of your GPS
- turn off your GPS. When you turn your GPS back on it should return to its normal navigation mode.

Note that GPS Waypoints complement the routes in Walk! The South Pennines, and are not intended as an alternative to the detailed walking route descriptions.

### Personal Navigator Files (PNFs) CD version 3.01
Edited versions of Clarke Rogerson's original GPS research tracks and waypoints are available as downloadable files on our PNFs CD, which also includes all the edited GPS tracks and waypoints for all the Walk!/Walks guide books published by DWG along with GPS Utility Special Edition software. See DWG websites for more information
www.walking.demon.co.uk & www.dwgwalking.co.uk

### GPS The Easy Way (£4.99)
If you are confused by talk of GPS, but are interested in how this modern navigational aid could enhance your walking enjoyment, then simply seek out a copy of GPS The Easy Way, the UK's best selling GPS manual.

A twenty minute train journey from **Manchester** brings us to the delightful village of **Broadbottom** where our walk starts. The first part of our steady uphill journey takes us along the **Etherow Valley** with excellent views of the **Peak District**. From the valley we climb to **Hollingsworthall Moor** trig point, which provides stunning views over **Manchester** and the **Pennine Horseshoe**. Crossing the moor, we drop down to the **Swineshaw** reservoirs then head into the **Tame Valley** before joining the **Huddersfield Narrow Canal**. Our walk ends at **Stalybridge**, noted in the Guinness Book of Records for pubs with both the longest and shortest names. Finally, we travel back in time to visit the **Station Buffet Bar** purveyors of cask ales and live music.

**Access by train:** from **Manchester Piccadilly** to **Broadbottom** station. Return by train, from **Stalybridge**.

**Access by car:** Leave the car at **Broadbottom** and return on the N°239 bus from **Stalybridge** station.

Ignoring the steps, we walk uphill through the station car park (Wp.1 0M) heading (E) towards the 'Etherow Centre & Riding Arena'. On reaching **Market Street** we cross the road, continuing downhill towards the railway viaduct (Wp.2 4M) where we turn left into **Gorsey Brow** and cross the road, heading after a further 45 metres onto **Hague Road** to begin leaving the village behind.

As we stroll along this wooded lane, splendid views of the Peak District open up, and after passing a small collection of buildings including **The Hague** (11M), we ignore a stile on the left and continue (NE) until we come to farm buildings (Wp.3 19M). To the right of the barn, almost hidden at the side of the metal gate, a small gap waymarked 'Tameside Trail' leads us downhill. Then, just before reaching a cottage, we come to a stile on our left, adorned with several waymarks. Crossing the stile, we climb a few steps to follow the grassy path at the rear of the barn. After descending steps at the end of the path we turn right (NE 24M) on the wide track to reach **Pear Tree Farm**.

Following the 'Woolley Bridge' sign through elaborate wrought iron gates, we pass farm buildings on our right. Ahead of us, between a stone wall and wooden fence, the grassy path leads us on our north-easterly trek. Dropping down to a stile (Wp.4 29M) we swing left (N) to follow a faint path across open fields. A waymarked post indicating 'Etherow Goyt Valley' in the middle of the field points us towards a finger post and stile. After crossing the stile we leave the **Etherow, Goyt Valley Way**, and turning left (NW), we head up the wide grassy lane towards a double width metal gate. Passing through the gate (Wp.5 36M) we turn right (NE) and uphill on a stony track to a dairy farm. Our route takes us through the farm yard and several gates then downhill on the tarmac road. Passing **Willow Bank Farm** and several other

buildings, we come to the busy A57. Crossing with care, we then turn right past a stone terrace and the 'Cartwheel Motor Company', to reach the **Coach Road** (Wp.6 47M). We turn left (NNW) and walk uphill past **Hollin Hey Terrace**. Quickly leaving the traffic noise behind, we head once more into countryside, passing more cottages as the track reverts to stone, leading us to **Nettle Hall Farm**.

As the track swings left into the farm, our path is directly ahead (NNW) between hawthorn bushes on the wide stony track of the old coach road - you can only hope the track was in better repair when the last coach travelled this way! As we approach the top of the rise, **St Michael's Church** of **Mottram in Longdendale** comes into view (W), its tower dating from 1486. The track levels at stone buildings; we follow the wall until the track opens out at **Ivy Dean Cottage** (Wp.7 61M).

**Longdendale**

Almost opposite the gate to Ivy Dean, we follow the track to our right (N) with a stone wall on the left, and head for **Clatterways Cottage** on **Rabbit Lane**. Strolling uphill, we pass several renovated cottages and views of the Pennines open up once more. Further along we come to a junction (**Dewsnap Lane**) and follow the road down to our right which brings us to **Lumb Farm** (Wp.8 72M) and then past **Hard Times Farm** before coming to **Higher Landslow Green Farm** (Wp.9 79M). Ignoring the footpath sign to our right, we continue on to **Hobson Moor Road** where we turn right heading downhill.

**The carved gates at 84 minutes**

Passing a wooden gate 'Private Road' we come to a building on our right with beautifully carved gates(84M). We come to **Ash Tree Farm** and the gate to **Hollingworth Hall Farm** and a clear sign provided by the Peak & Northern Footpath Society (Wp.10 87M) points our way left (NW) to 'Stalybridge via Shaw Moor'. Climbing a couple of stone steps onto a narrow uphill path, we leave the well-made tracks to head onto the moors. At the top of this climb we turn left (WSW) towards a footpath sign and a stile.

We cross it, then take a diagonal route across the field towards farm buildings (WNW). Leaving the field through a metal gate, we cross the gravel area in front of the buildings, another gate bringing us onto a road with six stone steps ahead of us (Wp.11 100M) The steps brings us up onto a grassy bank with a stile ahead; take time here to look back at the view before continuing uphill across **Hobson & Shaw Moors**. Crossing the stile, we follow a vague track towards a post, more posts marking our sometimes damp path to a wooden footbridge. Over the bridge, we follow the fence line to a stile with gate and finger-post. from where we follow a clear stone path straight ahead. A small dip at **Gallows Clough** brings us to the final climb to **Holligworthall Moor**. Rising up to a stone cairn (Wp.12 113M), we take the broad track to our right (NNE) heading uphill past pylons.

N.B. In the event of poor weather take the track left, dropping away from the moors towards civilisation.

Beyond the pylons we come to a trig point (Wp.13 116M 399 metres), its spectacular panorama truly the high point of our journey. From here you'll see why I refer to the area as the **Pennine Horseshoe**. Looking west below us, set in a bowl, is the sprawling mass of the **Greater Manchester** metropolis; individual buildings and town centres are identifiable. Surrounding the urban sprawl we have the **Pennine Spur**, and scanning from the north to the west we can see **Windy Hill** transmitter, **Hartshead Pike** and in the far west, **Winter Hill** transmitter. Continuing to scan, we can clearly see the three **Audenshaw** reservoirs, while further round beyond **Stockport** you should see planes land and take off at **Manchester** Airport with amazing regularity. Further south, **Jodrell Bank** radio telescope is visible. In fact, there's so much to the west that it's easy to forget that just behind us is the **Peak District National Park**.

Leaving the trig point, we take a clear path (NE) across 'Access Land'. As the first reservoir comes into view we use a metal post (the water authority sign having long since vanished) to guide us across the moor. The track tends to split and rejoin as we head towards a stile (with a hazardous drop on the far side). Next we make for a gate (Wp.14 127M) and continue our descent to a stile (Wp.15 134M) with the reservoirs ahead of us. The path can at times be indistinct, but it does carry straight on. Passing a ladder stile (Wp.16 140M) we follow the finger post with 'Swineshaw' carved on it. Travelling NNE to the next gate and stile, we cross into a field where our path all but disappears, but going straight ahead we aim for a stile in the far wall. Crossing the stile we head left (NNE) on a clear path bringing us to a waymark post (Wp.17 148M) above **Lower Swineshaw Reservoir**. Descending more rapidly with a wall to our right and the land dropping sharply on the left, we come to a fingerpost (Wp.18 156M) where we turn left (NW) on the **Tameside Trail** towards the reservoir.

Following 'Pennine Bridleway' (PBW) signs we pass a metal gate and cross the dam between **Upper** and **Lower Swineshaw Reservoirs**. The gates on the **PBW** have ingenious catches allowing horse riders to open them without dismounting. After crossing the dam (Wp.19 163M) we follow the 'PBW' sign down the tarmac road to **Brushes Valley**. (There's the option to extend the walk to **Greenfield** from here, by following Walk 21 from Wp.9). Rounding a bend in the road, we come across the disused quarry that supplied stone for the dam (171M). The road leads down to a plethora of gates (Wp.20 184M) at the head of **Walkerwood Reservoir**. Staying on the **PBW** towards **Carrbrook**, we head uphill to our right (NW). As the tarmac road swings right we continue ahead on the **PBW** at the now familiar metal gate. We reach the top of a rise (190M) with**Stalybridge** to our left, and continue north on the green lane, with views of **Hartshead Pike** above **Mossley**, while below us is the spire of **St James' Church** at **Carrsbrook**.

As the **PBW** meets a tarmac road (Wp.21 203M) we turn sharp left (SW) and head downhill to **Lower Hyde Green Farm** (Wp.22 208M). Although basically straight on, we do a quick right and left to take us between the farm buildings. Just past the last barn, on the right, the land drops and we cross a stile and head towards school buildings further down the slope. Half way down a post guides us under the pylon to **Huddersfield Road**.

Crossing the stile we turn left (SW) and pass **St James' Church** before crossing the road and passing a stone terrace. Turning right onto **Oxford Street**, **Millbrook**, we head for a finger post. Our path leads us down the side of **Staly Cricket Club** and along the side of the pitch (Wp.23 221M). This is the low point of our walk as we pass through a nasty little rubbish strewn area with a derelict mill and chimney on the left. Hurrying down the sett-paved road to a metal barrier we leave this area. Turning right we travel a short distance to a sign for the 'Tame Valley Staly Way' where a finger post guides us left (SSW) to **Stalybridge** along the **Huddersfield Narrow Canal**.

A twenty minute stroll with the canal on our right brings us to lock gates (Wp.24 249M) and **Stalybridge**. Staying by the canal, we drop down steps to take us under the new (built in 2000) road bridge past Tesco and into **Armentieres Square**. At the second lock gates we swing back towards a church to pass **Victoria Market** on **Trinity Street**. Passing the library and art gallery we cross the **Tame** on **Victoria Bridge**. As we meet the railway arches with the **Q Bar** straight ahead, we continue and turn right under the railway bridge. **Stalybridge Station** is across the road (Wp.25 269M). Go up the sett-paved ramp to visit the **Station Buffet Bar**.

# 2 SMITHY BRIDGE to LITTLEBOROUGH ( CLEGG HALL & HOLLINGWORTH LAKE)

From **Smithy Bridge** our stroll takes us to **Clegg Hall**, an outstanding example of early 17th century architecture with Grade II listing. The Hall, soon to be renovated, sits in a 19th century industrial complex by the **Rochdale Canal**. A renovated farm, and row of three-storey weavers' cottages are typical of the South Pennines. This conservation area charts the development from agrarian village to early industrialisation. From here our walk takes us to **Hollingworth Lake** at the foot of **Blackstone Edge**.

The lake was built in 1801 to supply water to the **Rochdale Canal** and became known as 'The Weighvers Seaport', being a traditional leisure destination for local millworkers. In its heyday several hotels, dance halls, a roller skating rink and boating on the lake provided a holiday atmosphere. Captain Webb is reputed to have used the lake as a training ground for the first Cross-Channel Swim, and today the lake remains a thriving centre for water based activities and family days out. With light refreshment available at the two modern day visitor centres, this easy walk ends with the option to sample great local pub hospitality.

* linear, or circular if travelling by car

**Access by train:**
From **Manchester Victoria** to **Smithy Bridge Station**

**Access by car:**
A58 from **Rochdale**, following 'Littleborough' signs, and turn right at 'Station' sign into **Smithy Bridge Road**. The car park is on the left after the level crossing.

| **Short Walk Option** |
| Park at **Hollingworth Lake Visitor Centre**, signposted from **Rochdale**, for the 2.4km walk around the lake. |

Leaving the station (Wp.1 0M) we cross the road to the station's car park and drop down to the right, bringing us onto the **Rochdale Canal**. Turn right (SW) and passing under the road bridge, canal on our left, we stroll along the towpath. As we approach a bridge, with **Clegg Hall** on the opposite bank, we come to a gap in the wall (Wp.2 14M). Through the gap, we take the path leading up to the bridge at **Clegg Hall Lane**. After crossing the bridge and passing the newly renovated **Clegg Hall Farm** we turn left (NW).

The road takes us past **Clegg Hall Cottages** (19th century weavers' cottages) and **Clegg Hall** itself. As we pass derelict mill buildings (19M) we turn right (SE) into **Branch Road**. Travelling along this straight, wide track, we have the grassy bump of **Owl Hill** to our left and a small reservoir on the right.

The track brings us to **Wild House Lane** (Wp.3 27M) which we cross to continue (SE) up the tarmac road opposite. As the road swings right we follow a footpath sign (Wp.4 30M) left (E). The gravel track takes us past cottages dated 1787, bringing us to a metal gate. Through the swing gate our path takes round the edge of the field, with the wall to our right, and brings us to a stile (Wp.5 37M) which we cross, then heading N to the well-hidden stile in the top left of the field (Wp.6 38M).

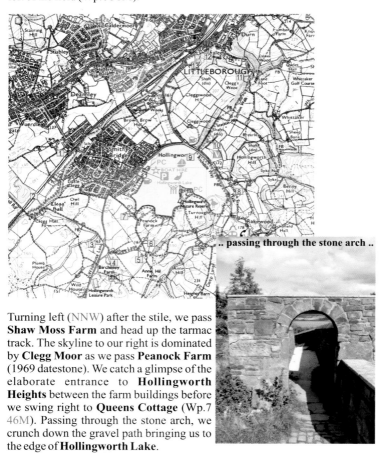

.. passing through the stone arch ..

Turning left (NNW) after the stile, we pass **Shaw Moss Farm** and head up the tarmac track. The skyline to our right is dominated by **Clegg Moor** as we pass **Peanock Farm** (1969 datestone). We catch a glimpse of the elaborate entrance to **Hollingworth Heights** between the farm buildings before we swing right to **Queens Cottage** (Wp.7 46M). Passing through the stone arch, we crunch down the gravel path bringing us to the edge of **Hollingworth Lake**.

At the lake side we turn right (NE) to stroll the perimeter of the lake. Ahead of us we can see **Rakewood Viaduct** carrying the M62 across the **Longden End Valley**.

Continuing around the lake we pass **TS Palatine**, the Sea Cadets NW Inland Training Centre, and soon arrive at a visitor centre (61M). The centre with its **Pavilion Café**, toilet facilities and picnic benches provides a pleasant area to take a break before resuming our lakeside stroll, soon passing through a bird sanctuary before arriving at a bridge (Wp.8 70M). We turn left (NE) to walk along **Rakewood Road**, a **Pennine Bridleway** finger-post pointing the way to the main visitor centre. As we cross the embankment we enjoy views to the right of **Blackstone Edge**, then at the end of the embankment (Wp.9 79M) turn right (NE) into the visitor centre.

Passing the centre (Wp.10 82M), we continue (NE) through the car parks and take the track between 'No Entry' signs. As the track swings right, we continue straight ahead on the path through a picnic area. Passing through four kissing-gates, with **Hollingworth Brook** on our left, we come to a stone footbridge (Wp.11 92M) and turn left (NW) onto **Shore Lane**. We continue down this leafy lane with the terraced **Cleggswood Hill** and **Ealees Brook** on our left. Passing two cottages, we come to the buildings and metal fence of **Fothergill's Mill**.

The Red Lion

Heading right towards stone houses we come to **Ealees Road** with **Stone Terrace** on the left, and less attractive modern housing on the right. After crossing the bridge over the **Rochdale Canal**, we drop down to the A58 **Halifax Road** (Wp.12 99M) and turn left (SW) to come to **The Red Lion**. Its eclectic décor and range of cask ales will delight those who value the true 'Local Pub'.

From the **Red Lion** we continue SW into **Canal Street** as the Halifax road heads under the railway bridge. Passing stone industrial buildings, we arrive back at the **Rochdale Canal** and, on the opposite side of the road, **Littleborough Station** (Wp.13 103M). Those travelling on a Day Ranger ticket can return to **Manchester Victoria** from here. To return to the car park at **Smithy Bridge Station** take the path by **The Waterside Restaurant** and pass under the road bridge for the stroll back along the canal to the car park (Wp.1 121M).

Here's a favourite walk to build up an appetite for Sunday Lunch at **The Rake Inn**. With **Littleborough** being on the **York** and **Selby** line there is a regular service, even at weekends. Our walk takes us out to **Hollingworth Lake** which can be quite crowded with visitors at the weekend, but we soon leave the crowds behind as we head away from the lake. We pass the award winning **Syke Farm** as we come on to the edge of the moors below **Blackstone Edge**. With good views along the way, the final descent has a little hidden surprise before we arrive at **The Rake Inn**. With genuine home cooked food made with local produce, real ale and fine wines, **The Rake** provides a congenial atmosphere for a relaxed lunch.

**Access by train:** From **Manchester Victoria** to **Littleborough Station**

**Access by car:** A58 from **Rochdale** following **Littleborough** signs. Turn right towards the station at the mini roundabout; there are several car park options.

Leaving the station (Wp.1 0M) via the subway (SW), we head away from the town onto **Canal Street**. Crossing the road, we turn left (NE) to walk along the canal to the first lock where we cross the canal and continue on the opposite bank. Following the path round in front of cottages we emerge by **Fothergill's Mill** and carry straight on (SE) with the metal fence to our right. As we continue along the cart track, we pass the **Old Mill Cottage** to the babbling sound of **Ealees Brook** on our right. We turn right (SW) at the stone footbridge (Wp.2 13M) and follow the finger-post to **Hollingworth Lake**.

**Blackstone Edge**

After passing through four kissing-gates we swing right across the first footbridge into the picnic area. Joining a tarmac track, we continue (SW) uphill past the car park to the **Visitor Centre** (24M), from where we stay on the road until we reach **Hollingworth Lake** (Wp.3 26M).

Here we turn left (SE) to walk across the embankment. On the far side we follow the **Pennine Bridleway (PBW)** fingerpost, to **Summit**, on the uphill track (28M).

As we climb **Bear Hill** we pass **Hollingworth Fold** and have a good view of **Rakeswood Viaduct**. Beyond the white cottage (dated 1755), we pass the **Warden's Cottage**, set back on the left, and follow the **PBW** fingerpost straight ahead. Ignoring a footpath to our right, we continue past a cottage and take the path to the left of the bungalow. Following the signs for **Syke & Sheep Bank Farms** we cross a cattle grid and drop sharply downhill on the gritstone cart track, to the renovated buildings of **Syke Farm** (Wp.4 39M).

Crossing the stone footbridge with its iron cartwheels, we again start to climb. The grass-covered hummocks are spoil heaps from coal mining in the area. Climbing the gritty track, with the intriguingly named **Benny Hill** to our right, we pass between gritstone gateposts. We can only imagine that the out of place yellow 'driveguard' is designed to slow speeding riders.

The rather dull climb, after the driveguard, brings us to a fork (Wp.5 50M) where we follow the **PBW** waymarker left (NE) heading up towards pylons. Rising up to a wide track (Wp.6 54M) we turn left (N) to stroll down hill. During this downhill stretch we can enjoy the contrast of the rolling umbers of **Syke**, **Clegg** & **Whittaker Moors** with the craggy outline of **Blackstone Edge** to our right. On our left we have **Littleborough** and **Rochdale** in the distance. The lush greens of **Whittaker Golf Course** just below us lead the eye up the valley to the gorge at **Summit** and the **Rossendale Moors** ahead.

We continue our downhill stroll northwards as we meet a tarmac track (Wp.7 67M) bringing us down to the rear of **Lydgate Farm** (Wp.8 74M). Turning left (W) on **Blackstone Edge Old Road**, we pass through the hamlet, and ignoring the path to the right at **Lydgate House**, we follow the fingerpost (Wp.9 78M) which directs us over a stile to the right (N) for the last climb of the walk, following an indistinct uphill path with a fence to our right and a steep drop to the valley below. Across this narrow valley, **Stormer Hill** rises up with the **PBW** following the line of pylons. Beyond **Stormer Hill**, **The White House Inn** nestles by the side of the A58.

As we reach the top of the climb the fence falls away to the right and we continue (NNW) down to a gap in a broken down wall (Wp.10 86M) which we follow left (SW) until we reach a dilapidated gate and stile and continue between two stone walls towards houses. This track brings us back to **Blackstone Edge Road** which we cross in front of **Gatehouse Cottages** (Wp.11 92M) and take the right hand path (W) to the side of a double garage.

Descending the steps towards metal gates, more steps to the right of the gates take us down a grassy path at the rear of houses. Just as you think the path can't get any worse, we come to a kissing-gate by a double stone garage (97M).

Going straight across to the gap ahead, we have the feeling of entering someone's garden as we go down the well tended grass slope in front of a grand stone mullioned house dated 1653.

At the bottom of the slope we descend six stone steps to arrive at **The Rake Inn** (Wp.12 105M). Open seven days a week, the inn offers home cooked local produce, cask ales and an extensive range of wines. Food is served all day at weekends, but check by phone (01706 379689) if you want a meal mid-week.

From **The Rake**, we continue a short distance downhill and turn left (SW) to walk along **Westview**. At the cottages on **Ealees Road** (Wp.13 109M) carry straight on and retrace the path, we set off on, to the canal and station (Wp1 113M). An alternative route to the right at this point takes us over the canal to the A58 with **The Red Lion** to the left, beyond which we turn left into **Canal Street** with the station across the road on the right.

Our circular walk takes us from **Littleborough** along the **Rochdale Canal** towards the **Summit Pass**. The rail tunnel at **Summit** opened in 1841 and was the longest (over 2,500 metres) ever built at that time. As we head up the west side of the gorge, cut by glacial meltwater, following old trans-Pennine routes we have wonderful views of the canal below and moors ahead and to our right. Crossing the valley floor we climb up to join the **Pennine Way** leading us to **The White House**, the most easterly pub in Lancashire. Next we head for the **Aigin Stone**, an ancient marker for travellers, before we descend the **Roman Road** on the return to **Littleborough**.

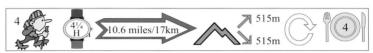

**Access by train:**
From **Manchester Victoria** to **Littleborough Station**

**Access by car:**
A58 from **Rochdale** following **Littleborough** signs. Turn right towards the station at the mini roundabout. There are several car park options.

**Short Walk Options:**
(1) On reaching A6033, **Todmorden Road** (Wp.6 101M) return to **Littleborough** by bus. Approximately 5.5 km.

(2) Or return by continuing along **Rochdale Canal** from **Warland Upper Lock**, No 35. Approximately 10.5 km.

Leaving the station (Wp.1 0M) via the subway (SW) we head away from the town onto **Canal Street**. Crossing the road, we turn left (NE) to walk along the canal towpath. We soon have views ahead of the hills that we'll be climbing during this canal section, and as we walk we pass lock N°s.48 to 44 before passing mill buildings, the one on the right having a clock tower. After we pass the sixth set of locks, N°43, by looking over on the left we catch sight of the **River Roch** as it crosses the railway in an iron trough. Just before the 7th set of locks we cross the car park (Wp.2 24M) to our left, bringing us to **Todmorden Road**. Crossing the road, over the wall we can see the entrance to the **Summit Rail Tunnel**, and turning left we come to a bridleway sign, just before cottages, where we turn right (NW) and start our first climb.

We follow the path as it curves right between spoil-heaps and continue until we emerge by **Stansfield Hall**, crossing the road and heading straight on (NW) up **Moor Road**, passing **Mawrode Farm**. At the next road we continue our north-westerly climb on the bridleway towards white painted cottages at higher **Calderbrook**, pausing to look back at **Blackstone Edge** before we reach the road by the cottages where we turn right (N), following the **Pennine Bridleway (PBW)** towards **Summit**.

At the second **PBW** sign (Wp.3 38M) we bear right for a downhill stint, the tarmac soon giving way to a stone path. To our right, across the gorge, the **Pennine Way** runs along the top of the moors the route for our return journey. Coming down to a road by one of the many ventilation shafts we'll see, we continue north on the **PBW**.

At the next **PBW** finger-post (Wp.4 48M) we bear left (NNW) following the 'MT (Mary Townley) Loop East' sign. Climbing the rough track, we soon look down into the valley to see the **Rochdale Canal** and **Todmorden Road** snaking through the valley. As the track curves to cross a stream we leave **Lancashire** for the **West Riding of Yorkshire**. As we climb the stone slabs of the **Reddyshore Scout** packhorse track, we catch sight of **Steanor Bottom Toll House** on the **Calderbrook** and **Todmorden Turnpikes**. Approaching pylons, taking the short route to the **Pennine Way**, we see **Coal Clough** wind farm in the distance ahead of us. To the right of the wind farm we can also see **Great Bride Stones**.

Passing through he gate beyond the pylons, we come to a **PBW** fingerpost (Wp.5 86M) taking time to look at the milestone just ahead, before we start the descent to the right (N). The track, part stone-paved, part quagmire, brings us down by our final ventilation shaft. Passing through a gate we cross a pseudo-cobbled track to continue our north-westerly descent to **Todmorden Road** (Wp.6 101M). Crossing the road and turning right (SE) brings us to a bridge crossing the **Rochdale Canal**. A bus stop here provides the return to **Littleborough** for the first short walk option. By the side of the bridge we turn left and take the steps down to the towpath where we turn right (SE). Approaching **Warland Lower** lock N°34 we look up, to the left, to see the ostentatious castellated walls of the farm above.

The county boundary markers

Continuing to the upper lock we cross back into **Lancashire** marked by the new boundary stone on the opposite bank. At the swing bridge (Wp.7 111M) we turn left (NE) to commence our climb to the **Pennine Way**. Following the road as it swings up by 17th century **White Cottages** behind the four-storey houses.

We continue the steady uphill climb and take the right hand fork towards **Calf Lee House** following the **Calderdale** waymark. A faded sign points the way as we swing right towards wrought iron gates. Passing through the small pedestrian gate on the left, we pass **Calf Lee** house and swing left past the kennels and garages. At the gate ahead (Wp.8 126M) we cross the stile. Following the waymark taking us right (E) in front of the second building, we make our way to the far rear corner of the building and climb over the high stile. Back on moorland, we follow waymarks uphill and across another stile to bring us onto a clear stone track which takes us up to the **Warland Reservoir** dam. At the dam we turn right up a wide track (Wp.9 139M) taking us to the edge of the reservoir.

We swing right (SSE), by the reservoir, on the **Pennine Way**. After our uphill climb the wide, well made track passes **Light Hazzles Reservoir** and allows us to enjoy the views. On rare clear days you may see **Jodrell Bank** to the south, **Winter Hill** and the **Welsh Mountains** to the west. **Manchester**, **Rochdale** and **Hollingworth Lake** in the basin below are usually visible.

**View to Littleborough**

Behind us on the skyline is **Pendle Hill**. Ignoring all paths to the left, we pass under pylons, having taken their shortcut across the valley, and follow the track on past the rocks of **Cow Head** until we reach **Blackstone Edge Reservoir**. Following the dam wall, we emerge on the A58 **Halifax Road** and turn right (SW).

We pass **The White House Inn** (Wp.10 170M), serving food and a range of cask and bottled beers, a pleasant stop on a foul day. Turning left (S) and crossing the road just before the anemometer we start the last real climb following the **Pennine Way** sign for 'Blackstone Edge'. At the top of the rise we follow the broad path with the drain to our left. Passing the first narrow footbridge over the drain we continue to a second footbridge (Wp.11 183M) taking us left (E) over the drain.

Following one of several paths, more typical **Pennine Way**, diagonally (E) uphill towards fence posts on the horizon. (Note: in bad weather - when you can't make out the fence posts - you may want to miss this section to the **Aigin Stone**, in which case keep by the drain until you reach the wicker gate and turn right, downhill, before it.) Our route changes to stone-paved and back to rough track finally bringing us up to the **Aigin Stone** (Wp12 193M) a medieval guide stone for travellers.

Turning right (WSW) to head downhill on the **Roman Road** which becomes a well paved dual carriageway of its time. Proving there is nothing new; age old graffiti can be seen carved into the centre drain. Dropping down, we cross a stone footbridge over the drain channel, by a wicker gate to continue downhill.

The stone paving peters out on the steady descent, reverting to a rough track. We come down to a farm track (Wp.13 205M), just short of the **Halifax** road, and carry straight along the path ahead. With **Hollingworth Lake** ahead, we follow the track, by a stone wall, to bring us down to the hamlet of **Lydgate** (Wp.14 218M). Passing in front of the cottages, we turn left (S) after the white farm building of **Lydgate Farm** to rejoin the **PBW**.

When the road forks (Wp.15 224M) we take the right hand track heading for **Whittaker Golf Course**. Going through a kissing gate and stile, we pass a sign warning of 'low flying golf balls'. As the track swings right to **Owlet Hall** we follow the path straight on through the golf course. Waymarks and **Hollingworth Lake** ahead guide us across the fairways. Leaving the course at a kissing-gate we cross a stone footbridge and following a waymarker turn left (W). Dropping down through young oak trees, **Shore Lane Brook** below us, we cross a wooden footbridge (Wp.16 236M). Coming up behind a cottage, a waymarker points us right; this down hill stretch finishing with wooden steps to take us onto **Shore Lane**.

Turning right, we continue down the lane and pass between two cottages, continuing past buildings and the metal fence of **Fothergill's Mill**. We then head right towards stone houses to reach **Ealees Road** with **Stone Terrace** on the left and less attractive modern housing on the right. Crossing the bridge over the **Rochdale Canal** we drop down to the A58 **Halifax Road**. We turn left (SW) and come to **The Red Lion** (Wp.17 247M)., then continue SW into **Canal Street**, as the **Halifax Road** heads under the railway bridge. Passing stone industrial building brings us back to the **Rochdale Canal** and **Littleborough Station** (Wp.1 250M) on the opposite side of the road.

If you'd like to finish with a meal, turn right at the stone terrace past the less attractive houses on **West View** taking you to **Halifax Road**; turn right to see **The Rake Inn** (Walk 3) a short distance ahead.

Starting at **Rose Hill Station**, we walk a section of the **Middlewood Way** a disused railway line to **Macclesfield**. Crossing **Marple Golf Course** we join the **Macclesfield Canal** (part of the 'Cheshire Ring' of canals) bringing us to **Marple Locks**. Descending the flight of 16 locks, our walk takes us along the **Peak Forest Canal** and over **Marple Aqueduct** as it crosses the **River Goyt**. It's hard to believe today that in the 1960s, the canal was un-navigable and the aqueduct, now a listed structure, was close to ruin.

Leaving the canals behind we travel through **Kirk Wood** to arrive at **Chadkirk Chapel** with links back to the 7th century when St Chad set up a monastic cell on the site. With so much to see and learn from the information boards, and plenty of opportunities to stop along the way, few people will complete this walk in the suggested two hours. The excellent web sites (see appendices) also provide the opportunity for a virtual tour, providing a taste of what is in store on this walk.

**Access by train:**
From **Manchester Piccadilly** to **Rose Hill Station**.
Return to **Manchester Piccadilly** from **Romiley Station**.

**Access by car**
A626 **Stockport Road** to **Marple**. Follow station signs onto **Railway Road** and park at the station. Return to **Rose Hill** from **Romiley** by train.

> **Short Walk Option**
> The walk can be completed in two sections by travelling via **Marple Station** which is 200 metres downhill on **Station Road** from the canal at Wp.5.

Leaving the station we walk through the car park (Wp.1 0M) heading SSW towards the coal merchant's yard, and follow the 'Middlewood Way' sign left (S) onto **Railway Road**. Continuing south, we come to the disused railway line at the side of the refuse disposal depot. Having left the industrial environs behind, we stroll down the tree lined track bed passing under a bridge before coming to a five-bar gate (6M). Crossing the clearing, we pass through a second five-bar gate and continue south. Shortly after we pass a square chimney and buildings up to our left to come to a finger-post for the **Macclesfield Canal** (Wp.2 9M); here we turn left (E) and cross a stile onto **Marple Golf Course**.

Keeping to the edge of the course, we come to a few stepping stones on the left, taking us off the course. After a short distance we come back onto the course and continue to follow the perimeter until we come to a gravel path (17M) a waymarker takes us straight ahead (SE). Crossing a small wooden footbridge, we come to a finger-post guiding us to the 'Macclesfield Canal'. Taking care as we cross the fairway, we follow the line of a small ridge with the remains of a hawthorn hedge, until we come off the course onto the canal towpath (Wp.3 21M) where we turn left (NW) to follow the canal, passing under two bridges and by a mill on the opposite bank. At the third bridge (Wp.4 33M) our path curves up and round taking us over the canal, then dropping down to our left onto the other side of the canal opposite **The Ring O'Bells**. Continuing for a short distance to the next bridge, we rise up and turn left (N) heading for **Marple** top lock (35M).

After descending the first four locks, we pass under **Stockport Road** via an elliptically shaped tunnel (43M). For those wanting refreshment, **The Navigation Hotel**, one of several that supplied ale to the navvies, is 100 metres to the left along **Stockport Road**. Continuing along the canal, we pass a further four locks before coming to **Station Road** (Wp.5 49M). The short walk option ends or start here, with **Marple Station** just 200 metres away. Crossing the road, we drop down to our right and follow the footpath sign left to continue north along the canal.

**... an elliptically shaped tunnel ...**

We drop down past the remaining eight locks, each with a bench and picnic area providing us with ample opportunity to rest or enjoy lunch.

Passing the final lock, we rise up by bridge N°16 and cross over the canal heading under a railway bridge bringing us to **Marple Aqueduct** (Wp.6 67M). Crossing the aqueduct with the railway viaduct on our right we can look down on the **River Goyt** in the valley below. Continuing along the canal through a stone lined cutting and under a bridge we come to warning signs on tunnel safety and soon we have an excellent view through the 300 metre long **Hydebank Tunnel** (77M).

Our path takes us up steps to detour round the tunnel. Coming out onto a lane, we turn left (NNW) towards a row of white painted houses, the lane then dropping down at the side of **Hyde Bank Farm** (17th century dairy farm) which serves teas and ice cream. A further 25 metres brings us to a track that drops down to our left (Wp.7 80M) a finger-post for the 'Valley Way' guiding us onto a concrete path. Passing under a bridge, we cross the canal at the tunnel exit to continue our stroll along the towpath.

As we approach mill buildings on the opposite bank, we come to a gap and stone steps (Wp.8 82M) taking us left (W) on the **Midshires Way** through **Kirk Wood**. The pleasant walk through the woods brings us to two wooden posts (Wp.9 89M) at the head of a flight of steps. Descending the steps we continue along until the track splits and take the right hand path down more steps. A **Midshires Waymarker** (Wp.10 94M) takes us right (NW) and further steps bringing us to a finger-post where we turn right (N) towards the chapel.

**Chadkirk Chapel**

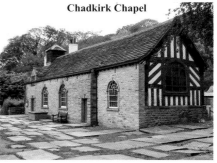

As our path leaves the wood we come to the walled garden of **Chadkirk Chapel** and take the steps down to our left (W) into the graveyard and pass the front of the chapel. Following the path round, we come to a metal gate leading onto a lane where we turn right (NNW) and follow the fingerpost for the farm.

Passing the farm, we rise up over a small bridge to head uphill past **St Chad's Well** (Wp.11 102M). Climbing past **Kirkwood House** the path levels out by a brick terrace, swinging right to pass under the canal as we continue uphill. As we see a sign for 'Gregory Avenue' we turn left (NNE) onto **Chadkirk Road**. At the sign for **Beech Lane** we continue straight ahead on **Church Lane** and past **St. Chad's Church**, bringing us to **Stockport Road** and **Romiley** village. Crossing the road to **The Railway Hotel**, **Romiley Station** is just to our right (Wp.12 117M).

A 20 minute train ride from **Manchester Piccadilly** brings us to the aptly named **Middlewood Station**, set in **Middle Wood**. It has no road link, yet does have a surprisingly regular rail service. From the station, our walk takes us through the woods to the **Macclesfield Canal**, the highest in the British Waterways system, which we follow for a short distance before heading cross-country to bring us into **Lyme Park**, whose medieval deer park became the family seat of the Legh family and is now owned by the National Trust. Our walk through the park climbs past **The Cage**, built in 1737, which was used to watch the progress of the hunt. From **The Cage**, we drop down to the north entrance of the hall before heading out of the park. Our return journey takes us back to the **Macclesfield Canal** at **Higher Poynton** where we join the **Middlewood Way** for the short stroll back to the station. The walk time doesn't include viewing time, which can be considerable; therefore it's worth planning your return journey with this in mind.

**Access by train:** from **Manchester Piccadilly** or **Buxton** to **Middlewood Station**. N.B. Trains stop more frequently on Sundays.

Leaving the station (Wp.1 0M) we head up the ramp to join the **Middlewood Way**. At the northern end of the bridge we follow the fingerpost 'Alternative LVIT route via Macclesfield Canal'uphill (E). After a short distance on the well-made track we come to a fork, where we follow the yellow waymarker straight on as we drop down into a field. Following the perimeter of the field, brings us to a waymarker taking us into the woods with the railway line below us to the right. A plethora of yellow waymarkers guide us along the clear if somewhat muddy path, as we meander through the woods.

Arriving at the **Macclesfield Canal** (Wp.2 12M) we turn right (SSE) to follow the towpath. At the first bridge, N°13 (Wp.3 16M), we rise up and cross the canal turning left (NE) by the concrete pillbox, following the LVIT waymarker along the opposite bank. After 100 metres or so, we ignore the waymarker pointing straight ahead, turning right to descend a few steps, then crossing the well-hidden stile to reach a metal gate. Through the gate, we drop downhill (NNE) on the clear path to a second metal gate, and continue towards the wooden footbridge (Wp.4 18M). Crossing the bridge, we follow the LVIT waymarker to climb steps with a stream to our left.

Coming to a stile, we cross into a field and head ENE on a reasonably well-trodden path. Following waymarkers, we cross another footbridge and continue through the fields. After passing a bijou black and white shack (Wp.5 25M), we come to a ladder stile and cross over into a lane. Just to our right we cross a second ladder stile, the uphill path bringing us to a warning sign as we reach the railway line. Heeding the warning, we cross the line and follow the LVIT waymarker downhill in a NE direction. Crossing a third ladder stile we continue NE, following the perimeter of the field.

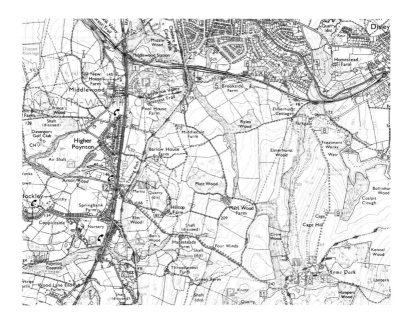

Crossing the next footbridge (Wp.6 32M) we follow the LVIT waymarker with a barbed wire fence on our left. Approaching farm buildings, we cross a stile and follow the LVIT up the farm track and between buildings, ignoring the track to our right and carrying straight on. Shortly before the track crosses a stream, we turn right (SE) over a stile (Wp.7 38M) waymarked 'Lyme Park via Bolling Hurst'. Following a fairly clear track, we pass under the railway and veer left (SE) to head uphill. Crossing the field diagonally towards what appears to be a small building, we come to a stone step-stile to the left of a substantial house.

Over the stile we turn left (NE) pass through a gate taking the path round the cattle grid and enter **Lyme Park**. Following the wide track downhill, we cross a stream and turn right (S) before the buildings to head uphill towards an old oak tree. Our path follows the line of four oak trees, at the fourth of which we veer left towards the tarmac access road (Wp.8 52M). Almost opposite us, we follow the wide grassy track uphill (SE). Rising up, we soon see a large square tower, **The Cage**. Taking the left fork as the track splits, we continue uphill to reach it (Wp.9 64M).

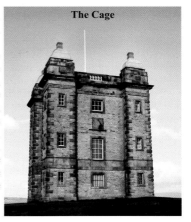

The Cage

With a 360 degree panoramic view, **The Cage** provides a pleasant location for a lunch stop. Taking time to admire the restoration we notice the three-piece sundial set high on the walls before resting on the stone seat on the western side. From here we can see over **Manchester** to the **West Pennines** (NW) then sweeping west over the **Lancashire Plains** we can see the **Welsh Mountains**, on a clear day. The **Cheshire Plains** lie to the south-west, and behind us sits the **High Peak**.

The Hall, Lyme Park

We leave **The Cage** in a southerly direction on the wide track, the downhill stroll steadily steepening as we approach the north entrance to the house, well worth a visit in its own right. There are also refreshment opportunities a short distance from here. At the main entrance gates (Wp.10 75M) we turn right (W) and head down steps to the car park and visitor centre.

Making our way across the car park to the access road, we head SW to pass through a gate at the side of a cattle grid. Heading uphill on the tarmac road, we take the right hand fork (W) onto a rough track as we reach the top of the rise. At the next fork (Wp.11 82M) we again take the right hand fork (NW) on the rough track. As we descend the hill with fine views ahead, we leave the park by a wooden kissing-gate.

Continuing downhill, we pass through another kissing-gate as we come to **Haresteads Farm**. As the track bottoms out, at a cattle grid, we start to climb again on a tarmac track. The track passes under pylons and brings us to another cattle grid. Passing through the kissing-gate we follow the yellow waymarker passing **Woodside Cottage** as we head down **Lyme Road** to the **Macclesfield Canal**.

After crossing the canal, we head down the road past the white cottages of **Mount Vernon**, reaching a visitor centre with an interesting sculpture depicting the local mines and giving details of over 70 local pits with such interesting names as 'Higher Reform' & 'House of Correction'. Further down the road we cross the bridge over the **Middlewood Way** (Wp.12 106M) with **The Boar's Head** directly ahead, and turn left to drop down to the picnic area at what was once **Higher Poynton Station**. With **The Original Coffee Tavern** and refreshments available near the canal, **The Boar's Head** isn't my first choice for refreshment.

At the bottom of the cobbled slope we turn left (N) to head towards bridge N°15 as we start the final leg of the journey. A pleasant stroll along the tree-lined track bed takes us under three more bridges before we arrive back at **Middlewood Station** (Wp.1 136M) for our return train journey.

This gentle uphill route takes us to **Marple Ridge**. **The Romper**, just before the ridge, with its decked and terraced outdoor areas provides a beautiful spot for refreshment. Providing a good range of food and cask ales, the **Romper** has fine views towards the **Peak National Park** from the terrace. On cooler days it provides a cosy interior and good service.

The second part of the walk takes us over the ridge with more views to enjoy as we stroll downhill to the **Peak Forest Canal**. Descending from lock N°16 down to N°9 on the **Marple** flight, we are a short distance from **Marple Station**. If you want to extend the walk, you can continue to **Romiley Station** by following Walk 5 from Wp.5.

**Access by rail:**
From **Manchester Piccadilly** or **Buxton** to **Middlewood Station**. Return via **Manchester Piccadilly**.

**Extension**
Follow the **Rose Hill** to **Romiley** route (Walk 5) from Wp.5 for the remaining eight locks and on to **Chadkirk Chapel**.

As with Walk 6, we leave the station (Wp.1 0M) heading up the ramp. At the northern end of the bridge we follow the fingerpost 'Alternative LVIT route via Macclesfield Canal' uphill (E). After a short distance on the well-made track, we come to a fork where we follow the yellow waymarker straight on as we drop down into a field. Following the perimeter of the field, we come to a waymarker taking us into the woods with the railway line below us on the right. Meandering through the woods our path, often muddy, is well waymarked

Arriving at the **Macclesfield Canal** (Wp.2 12M) we cross the wide track and turn left (N) to stroll along the towpath with the canal on our right. Our amble along the canal takes us over a humpback bridge as the canal branches into a marina on the left. Passing the **Bull's Head**, a little too soon to stop and enjoy its hospitality, we pass under bridge N°11. Our stroll takes us under bridge N°10 before we reach bridge N°9 where we take the steps (Wp.3 29M) up to our left.

At the top of the steps we turn right (SE) over the footbridge, to head uphill on **Andrew Lane**. Crossing the road we come to a sign for the **Scotch Produce Centre** (Wp.4 32M) and turn left (NE) and left again after 50 metres to follow the yellow waymarker to **Cawkwell Fields**. The tarmac track takes us to **Lumber Hey Farm** where we carry straight on towards a five-bar gate and a stile, tucked away on the left. After crossing the stile, a fingerpost points us straight on (NNE) to **Marple Ridge**.

Following the path, holly on our right, we come to another five-bar gate and pass through the kissing-gate, still heading NNE.

As our path drops out onto a wider track we ignore the track to the left and maintain our NNE course, passing through another gate. The track starts to rise and veers right (E), and continuing up the track, we approach a modern farm building to our left where we carry straight on (E), crossing a stile to enter a field.

Staying on the field's perimeter, our path veers left (NE) towards a metal kissing-gate (Wp.5 45M) which we pass through, staying on the perimeter of the next field to reach another stile by a metal gate.

Over this stile, a fingerpost points the way to the **Peak Forest Canal**.

As the muddy track swings left (NE) we follow it, ignoring the stile that goes straight on. Finally leaving the muddy track behind, we come onto tarmac passing between cottages.

The climb uphill past **Ivy Cottage** brings us out at **The Romper** (Wp.6 52M). Open for lunch mid-week and all day at weekends, we can enjoy the views and the refreshments.

Leaving **The Romper** in a north-easterly direction up the road, we carry straight on (NE) as the road veers left. Resist the temptation to visit the viewing point shown on the OS map, which in reality is a tatty little car park with a bench - the views as we carry on past cottages on **Hollinwood Lane** are just as spectacular. Dropping down the well-made path, we come down to a bridge over the **Peak Forest Canal** (Wp.7 61M). We turn left (NNW) as we cross the bridge to join the canal towpath.

The gentle stroll along the canal takes us under a footbridge and a road bridge, and then swings up and over the canal to follow the towpath on the opposite side, following a fingerpost for the 'Goyt Way'. Passing a marina with the **Marple Forces Social Club** on the right hand side we come to bridge N°1 (Wp.8 82M) at the junction of the **Peak Forest** and **Macclesfield Canals**. Rising up, we continue over the bridge (N) to follow the **Marple Lock** flight downhill.

We reach **Stockport Road** at the fourth lock, and our last chance for refreshment before **Marple Station**. **The Navigation** is 100 metres to the left on **Stockport Road** and serves Robinson's, one of the four remaining family-owned **Manchester** breweries.

**The renovated warehouse**

Passing through an elliptically shaped tunnel, we carry on along the canal. After three more locks we pass a renovated canal warehouse (now offices) on the opposite bank.

**Leaving lock N°9**

At lock N°9, the eighth of our descent, we come to **Station Road** where we turn right and head downhill, crossing the road to arrive at **Marple Station** (Wp.9 96M).

This walk offers the choice of starting at **Newhey Station** or **Ogden Reservoir**, gateway to the South Pennines, and passes through a landscape shaped by industry - but don't be put off, as the industry has largely gone, and nature (with a little help from local wardens) has reclaimed the area for our enjoyment. Reservoirs may have displaced a number of farms, but livestock still graze the moors, which are full of wildlife. Look out for the **Lancashire & Yorkshire Railway Cotton Warehouse**, the trig point designated as a monument, and the waterfall in the quarry as we circumambulate **Piethorne Valley** & **Crompton Moor**.

**Access by train**: from **Manchester Victoria** to **Newhey**. Return from **Newhey** to **Victoria**.

**By car:** from junction 21 M62, follow 'Shaw & Huddersfield' signs to **Newhey**. Turn left on the A640 towards **Huddersfield** and right into **Railway Street** just after the station where street parking is available. Alternatively, continue along A640 and turn left into **Ogden Lane**, take the left hand fork at the cemetery and park at **Ogden Reservoir** car park.

Leaving the station (Wp1 0M) on the uphill ramp we turn right as we reach

**Huddersfield Road** and almost immediately right (SE) into **Railway Street** following a footpath sign. Crossing a footbridge at the end of **Railway Street** brings us to **Two Bridges Road** where we turn left (NE) to walk through a small estate. We turn right (ESE) in front of the **Wheatsheaf Hotel** pub onto **Hague Fold** and pass between cottages; the dates on **Hague Terrace** on the left (SE) showing that it was built nearly 100 years after **Hague Fold** cottages on the right.

Noting a track to our right (Wp.2 6M), our return route, we continue up **Hague Square**, passing three-storey weavers' cottages at **Kiln Gardens**, bringing us onto **Bethany Lane**. We follow the tarmac road as it climbs and swings left (NE 8M) until we reach the A640 (Wp.3 14M). Crossing the road, we head past the sign for 'The Bull's Head' onto **Ogden Lane** and continue past **Greenhalgh's Dye and Bleach Works**. As we come to a cemetery on the right we take the left fork (NE), ignoring the footpath on our left, to continue up the road towards **Ogden Reservoir**.

Approaching the dam (Wp.4 21M), we turn left before the car park (NW) through a gap in the wall, to climb the steps up to the dam wall. The car park, the Gateway to the South Pennines has an information board and toilets, and is an alternative start point for those travelling by car. Strolling across the dam, we cross a small footbridge by the reservoir overflow.

The reservoir overflow

The path up to the right takes us up steps to pass through a gap in the wall where we turn right (NNE) to follow the yellow waymarker. Passing through a kissing-gate, we continue straight on following the waymarker, ignoring the track down to the right. As the track splits we take the right hand fork onto a short section of surfaced path before we turn right (E) at a yellow waymarker to cross a footbridge (Wp.5 33M). Climbing steps made from reclaimed stone and cobbles, we reach the ruins of **Raghole Farm**.

Passing the ruins, we swing left (NE) between drystone walls and ascend to a wide track. Turning right (SE) following a white waymarker, we take the wide track towards power lines, ignoring yellow waymarkers, first right, then left, to reach a five-bar gate. Crossing the stile by the gate, we stay on the track, the water treatment plant below **Piethorne Dam** ahead of us. Another stile brings us to the dam (Wp.6 49M) where we turn right (SSE) and stroll across the dam wall, enjoying views (on a clear day) of **Windy Hills** and the radio mast on the left; and down the valley back towards **Newhey** on our right.

We cross the broad track at the far side of the dam, following the tarmac as it swings right towards a cattle grid (Wp.7 54M), just before which we follow the right-angled yellow waymarker to the left (SSE) to climb steps and pass through a gate. Keeping the field boundary to our left, we start the stiff climb over **Ogden Edge**. At the top of the first rise we follow a yellow waymarker left and diagonally to the next marker. Ignoring the two downhill paths, we carry straight on to cross a stile., then turning right (S) uphill. The boundary, now on our right, leads us to the next stile (Wp.8 72M) from where the antennae above **Crow Knowl** on **Crompton Moor** is visible, our objective.

Piethorne and Kitcliffe Reservoirs

After taking time to catch our breath and enjoy the views over **Piethorne** and **Kitcliffe Reservoirs**, we cross the stile. Over the 2nd stile, we continue south on a left hand diagonal across the field to cross a 3rd stile, then heading slightly to the right of the building to a 4th stile, which drops us onto a track.

Here we turn left, then immediately right to continue south to the A640 **Huddersfield Road** (Wp.9 81M) at the border between **Saddleworth** and **Denshaw** on the left and **Milnrow** on the right.

Crossing the road, we carry straight on (SW) up the track opposite to a fingerpost where we take the right hand fork (SW) following the **Oldham Way**, the tarmac soon giving way to a rough track. As we pass under power lines we leave the **Oldham Way** to go through a gate and across a stile immediately on the right, then head west, aiming for the right hand mast and a gap in the fence. This direct route, climbing over rough grass, can be avoided by following the track round and up to the masts.

Passing through the gap in the fence, we continue towards the mast until we meet a track, then turn left and left again to pass the largest mast, bringing us to the trig point (Wp.10 93M) bearing a plaque describing it as a 'Monument forming part of the OS National GPS Network'. If you're tempted to stop here for lunch, I'd suggest walking a little further to the picnic area at **Brushes Clough**.

Leaving the trig point, we head SW down the wide gravel access road following the fence line for less than 100 metres, and go through a gap in the fence on a fairly clear path. Passing to the right of a hummock, we pass through another gap in a fence and continue downhill towards **Crompton Fold**. Passing a gate with a 'No Motorcycling' sign, we ignore the track to the left and continue downhill. As the track splits we take the left hand fork following **Oldham Way** markers again, to head between two small plantations. Dropping down to the upper edge of **Brushes Clough Quarry**, we follow the path down and pass through a gate to a viewpoint and picnic area (Wp.11 109M). Ignoring the urban muddle below us, we can enjoy the views to the distant hills which are clearly marked on the Toposcope.

Retracing our steps back through the gate we take the **Oldham Way** sign down to our left and follow the track down into **Pingot Quarry**. We are greeted by a waterfall - maybe not Malham Cove, but spectacular none the less. Following the path round to the west, we leave the quarry and waterfall behind. Coming to a tarmac road, and a profusion of 'Oldham Way' markers - none of which point our route out - we head uphill to the right (NW). At the metal gate we leave the road to slip through a gap and head for what appears to be a garage, where we swing left to head for the large metal box structure and a barbed wire fence.

Crossing a crude stile at the barbed wire fence, we continue NNW with a stone wall on our left, passing through a gap in a fence we once again follow **Oldham Way** markers to another crude stile. With the spire of **St Thomas' Church** at **Newhey** now in sight we pass through the gate, and by the sheep pen made of Armco, we come to a track. Across the track and over a stile, still on the **Oldham Way**, we walk between a barbed wire fence and drystone wall. As the fence swings away to the left (Wp.12 128M), we leave the **Oldham Way** and stay by the wall as we drop downhill on an indistinct path towards a footbridge.

Over the bridge and across a stile, we follow a yellow waymarker across fields towards farm buildings. Another stile and waymarker guide us along as the path curves to the right uphill to a metal gate; coming out on a farm track, we continue straight ahead between the farm buildings and follow the tarmac road towards **St Thomas' Church**. As the road drops down to **Garden House** (Wp.2 145M) we turn left (W) to retrace our outward route to the station. Those who left cars at **Ogden Reservoir** need to turn right up to **Hague Square** and follow the early part of the walk up **Bethany**, with the possibility of refreshment at **The Bull's Head**.

Passing the stone cottages, we swing left at **The Wheatsheaf**, through the small estate and turn right into **Railway Street** bringing us back to **Huddersfield Road** and the station on our left (Wp.1 151M). If you require liquid refreshment, continue down **Huddersfield Road** and turn right on **Newhey Road**; **The Waggon and Horses** is on the right - part of the J.W. Lees estate, the pub provides a warm if basic welcome, and fine local ales.

# 9 STRINES CIRCULAR

This circular walk around the picturesque **Goyt Valley** takes us along the **Peak Forest Canal** to **New Mills** above an impressive gorge. The **River Sett** joins the **Goyt** where the remains of old mills in the gorge are evident, and where you may see climbers practising their skills on the sheer rock faces. The gorge is crossed by several bridges and our route takes us over the **Millennium Walkway** (slightly vertiginous) before returning along the **Goyt**. Leaving the river, we climb up from **The Toll at Hague** bar to **The Fox** at **Brook Bottom**, a traditional pub serving Robinson's beers and snacks. Sitting by the fire among cobbler's lasts and horse brasses is one of the joys of a winter walk. Closing at 3 p.m. during the week, the **Fox** opens all day at weekends and bank holidays.

**Access by train:**
From **Manchester Piccadilly** and **Sheffield** to **Strines Station**.

**Access by car:**
From **Marple** or **New Mills**, turn into **Station Road** and park at the station.

**Short Walk Option**
Take the steps up to **New Mills Town Centre** from Wp.6, for a return by bus or train (1½ hours, 4 miles/6.5km).

Leaving **Strines Station** on the downhill ramp (Wp.1 0M) we turn left (W) to pass under the railway, heading downhill on the sett-paved road. Passing the car park exit, we follow the 'Goyt Way' fingerpost.

... passing a large dovecote ...

As the road levels out we ignore the **Goyt Way** to the right and follow the tarmac road behind **Strines Hall** and the entrance to **Whitecroft Farm** caravan site, passing a large dovecote in the mill pond before we cross the **River Goyt** on a bridge, built to replace one lost in the 1872 floods. Shortly after, we come to **Strines Road** (Wp.2 8M).

Crossing the road, we head up the rough track opposite, ascending past **Springfield Copse** and the cottage built by Peeres Swindles (1694), then on towards the canal bridge. Shortly before the bridge (Wp.3 13M) we turn right (NW) to climb steps up to the **Peak Forest Canal**. Turning left (SE), we amble along the towpath with the canal on our right, enjoying the views to our left and passing a variety of bridges, including a hand operated cantilever bridge and swing bridge (29M). Further along, we're met by the aroma from Matlow's sweet factory. After passing under bridge N°28, we go through a marina and the views once again open up. We pass the first of several

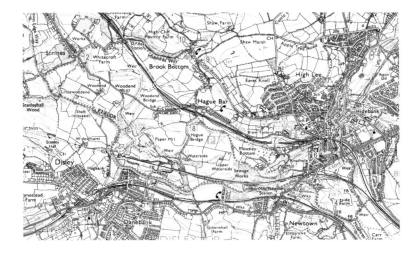

entrances to **Torrs Riverside Park** before rising up towards bridge N°29 (Wp.4 64M), where we leave the canal and take the downhill track straight ahead (SE).

**The railway viaduct**

As we descend, crossing three stiles, take time to look at the railway viaduct which we'll soon pass under on our return journey. Passing another entrance to **Torrs Riverside Park**, we cross the **River Goyt** on a metal footbridge, then turn left (NNW) on the **Goyt Way** where the path soon opens out into a track.

Turning left (NW) at the last building, we continue on the **Goyt Way** towards and under the viaduct, following the track (73M) to enter another section of the riverside park. With picnic benches by the river you may be tempted to stop for lunch, but don't worry if they are occupied as there are other places to stop as we pass through **Torrs**.

After 200 metres the track starts climbing, and we turn left on the path down by the river at a broken finger-post (Wp.5 79M). Our path takes us under a twin arched bridge and along the **Old Mill Leat**, once used to divert the river to power the mills in the gorge. Crossing the **Millward Memorial Bridge**, we swing left (NW) to head under the four-arched bridge. It's at this point that the **River Sett** joins the **Goyt** in the wonderful gorge below **New Mills**.

We soon pass signs and steps (Wp.6 86M) leading up to the **Heritage Centre**, and to the bus and railway stations in the town which provide a return route for those taking the Short Walk Option.

Following the path round from the steps, we come to the spectacular **Millennium Walkway**, which we cross as it swings around the rock face and the retaining wall for the railway above us. Leaving the walkway, we continue along the path by the river which soon climbs to a road (96M).

Keeping the river to our left, we follow the road which becomes a track after a short distance. Through a kissing-gate (Wp.7 99M) we turn left (S) on the **Goyt Way** and pass through a small copse. At a broad track we turn right over the stone steps by a gateway, still on the **Goyt Way**. Soon after the step stile we swing left off the track and stay by the river, following 'Goyt Way' signs. Along the way, on our right, we pass a marker for the 'Midshires Way' (109M) which informs us that we're 210 miles from the Ridgeway.

Staying by the river, we follow a 'Goyt Way' sign left as stroll through fields, passing through the first of three kissing-gates. Soon after the 3rd gate, we climb steps up on our right heading NW (Wp.8 118M), to follow the path as it zigzags up to a car park and picnic area. Leaving the car park we turn right uphill (NNW), and cross over the railway which brings us to **Hague Bar**. Crossing the road, we pass **Toll Cottage** as we head up **Hague Fold Road**, a stiff climb on the tarmac taking us up past **Lower** and **Upper Hague Fold Farms**, where the tarmac gives way to a rough track up to **Brook Bottom Road** (Wp.9 132M).

Turning left (NW), we come to a bench which unfortunately faces the wrong way, but does provide a place to catch our breath and enjoy the views. To the south is the **Cage** at **Lyme Park** and to the west (on a clear day) you should see the cooling towers at **Fiddler's Ferry**, and the mast on **Winter Hill** in the **West Pennines**.

Continuing NW, we look forward to refreshment at **The Fox Inn**, train and opening times permitting, as we stroll down the road. If not stopping at **The Fox** (Wp.10 137M), turn left (SW) just before reaching it to head down the rough tree-lined track on the **Goyt Way**. Coming down to the railway bridge, the ramp for the **Sheffield** platform is on our left. Pass under the bridge to come to the car park entrance which rises up sharp left to the **Manchester** platform (Wp.11 142M).

This pleasant stroll along a section of the **Peak Forest Canal** takes us through **Woodley Tunnel** (torch useful). **The Navigation Hotel** (Robinson's Beer) provides a refreshment opportunity as we leave the tunnel. From **Woodley** our route takes us into the **Tame Valley** and through the **Haughton Dale Nature Reserve**. We cross over the canal on **Captain Clarke's Bridge**, originally named **Wood End Bridge**, said to have been built to divert horse traffic so that the Clarke family wouldn't be disturbed by the barges. Being sheltered, it makes an ideal walk for those days when the weather doesn't tempt you out onto the hills.

**Access by train:**
From **Manchester Piccadilly** to **Romiley**, return from **Hyde** to **Manchester Piccadilly**

**Extension**
Extend the walk from **Hyde** to **Stalybridge** on the next walk (Walk 11).

**Short Walk Options**

**(a)** Finish the walk at **Woodley** (Wp.5), cutting times and distance in half.
Exit to **Woodley Station**: leave the canal at bridge N°11, turning left up steps and left again to cross the bridge. Over the bridge, swing left towards a triple garage and pass up the side of the garage (ENE) on a sett-paved track. At the top of the rise, cross **Gravelbank Road** towards **Hall Lane** to reach **Hyde Road**. **Woodley Station** (Wp.5) is just to the left on **Hyde Road**.

**(b)** Start the walk at **Woodley** (Wp.5), cutting times and distance in half.
To join the walk from **Woodley Station**: Cross **Hyde Road** (WSW) towards **Spring Bank Court** continue down **Gravelbank Road** and pass the **Olde House** on the right. Following the sett-paved road downhill to **Manor View**, swinging left and then right to cross a bridge and take the steps down to the canal. Turn left following the fingerpost to 'Hyde'.

Leaving **Romiley Station** (Wp.1 0M) via the subway, we cross **Stockport Road** heading SW to **Church Lane** and follow the fingerpost to 'Chadkirk Chapel'. Passing **St Chad's**, we continue onto **Chadkirk Road** and pass **Gregory Avenue**, following the road down to our right (WSW). We pass **Sterndale Road** before going under the canal, swinging left to continue by the terraced row, soon turning left (N) up steps (Wp.2 8M) and left again (WNW) at the canal to start our stroll along the **Peak Forest Canal**.

The first part of the walk needs little description, as we stay by the canal, enjoying the surroundings and the various bridges that we pass under. We come to a tunnel of about 200 metres in length (Wp.3 36M), and although a torch is useful here, it's not essential as we can literally see the light at the end of the tunnel as we enter it. The surface under foot is sound, and a guard rail ensures we don't fall into the canal. Coming out of the tunnel, we have the opportunity to take the ramp up to **Hyde Road** and **The Navigation Hotel** for refreshment.

Continuing along the canal, we pass under a railway bridge (N°12) before

coming to bridge N°11 (Wp.4 42M) which is the exit point for the Short Walk Option to **Woodley Station** (Wp.5).. A finger post points us on towards 'Hyde' and again the walk requires little description but takes us past two sections of the **Haughton Dale Local Nature Reserve**, an interesting area to explore.

**Haughton Dale Local Nature Reserve**

Soon after passing **Haughton Dale**, we rise up and cross over **Captain Clarke's Bridge**, to continue on the opposite side of the canal (74M). When we begin to enter the industrial environs of Hyde, and pass a finger post for 'Alexandra Street' towards the end of a large industrial building (Wp.6 76M), and just before the footbridge, we turn left up steps and cross over the bridge to continue with the canal on our right. Looking across the canal we can see the building erected by Joseph Adamson & Co. in 1885 and extended in 1898.

As we come to a kissing-gate bringing us out onto **Manchester Road**, take time to read the blue plaque detailing a mining disaster. Turning right (E) on **Manchester Road**, we pass **The Cheshire Ring** pub on the opposite side before turning right (SE) into **Great Norbury Street**. The steps up to **Hyde Central** (Wp.7 94M) are found just before the bridge on **Great Norbury Street**.

This linear walk takes us along the final stretch of the **Peak Forest Canal** into **Portland Basin** where it meets the **Ashton & Huddersfield Narrow** canals. The converted warehouse now houses a museum and café; a pleasant point to take a break and discover our industrial heritage. Leaving the basin we take a small diversion by the **River Tame** before we join the **Huddersfield Narrow Canal** at the first lock. The second half of the walk, though not through the prettiest of areas, is made worthwhile by the choice of several pubs and the buffet bar at **Stalybridge Station**.

**Access by train:**
From **Manchester Piccadilly** to **Hyde Central**. Return from **Stalybridge** to **Manchester Piccadilly** or **Victoria**.

Leaving **Hyde Central** (Wp.1 0M) we head down the ramp in a northerly direction. Passing under a bridge we continue towards **The Cheshire Ring**

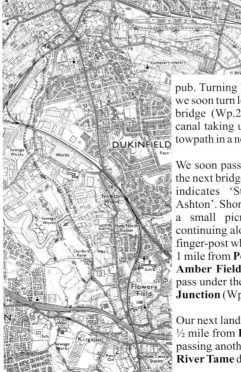

pub. Turning left on **Manchester Road** we soon turn left again onto the old canal bridge (Wp.2 6M) that curls over the canal taking us under the road onto the towpath in a northerly direction.

We soon pass under a motorway and at the next bridge (Wp.3 17M) a fingerpost indicates 'Stalybridge 4 miles via Ashton'. Shortly after the bridge we pass a small picnic area and car park, continuing along the canal past the next finger-post which informs us that we are 1 mile from **Portland Basin** and that **Jet Amber Fields** are to our left. We then pass under the railway at **Guide Bridge Junction** (Wp.4 37M).

Our next landmark is a cantilever bridge ½ mile from **Portland Basin**, then after passing another picnic area we have the **River Tame** down to our left.

**The footbridge at Portland Basin**

Soon after the next railway bridge we cross the **Tame** to head towards a footbridge at **Portland Basin**, bringing us to the end of the **Peak Forest Canal**. A visit to the museum and café in the converted warehouse offers the opportunity for education and refreshment, or you may want to continue with the route if a pint is your preferred tipple.

Leaving **Portland Basin**, our route takes us away from the canal which soon passes under an Asda store. Crossing the stone footbridge (1835) (Wp.5 51M) into **Portland Basin Marina** we head up the ramp lined by white rails, at the top of which we pass between buildings and continue (quickly!) through a messy industrial area on **Station Street**. At **Wharf Street** we turn left (E) and walk up the road towards the traffic lights where we cross the road and turn left, down to **Cooper Street** where we turn right, then crossing the road and head into **Cooper's Ride** (Wp.6 58M). The well-made path changes to a grass surface as we approach the railway viaduct and swing round by the river until we come out on **Bow Street** (Wp.7 66M). **The Park** pub on **Furnace Street** is less than 100 metres off route.

Turning left (E) at **Bow Street**, we cross both the river and the border between Lancashire and Cheshire on **Dukinfield Bridge**. Turning left down steps at the end of the industrial building, we rejoin the canal where we turn right (ESE) under the road bridge. Through the horse bridge with the fancy brick arch, we come to the first locks on the **Huddersfield Narrow Canal**.

**... through the horse bridge ...**

Our path takes us through the long narrow cutting of **Whitelands Tunnel**, once covered. Moving quickly through the industrial environs of **Ashton**, we pass two more locks and enjoy views ahead of **Hollingworthall Moor** before passing **Wray Mill** (Wp.8 81M). Continuing by the canal, we make our penultimate crossing of the **Tame** and pass under three more bridges (two of which are dated 2000 AD) as we make our way into **Stalybridge**; after the second bridge thus marked, (Wp.9 98M) we climb steps and turn left onto **Melbourne Street**. Crossing the **Tame** for the last time, we turn left (WNW) at **Market Street**, continuing past **Central Hall**, noticing the billiard tables on the wall. After the bus station we pass **The White House** and **Q Bar** in quick succession, both selling Hydes Beers, before we go under the railway and turn left into **Stalybridge Station** (Wp.10 105M) with its buffet bar - there's no shortage of refreshment choices as we finish our walk.

**Stalybridge** got its name when a bridge was built over the **Tame**, though today it has more than its fair share of bridges, most of which were rebuilt in 2000. There's a gentle ascent from **Stalybridge** to **Greenfield** on the **Huddersfield Narrow Canal** through pleasant countryside, and we pass through the **Scout Tunnel** (torch advisable) where rock bolts stabilise its roof.

The sculptures along the way were inspired by ideas from school children and designed by local artists, and the rest of the sculpture trail can be seen on Walk 13, Greenfield via Diggle.

With more than enough places to stop for refreshment, the route can be split into two shorter walks.

**Access by train:**
From **Manchester Victoria** or **Piccadilly** to **Stalybridge**, return from **Greenfield** to **Manchester Victoria** or **Piccadilly**.

---

**Short Walk Options**

Start or finish the walk from **Mossley** (Wp.6), cutting time/ distance in half.

**(a)** Finish at **Mossley Station**
Turn right (E) at the bridge dated 1865 (Wp.6) by the metal fence and walk up the rough track. At the end of the wall, reverse direction to cross over the canal and the **Tame**. Cross the road and take the right hand fork for the steep but short climb to **Mossley Station** (Wp.7), on our right across the road. With **The Commercial Hotel** opposite and further along on the right, **The Station Café** and **The Brittania**, which offers fine ales and reasonably priced food, there are plenty of choices for refreshment.

**(b)** Start at **Mossley Station**
Exit the station (Wp.7), turn right and cross **Manchester Road** at the pelican crossing, then head down **Mill Street** (NE) with fine views of the hills ahead. At the bottom of **Mill Street**, swing left across the **Tame** and the canal, before crossing the road and reversing direction at the end of the stone wall. Descending between wall and metal fence brings you to the canal; turn right (NNW) under the bridge, with the canal on the left.

---

Leaving **Stalybridge Station** (Wp.1 0M) by the ramp, we turn right (SE) into town. Passing the **Q Bar**, **White House** , bus station and **Central Hall**, we turn right (S) into **Melbourne Street**. After crossing the **Tame** we pass **Castle & Corporation Street** which brings us onto the canal bridge (Wp.2 6M), where we take the steps down to the right, then turn right again at the bottom under **Oldham's Bridge**, with the canal on our left. Passing our first lock, we continue through **Armentieres Square** heading towards the Tesco store.

Staying by the canal, we pass under a number of new bridges and come up by our second lock and the preserved remains of a canal-side crane (Wp.3 13M).

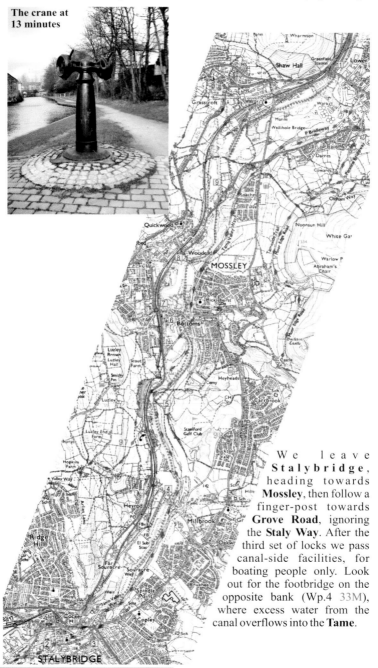

**The crane at 13 minutes**

We leave **Stalybridge**, heading towards **Mossley**, then follow a finger-post towards **Grove Road**, ignoring the **Staly Way**. After the third set of locks we pass canal-side facilities, for boating people only. Look out for the footbridge on the opposite bank (Wp.4 33M), where excess water from the canal overflows into the **Tame**.

**The Scout Tunnel**

We pass another three locks before arriving at and passing through the 188 metre-long **Scout Tunnel** (Wp.5 48M).

Continuing beside the canal, we pass one more bridge after lock N°12 before coming to another dated 1865 (Wp.6 64M), the exit to **Mossley** where the Short Walk Options leave/join us from Wp.7.

There are opportunities for refreshments here, and a picnic area ahead provides an alternative lunch stop.

Continuing under the 1865 bridge, we stroll on towards **Greenfield**. We cross the canal at lock N°14 (Wp.8 71M) with its small picnic area, and follow the finger-post for 'Roaches ½ mile', the canal now on our right and the **Tame** to the left. Our very gentle uphill stroll continues past **Roaches Lock** and a pub and canoe trail to our left, following a finger-post '1 ¾ miles to Greenfield'. Look out for the giant shuttle sculpture as we come to **The Tollemache Arms** (Robinson's Beers and bar snacks) whose garden overlooks the canal (Wp.9 86M).

'Hill Shelter'

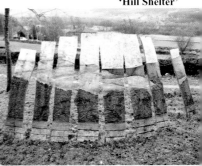

We cross the canal soon after the **Tollemache** at lock N°16 to continue with it on our left. Along the way we pass sculptures and see the antennae on **Wharmton Hill** above **Greenfield** ahead as we pass locks N°s 17, 18 and 19. At **Manns Wharf Bridge** (Wp.10 101M) we pass under **Well-i-hole Road** and come to the sculpture 'Hill Shelter' made of oak depicting the hills to our right.

The sight of the obelisk at **Pots and Pans** indicates that we're on the final stretch to **Greenfield**; the Phillip Greenwood stand at the rugby club, and the house with the lovely balcony above its conservatory are near our exit point. Leaving the canal by steps at the square-shaped bridge, we climb onto **Chew Road**. Turning left, we head west uphill and cross the road with care before swinging round the hairpin bend on the 'Oldham' sign. A few more steps and we pass **The Railway** pub (a Free House serving a range of beers and offering accommodation) to cross the road to **Greenfield Station** (Wp.11 114M).

# 13 GREENFIELD VIA DIGGLE

This varied route takes us along the **Huddersfield Narrow Canal** (a Site of Special Scientific Interest for its rare aquatic plants) to Britain's highest, longest and deepest canal tunnel at **Standedge** (3¼ miles long). There are sculptures along the way by local artists, inspired by local children, and the museum at **Uppermill** is worth visiting (see Diversion); and just before **Diggle**, there's a game of dice and hopscotch. We pass the entrance to three rail tunnels before starting our return route, a little more demanding but with efforts well rewarded.

Refreshments can be had at the **Cross Keys**, or try the range of beers at the **Church** inn brewed in the adjacent micro-brewery. Both serve food and have pleasant beer gardens.

The first **Saddleworth Church** (1215) was replaced with the present **St Chad's** built 1831; the village stocks (1698) are just by the gate. Visit the grave of William Bradbury (Bill o' Jack's) and his son Thomas (Tom o' Bill's) in the sadly overgrown graveyard, both brutally murdered at **Moorcock Inn** in 1832; an account of which (in verse) is found on the large raised stone in the graveyard's south-west corner. Our final leg along the disused rail line takes us back to **Greenfield** and more refreshments at **The Railway**. The only downside to this walk is that trains no longer stop at **Greenfield** on a Sunday.

**Access by train:**
From **Manchester Victoria** or **Piccadilly** with a change at **Stalybridge** to **Greenfield Station**. Return from **Greenfield** to **Manchester Victoria** or **Piccadilly** with a change at **Stalybridge**.

**Access by car:**
Parking is very difficult, especially at weekends. Try the **Brownhills Centre** or **Wool Road**. Better still, park at **Diggle** and do the uphill section first, then return to **Diggle** on the outward canal section.

**Short Walk Options**
**(a)** Walk to **Diggle** 2½ miles/4km and either retrace your steps from the **Diggle Hotel**, or return by bus from **Huddersfield Road**.

**(b)** Park at **Uppermill**, **Brownhill** or **Wool Road** and return from **Ryefields** (Wp.10), cutting the walk time and distance in half. Continuing straight ahead down **Ryefields Drive** to **High Street**. **Uppermill** is to the left, **Brownhills** and **Wool Road** right.

From **Greenfield Station** (Wp.1 0M) we cross the road towards the **Railway**, turning right (SSW) to head downhill. Following the road round the hairpin bend, we continue down **Chew Valley Road**, crossing the side road to continue straight on over the canal and taking the steps down to our left (Wp.2 3M). With the canal on our left and the obelisk at **Pots and Pans** up to the right, we start the very gentle uphill walk to **Diggle.**

Coming to **High Street Bridge** (Wp.3 13M) we climb steps and cross the road to rejoin the canal. There's an optional diversion to visit **Uppermill Museum** before rejoining the main route (see box). With the canal on our right we follow the finger post, 'Diggle 2 miles'. At the next bridge we cross the canal, following the fingerpost for 'Brownhills', soon passing a sculpture and stepping stones over the **Tame** (visitors to the museum rejoin us here).

**Diversion to Uppermill Museum**
Turn right at **High Street** (Wp.3) and walk the short distance to the museum. After your visit turn left and continue along **High Street**, turning left by the library, through the grounds and over the **Tame** on the **Stepping Stones**. Turn right to continue along the canal on the main route.

Sculpture and Stepping Stones

Passing lock N°22, we continue under the railway viaduct with its skewed arches (Wp.4 26M), and ascend to lock N°23, crossing the **Tame** for the last time as it swings away towards **Delph**.

The railway viaduct

Passing the **Brownhills Visitor Centre**, (toilets and picnic benches), we follow the fingerpost to the 'Transhipment Shed and Standedge Tunnel 1 ¼ miles'. Our path briefly swings away from the canal as we pass through a car park at the **Wool Road Transhipment Shed**.

Back by the canal, we pass under a bridge with the mural 'Past Present & Future' by Mark Whyatt. Approaching lock N°24 (Wp.5 33M) we ascend gently as locks come thick and fast. At lock N°29 is Shaw's 'Pallet Works' at the former **Dobcross Loom Works** built in 1861. The sculpture at Geoffrey Dickens' lock N°31, 'Through Heathered Hills' was designed in collaboration with the pupils from **Diggle Primary School**. At lock N°32 we cross the canal and pass a clever revolving dice and a hopscotch game before arriving at **Diggle Portal** (Wp.6 55M). Continuing through a car park we turn right (NE) on **Station Road** heading towards **Diggle Hotel** (Short Walk **(a)** returns from here). Turning right over the railway, we can see the three rail tunnel entrances before reaching the hotel.

From the **Diggle Hotel** we turn right (SSW) following the **Pennine Bridleway** (PBW) fingerpost to 'Uppermill 1 ¾ miles' into **Kiln Green** to **Lee Side Lane**. There's a bit of an up and down tarmac slog as we head out with the former **Diggle School**, now **St Chad's** on the left. With PBW markers guiding our way to 'Holly Grove Farm' we leave the PBW to follow the **Oldham Way**, soon leaving the tarmac as we head left (E) uphill between dry stone walls (Wp.7 74M). A short, stiff climb brings us out on **Running Hill Lane**. Turning left, we walk a short distance to follow the **Oldham Way** over a step stile on our right (S).

Now on an indistinct path, we see **Saddleworth Church** ahead and make our way as best we can down the dip, swinging left across a footbridge and then right, 'Oldham Way' markers guiding us along a clear path. Heading uphill along the line of a wall, we keep to the higher ground towards buildings, from where we continue (S), heading for and crossing a second stile to follow the line of a broken down wall. This takes us to a footbridge and our third stile, then by a clear path to the next stile (Wp.8 92M) and back onto tarmac.

With the church below us to our right we head uphill, leaving the **Oldham Way** as we turn right (SSW) at **Ivy Bank**. Ignoring a footpath to the right we pass **Briggs House** before following a footpath sign right (N) down steps into the car park of **The Cross Keys**, HQ for the Oldham Mountain Rescue Team, provided by J W Lees and the landlord of the time. The pub provides a warm welcome, good beer and food all week.

Leaving the car park at its bottom left hand corner, we head NNW down steps towards the church, then onto a clear path into the square housing **St Chad's** and **The Church Inn**, a micro-brewery selling a good range of beers and food. We head to the left of the church by the graveyard, with the Bradbury grave in its south-west corner, then turn left (W) at the end of the graveyard (Wp.9 101M) on a rough downhill path which descends to a stile. We stay by the fence as far as the next gap stile, where we turn immediately left through another gap stile. Ignoring the path up to the right at the next stile, we stay on the edge of the field; we're on the **Oldham Way** again.

Pausing to look back at **St Chad's** and **Pots and Pans**, we continue on the upper perimeter of the field. Passing through a stone gap stile, we head for the metal gate and pass through the kissing-gate on the right. A broad track takes us through a second kissing gate to come out at **Ryefields** (Wp.10 115M; Short Walk Option **(b)** returns from here), where we turn left (SW) on the **Saddleworth Linear** bridleway, following PBW waymarkers as we head south, now following the line of a long-abandoned railway. We veer left still following the PBW as we head towards a school and across two wooden bridges that replaced the original railway bridges on this pleasant track. Passing through the car park at **Saddleworth Swimming Pool** we continue on the PBW until we emerge at **Higher Arthurs** (Wp.11 137M).

We turn right (NW) into **South Lane** and zigzag left, right, left through a small housing estate, then walk down **Shaw Street** which brings us to **Chew Valley Road**. Turning right (NW), we pass **The Wellington**. Across the **Tame** and the canal, it's over **Chapel road** to head uphill and right, round the hairpin bend to **The Railway** inn and **Greenfield Station** opposite (Wp.1 149M).

# 14 MARPLE TO STRINES VIA ROMAN LAKES

From **Marple Station** we head through the picturesque village of **Marple Bridge** towards **Roman Lakes**. The lakes, originally built as mill lodges, fed Samuel Oldknow's Mill, long since demolished. Family owned for more than 100 years, **Roman Lakes Leisure Park** provides a number of attractions; prize winning carp and pike attract fishermen, though rowing is no longer allowed on the lake. In addition to refreshments, the café offers a range of publications on the area for walkers, mountain bikers and naturalists. Along the way we take a break to stand on the 17th century Roman packhorse bridge over the **River Goyt**.

2 | 1H | 2.8 miles/4½km | 106m / 90m | 2

**Access by train:** from **Manchester Piccadilly** to **Marple Station**

Return from **Strines** to **Manchester Piccadilly** (not Sundays). On Sundays, return to **Marple** by bus, or extend the walk via **Mellor** for a great day's walking, and return from **Marple**.

**Access by car:** Park at **Marple Station**. Return to **Marple** by train or bus from **Strines**.

We leave **Marple Station** (Wp.1 0M), crossing the car park to our left. At **Station Road** we turn left (NE) and head downhill towards the traffic lights. Crossing the road at the lights, we follow the sign to **Mellor** into **Town Street** heading south-east. Taking the right hand pavement we stroll through **Marple Bridge** with the **Goyt** down to our right. Shortly after passing **The Royal Scot** (a Robinson's pub), we leave the pavement and continue gently uphill on **Low Lea Road** (Wp.2 6M) past renovated cottages, views across the valley soon opening up.

Ignoring a sign to 'Longhurst Lane', we continue along the track and start a gentle descent with **Cage Hill** at **Lyme Park** ahead of us. Part way down, the track changes to **Bottoms Mill Road**, bringing us to a junction (Wp.3 18M) where we turn left (SSE) on **Lakes Road**. At the next junction we swing right, following the sign for 'Roman Lakes'; on our left are the splendid buildings of **Bottoms Hall**. The track soon brings us to the entrance to **Roman Lakes** (Wp.4 26M).

As we continue south on the broad track, the roar of the **Goyt** soon becomes audible as it tumbles over a weir. Passing under the railway viaduct (built 1865), we come to the tollhouse, once home to both the toll and the sluice keepers; the latter controlled the water flow from the river to the mill lodges. Ignoring a footpath to 'Mellor and Cobden Edge' we stroll on to **Roman Lodge** and **Strawberry Hill** (Wp.5 33M).

Roman Bridge

The finger-post to 'Strines Road' indicates our short diversion to **Roman Bridge** before returning to the track, the sound of the rushing river accompanying us as we continue our stroll (SSE) before swinging away from the water, the track now leading us towards the railway and through a tunnel (Wp.6 42M).

The track takes us through **Richmond Farm**, although the sign over the door says 'Windybottom'! Staying on the track, we ignore a bridleway on the left and continue as the track gets rougher and gently rises up. We cross a stile with the railway down to our right, and at the second stile (Wp.7 53M) our route drops into a lane.

We turn right (SW) towards **Greenclough Farm** where we swing left (S), ignoring the path ahead to stay on the tarmac lane following a 'Goyt Way' marker. Swinging right and then left as we cross the railway, the track heads downhill bringing us to a T-junction where we turn left to head up the sett-paved road. Turning right by the **Goyt Valley** Information board takes us into **Strines Station** car park and Platform 1 (Wp.8 59M).

There are no refreshments available at **Strines**, unless you fancy continuing under the railway and up the steep rough track to **The Fox Inn**, about 12 minutes climb on a rough track, which closes at 15.00 during the week but opens all day at weekends and bank holidays.

Starting with a stiff climb, this pleasant walk takes us through **Brook Bottom Conservation Area**. Passing **The Fox Inn** a little too soon for refreshment, we head out to cross **Mellor Moor**. **Primrose Lane** offers wide open views as we stroll along what must have been the equivalent of a motorway in the days of horse and cart transport. From the moor we head to **Mellor Church**, prominently placed above the village. Information on the Mellor Archaeological Dig and a reconstructed stone-age dwelling can be found here. A bench by the church entrance has fine views and provides an ideal place to enjoy a picnic. Our route takes us on to **Linnet Clough**, home of Greater Manchester Scouts. As we head down the cart track the carpet of *ramsons* (wild garlic) are a wonderful sight in the spring, but the smell may not please everyone. We finish the walk through **Marple Bridge** with plenty of refreshment opportunities before heading back to the station.

As trains don't stop at **Strines** on a Sunday, do consider doing Walk 14, 'Marple to Strines' first as the two walks together make a superb day's walking. Alternatively, park at **Strines Station**, complete this walk, and return to your car on the **Marple** to **Strines** walk.

**Access by train:**
From **Manchester Piccadilly** to **Strines**. Return to **Piccadilly** from **Marple**

We leave **Strines Station** (Wp.1 0M) by the downhill ramp and swing left and right before the bridge, following a bridleway sign. Our steady uphill climb on tarmac takes us past **Cliff Farm Cottage** (8M), the **Cage** at **Lyme Park** coming into sight after passing the next cottage. Enjoying the views across the **Goyt Valley**, we start to drop down into **Brook Bottom** as we pass the **Primitive Methodist School Chapel** (1874), following the road round to pass **The Fox Inn** (Wp.2 18M).

Ignoring the path to our left and the **Goyt Way** on the right, we pass a phone box and leave the village. A little further up the road we turn left at a green bench (Wp.3 20M NE) on a rough uphill track between dry stone walls. With **Lantern Pike** ahead, we continue uphill, ignoring paths off right and left as we pass the golf course. As we approach **Apple Tree Lane**, **New Mills Golf Club House** is to our right, and we turn left (N) into **Castle Edge Road**. We soon turn left (W) again towards **Stonypiece Farm**, following a footpath sign (Wp.4 33M), the road swinging right (NNW).

Passing the first gate by a stile, we ignore a path to the left and continue towards a metal gate, leaving the road just before the gate to cross the stile on the right across the verge, heading NNW with the fence on our left. The boundary changes to a stone wall and we follow the fingerpost straight ahead, our barely discernible path crossing tussocks to bring us to a broken down section of wall (Wp.5 42M), and a stile into the next field. With the wall on our right we cross this field and cross another stone step stile. Continuing NNE we head across the field (which can be muddy) and cross a stile into **Primrose**

**Lane** (Wp.6 51M). Enjoying the panoramic views from the stile, we turn left (NNW) between dry stone walls. Ignoring **Black Lane** to our left we continue along **Primrose Lane**, now broad and straight as we cross **Mellor Moor**. As the track comes out on **Bogguard Road** (Wp.7 59M) we continue straight ahead towards **Higher** & **Lower Birchenough Farms**, following a fingerpost. At the farm we pass to the right of a curved, corrugated farm building onto a short stretch of firm path before crossing a stone step stile into a field. Keeping the field boundary on our left, we head towards **Mellor Church** in the distance, passing through a gap stile at the bottom of the field (Wp.8 67M) and following the footpath sign towards and then alongside a stone wall ahead, keeping the wall to our right.

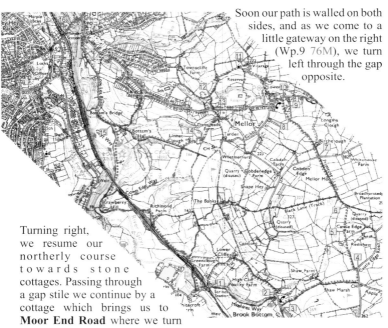

Soon our path is walled on both sides, and as we come to a little gateway on the right (Wp.9 76M), we turn left through the gap opposite.

Turning right, we resume our northerly course towards stone cottages. Passing through a gap stile we continue by a cottage which brings us to **Moor End Road** where we turn left (Wp.10 79M SW) towards **The Devonshire Arms** (winner of its brewery's best kept bar and cellar award) which makes a pleasant refreshment stop. There's also a public toilet just past the pub on **Church Lane**.

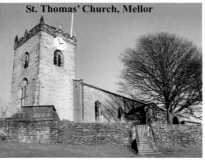

St. Thomas' Church, Mellor

We turn right (NNW) just before the pub and head downhill on a rough track, passing houses and climbing again to come onto **Church Lane**. We continue uphill as the road swings left, and a sign asks us to use the footpath which comes to an end by **Mellor Parish Centre** where we continue up the road. Our route turns left (WSW) at the end of the graveyard, taking us into **St. Thomas' Church**. You may want to take time here to read about the dig or visit the stone-age dwelling over a stile by the building ahead. We continue to the early 19th century church (Wp.11 89M), a bench before its entrance providing a fine view and an ideal place to stop.

Leaving the church (WSW) down steps between railings, we pass through a gate and head downhill, across a field to a stile. Taking a look back at the church, we cross the stile and continue with a fence to the right to reach another stile. A few steps to our left, we pass through a gap stile into **Knowle Farm**. Turning left (SSW) we head downhill for a short distance to find an unmarked path to our left (Wp.12 97M) which takes us through a gap and down steps

Following the ivy-clad wall down towards a stream we cross a footbridge and climb back up the other side of the small valley. After a short climb our path descends to cross **Longhurst Lane** (Wp.13 103M), following a fingerpost for 'Strines'. The tarmac track soon gives way to gravel, and the path swings right as we head for a metal gate. Across a stile, we follow the clear track to the next gate and stile, from w here we follow the boundary on our right as best we can, as the path is often muddy. Crossing a stile, we follow the left hand boundary but soon swing away as the path down to the next stile becomes clear. Following holly bushes to the next gate, we pass through a gap stile, cross a stream and swing right on a gentle uphill gradient to reach a scout activity area where we follow the waymarker (Wp.14 112M) left towards the scout hut.

Turning right (W) before the huts, we continue through **Linnet Clough Scout Camp** and pass their equipment storage barn. Ignoring a tarmac road to the left we turn right (WNW) before the next camping field, following a fingerpost to 'Marple & Marple Bridge'. A stone pavement on the left soon peters out and we follow a rough track down through the **Clough**. **Linnet Clough** is carpeted with *ramsons*, typical of damp ancient woodland. We soon leave the **Clough** behind as we come down to **Old Hall Farm** and a sign for 'Roman Lakes' (Wp.15 137M).

N.B. If you left your car at **Strines** you need to turn left here onto **Lakes Road**, follow the **Marple** to **Strines** route from Wp.3.

Continuing our route, we ignore a sign to the lake and carry straight on with a small lake to our right. As we pass a small channel of dressed stone (a remnant of Samuel Oldknow's Mill) we come to a fork where we go right into **Bottoms Mill Road** and climb the gentle hill, the road soon changing to **Low Lea Lane**. Ignoring a footpath to 'Longhurst Lane' we finish the climb and then drop down by a converted farm building on our left. The lane takes us down past cottages and brings us out at **Marple Bridge** where we turn left to head through the shop-lined street passing **The Royal Scot** (Robinson's), where refreshments can be had in pleasant surroundings while watching the traffic chaos, normal in this village. Other refreshment opportunities are **Christie's Coffee Shop and Tea Room**, **The Norfolk Arms** and **The Midland** as we turn left at the lights.

Leaving the village, we cross the road at the lights and turn left to head uphill to the station. Passing **Brabyns Park** and **St. Martin's Church** on the climb, we come to the station car park, turn right, and head for the ticket office (Wp.16 158M).

Our route starts gently uphill but soon drops down into **Brabyn's Park** and along the **River Goyt**. We pass the confluence of the rivers **Etherow** and **Goyt** to head over a preserved iron bridge on the stroll to **Etherow Country Park** alongside what could be the shortest canal in the country (½ mile/0.8km) where you can marvel at the efforts of George Andrews (or rather, his workers) in building a spectacular curved weir to feed the canal from the **Etherow**. Our route then starts a steady uphill climb of 150 metres in 1¼ miles up the side of the valley, enjoying stunning views of the **Dark Peak**.

Dropping back down to the river through **Back Woods**, you'll see the dye vats at **Hodge Fold** which dumped multi-coloured effluent into the river, much cleaner these days. One last climb brings us onto the platform at **Broadbottom Station**. Refreshments can be had in **Broadbottom**, but the extra effort may have you thinking the train home is a better option.

**Access by train:** from **Manchester Piccadilly** to **Marple**. Return from **Broadbottom** to **Manchester Piccadilly**

We leave **Marple Station** (Wp.1 0M), heading across the car park (SSE) to climb the steps to **Station Road**. Turning right (SW), we walk uphill to the end of the stone wall and turn right (NW), following a footpath sign. This path takes us alongside tennis courts, at the end of which we swing left onto a broader track. Turning right (NE) before some steps, we cross the railway ignoring a track to the right. We follow the well made track (NNW) downhill and turn left (NNW) onto a tarmac track. As we approach a building we turn left and follow the fence around it to the rear where we drop down to the right and follow the path as it descends into **Brabyn's Park**.

After the descent we follow a finger-post left (WNW) on the **Goyt Way**, heading towards the **Goyt** and following the path (ENE) round past benches. As the field gives way to a track look out for the **Etherow** joining the **Goyt** on the opposite bank. Approaching a house, we turn left (NNE) following GW marker towards a footbridge (Wp.2 26M). Taking time to read the history of the bridge (built at Salford Iron Works 1813), we then cross the **Goyt**. and head north from the bridge to follow the broad track of **Rollins Lane** to **Compstall Road** (Wp.3 34M)

Turning left (N) following the GW finger-post, we head towards **The George** (a Robinson's pub), and cross the road to continue north, crossing the **Etherow** and passing **Compstall Mill**. At the end of mill car park (Wp.4 38M) we turn right (E) into **Etherow Country Park** following the 'Valley Way' sign. Heading across the car park towards the visitors' centre we continue east, taking a small path at **Warren Lodge** with what turns out to be a canal on our right.

At the first footbridge (Wp.5 46M) we cross the canal right then left, to continue east. With the **Etherow** down to our right (note an information board for **Erncroft Wood** and the history of the canal), we cross a footbridge and walk through the picnic area towards the weir (Wp.6 55M) then head west towards a small building that houses sluice gear, used to feed the canal from the river. We go towards a cottage (ignoring the track, which would take you back down the canal) and swing right between the cottage and toilets.

The sluice gear

Following an 'Etherow Goyt Valley Way' marker we go right to start climbing up the valley. Passing **Keg Woodlands**, the uphill slog is rewarded with bird song. Ignoring a fingerpost to 'Keg Wood' we reach a perfect picnic spot with two benches. From here, on a clear day, you can see the distant **Longdendale Valley** in the **Dark Peak**. Having feasted our eyes we continue a short distance up the tarmac to a fingerpost (Wp.7 76M), leaving it to follow the **Valley Way**. We turn left (W) and pass a small, seated shelter; it may not boast views, but could be most welcome on a rainy day as an alternative lunch stop. Continuing our climb, we pass a small sign on the gatepost informing us that we are on a concessionary path. The clear path leads us along the upper edge of **Mortin Clough** which we leave, crossing two stiles in quick succession. Ignoring a third stile to our left we continue between hedge and fence to the next stile (Wp.8 83M). Turning left (N) we soon come on to tarmac, following a 'Valley Way' sign to continue north, enjoying excellent views as we reach the small cluster of buildings of **Beacom Houses**, (Wp.9 91M).

We pass through the farm yard to continue on a rough track, **Beacom Lane**, the masts at **Werneth Low** to the left and **Longdendale** ahead. Climbing towards the masts with a golf course on our left (now on tarmac again), we follow a fingerpost right (Wp.10 99M NNE) which takes us into **Werneth Low Park** towards **Cock Brow**. With the field boundary on our right, **Coombes Edge Rocks** is visible on the far side of the valley.

Longdendale

At a kissing-gate we leave the park behind (Wp.11 103M), turning right (SE) to start descending to **Etherow**. Following the finger-post to 'Mottram Old Road' we head down the concrete track. The track changes to tarmac, levels out and we come to some buildings (Wp.12 108M) where we turn right (E) following a finger-post for 'Back Woods'. This narrow path soon has us passing through a tunnel of holly bringing us over a track which crosses our route and over a stile (Wp.13 112M). As we follow the **Etherow Goyt Valley Way** (EGVW) our path soon becomes rough; you'll need to watch your step as there's a high 'stumble factor' on this section. At the next metal gate we cross a stile and stay on the EGVW heading east, following the broad track as it veers right towards a stile (Wp.14 118M) the EGVW marker leading us ahead to the next stile.

A clear path guides our descent on the upper edge of the **Clough** bringing us to steps down to a stream.

A footbridge takes us over the stream (Wp.15 128M), and we climb a few steps towards a fingerpost where we turn right (E) towards buildings. Once through the gate another fingerpost guides us right (SSE) to **Hodge Fold** on a rough track. After the buildings the track leads us back to the babble of the **Etherow** on our right. Ignoring a fingerpost to 'Woodseats' we continue to **Hodge Fold**, the track leading us away from the river, though there's a small feeder stream to our right. At the white building of **Leyland Farm** we continue straight ahead and across the stream, turning right again on tarmac (ENE) as we pass **Old Croft** with the initials 'RW, MW, GW' and the date '1676' on the wall.

**Hodge Fold Dye Vats**

The road soon swings left (Wp.16 141M) but we continue on the EGVW onto a rough track. At a fork we take the lower right hand track bringing us to **Hodge Fold Dye Vats** (Wp.17 145M), opened in 1805 by Samuel Matley and closed in 1913. We continue up the track to start the final climb to the station. At the top of the first rise we come to a row of three-storey cottages, and curving back and up at the first cottage we head NNW at the side of **Summer Cottage**.

Turning left at the rear of the cottage, we follow the yellow marker on the telegraph pole, heading uphill. Rising up to steps, we turn right to take the last uphill steps onto the platform at **Broadbottom Station** (Wp.18 159M).

# 17 MILLS HILL TO NEWHEY VIA TANDLE HILL

If you're not familiar with the South Pennines, there can be no better introduction than this walk. Although we don't start in the Pennines, we finish at the very foot of them. The climax of the walk provides the best panoramic view I know of. We travel back in time along one of the most important trade routes between Lancashire and Yorkshire. Starting at **Manchester Victoria** we travel on the rail route to **Leeds** (opened 1839) to arrive at **Mills Hill,** joining the **Rochdale Canal** (1804) which runs from the city centre to **Sowerby Bridge**. Along the way we cross the **River Irk**, reputed to be **Manchester**'s most feared river for its tendency to flash flooding. The opening chapter of the novel 'The Manchester Man', describes just such an event.

Leaving the canal, we head up **Thornham Lane** with its toll bar cottage, and **Tandle Hill Tavern** which has served refreshment en route since the 17th century. A friend once commented on how rough the road was to which the landlord responded, "We like it like that - it keeps the riffraff away." - and where else can you order free range eggs with your pint? Leaping forward in time we see the M62 opened in the 1970s as it cuts a swathe across the Pennines to the highest point of any motorway in England.

Apart from a tricky bit where you'll need a compass at the least, or better still, a GPS to get down into **Newhey**, most of the walk is easy going on gentle uphill tracks and paths. I feel sure that after this walk you'll be itching to head south and follow the rest of the walks as they take us northwards and westward as we circumambulate the **South Pennine Horseshoe**.

3 | 2¾ H | 6.9 miles/11km | 299m / 167m | 3

**Access by train:** From **Manchester Victoria** to **Mills Hill Station** and return to **Victoria** from **Newhey Station**.

**Access by car:** Park at **Mills Hill**, and return by train from **Newhey**.

We leave **Mills Hill Station** (Wp.1 0M) on the downhill ramp and turn right (E) under the railway on **Middleton Road**. We cross **Mills Hill Road** by the traffic lights and turn right on the far side of the canal bridge down steps. At the canal we turn right (N) under the road and stroll along the towpath. Passing steps up to **The Rose of Lancaster** (4M, Lees Beers and a pleasant conservatory restaurant), we follow the towpath as it loops around the contours.

Ignoring steps on the right down to the benign-looking **River Irk (**Wp.2 8M), we continue on the towpath to our first set of locks, N°63, noticing the plaques along the way, each with a 'fisherman's tale'. After lock N°61 we pass under a railway bridge (known locally as 'Th'iron Donger', see the photo on the next page), the monument on **Tandle Hill** soon visible on our right. After two more locks we pass under a skewed arch bridge.

With locks coming thick and fast now, we pass a *winding-hole* and notice a roller on the corner of the bridge as we go through a tunnel and come up behind **The Ship Inn** at lock N°55. We leave the towpath at lock N°54, **Slattocks Top Lock** (Wp.3 43M), taking the downhill path to the first of several **Rochdale** roads that we'll cross.

**'Th'iron Donger', after lock N°61**

**St. John's Church**

Crossing the road and continuing northerly we soon come to **Thornham Lane** where we turn right (ENE) up the very bumpy road. Look out for the notice board just after the **Richard Bentley Smalley Memorial Hall** detailing the Thornham Woodlands Project. The steady climb up the lane takes us past **Toll Bar Cottage**, **St John's Church** and the Primary School, surely one of the nicest locations to receive an education around **Manchester**.

As the road swings right and left to cross the motorway spur between **Oldham** and **Rochdale**, we have views of **Winter Hill** and **Holcombe Moor**.

Just a little further and we come to the **Tandle Hill Tavern** nestled between farm buildings (Wp.4 73M). Turning right (SSE) just before the tavern, we (unfortunately) head towards the aroma of the farm yard, and avoiding the slurry heap take the path straight on over a stile, following the field boundary for a short distance until we see the memorial and head for the gap in the fence slightly to our left.

From the gap our path takes us up steps to the memorial, trig point and toposcope on **Tandle Hill** (Wp.5 79M). The toposcope tells us we are 7½ miles from the city centre and details the surrounding view, our first real sight of the hills and moors we are to walk.

**Blackstone Edge from Tandle Hill (Wp.5)**

But there's more to come, so we leave the hill heading ENE on a sandy track that soon changes to gravel, following an 'Oldham Way' marker taking us down by **Oozewood Clough**.

It's important to keep track of time here as we leave the park through a metal gate and continue down the path until we come to an easy-to-miss 'Oldham Way' fingerpost (Wp.6 85M) pointing right (E) across a field.

The path is indistinct at first, but becomes clearer as we drop down to a stile. We continue east to the next stile and follow the field boundary heading towards white buildings. Just before the buildings we come to a gate and drop down to a lane taking us up to the buildings. The 'OW' marker on the gatepost appears to point to the centre of the earth as we continue past the stables on the red brick road. The driveway drops down to **Highgate Drive** and brings us to the second **Rochdale Road** (Wp.7 97M)

Crossing the road into **Springfield Lane**, by The Pleasant Inn, we hurry on through a housing estate until we come to **The Turk's Head** where we turn left (N) into **Castleton Road**, cross the road and turn right (ENE) after bungalow N°186 (Wp.8 104M) into **Pit Lane**. A 'Rochdale Way' marker points us down the track (sometimes very muddy) to find the third **Rochdale Road** (Wp.9 116M) to turn right (ESE) for a short uphill slog on tarmac. Crossing the road just before the **Collier's Return**, we head north-east over a stile (Wp.10 122M) with an 'Oldham Way' marker, then following the boundary on our left to another stile, following the **Oldham Way**, the boundary now to our right. We continue over and through stiles still following the boundary until we come to an 'Oldham Way' finger post (Wp.11 137M) at the corner of a field where we turn left (N), **Winter Hill** and **Holcombe Moor** ahead. The path swings onto a north-easterly course through a couple of gap stiles. At the second gap stile where the 'Oldham Way' points right (Wp.12 141M), we take a short diversion. After following the **Oldham Way** for a short distance we look for a trig point on the right (Wp.13 144M) over a stone wall and make our way over to it.

This is the climax of our walk, and no photograph can do this view justice. Laid out around us are the hills and moors that we shall discover in the rest of this book: the **South Pennine Horseshoe**. Sweeping round from **Winter Hill** in the west we have **Holcombe**, **Knowl Hill**, **Watergrove** and **Windy Hill** on through **Saddleworth** - and way off over **Kinder** into the **Peak District**. Below us, the metropolis of **Greater Manchester** stretches away into the **Cheshire** and **Lancashire** plains.

Now we come to the tricky bit. We need to make our way down to **Newhey**, and we can see where we want to get to, but the path is not so clear, and there are no waymarkings to guide us. Firstly, we retrace our steps to the last fingerpost (Wp.12 147M) from where we head north-west towards a dry stone wall, but there are several, so trust your GPS or compass. We then follow this wall to the right (NNE); it's broken down in parts but the line is clear.

As we come to a rough track we swing NW and head for another wall (Wp.14 151M) where we swing right (NNE), heading downhill with the wall on our left. Skirting round the hollow as we come towards the end of the wall we swing NNW where it has crumbled away. The path isn't clear at first, but becomes clearer as we head downhill, moving away from the wall on the left, aiming at a point where the M62 disappears from sight. Once again we start to follow the line of a broken down wall which brings us to a very clear track (Wp.15 156M).

Tricky bit over, we turn right (ENE) downhill with **Ellenroad** chimney and engine house to our left. At the bottom of the track we pick up speed as we pass through the grotty farm yard and cross a stream. Past **Ellenroad**, we continue by the old mill cottages on **Bentgate Street**, crossing it to continue to **Newhey Road** (Wp.16 151M) and turn right (SE), crossing the road to head into **Newhey**. After passing **The Waggon and Horses** (a warm welcome and Lees Beer) we turn left (ENE) at **Cotton Tree Corner**. A stone pillar commemorates the inn of the same name, sadly long gone.

We pass the former Newhey Educational Institute, now **Newhey Lodge**, cross the road and continue to the ramp down onto **Newhey Station** (Wp.17 162M). With its single track, trains in either direction will return you to **Manchester Victoria** on a loop line. But for those with a real thirst and a taste for the quirky, cross **Newhey Road** (Wp.16) and turn left (NNW) slightly uphill. Follow the pavement round to **The Free Trade Tavern** on the right. From 16.00 on Friday, Saturday and Sunday a free buffet is supplied, and the warm welcome is there every day of the week. The first time I visited the gents here, I thought I'd made a mistake - curtains, flowers and a choice of soaps is not what you expect in this part of the world. I'm told the range of products in the ladies is even more extensive.

This is a walk of amazing contrasts; from wide open views as far as the **Welsh Hills**, in the far distance over the **Manchester** metropolis, to secluded woodland dells. Starting at **Woodley**, we pass from leafy suburb walking on old tracks to the beautifully restored hamlet of **Back O'th Hill**. Then we climb up to **Werneth** (from the Celtic *Warnet*, "a place growing with alders"), valued at 10 shillings (50p) as waste land in the Doomsday Book. At **Hackingknife** we visit the **Cenotaph** and the first of two toposcopes where binoculars come in handy. Our route from **Werneth** takes us down into the tranquillity of two woodland areas for a flavour of the countryside several hundred years ago when **Longdendale** was a forest. Finally, we pass three-storey weavers' cottages at **Summerbottom** built in the 1780s, before our final climb to **Broadbottom** Station.

3    2¼ H    5.6 miles/9km    268m / 242m    1

**Access by train:** from **Manchester Piccadilly** to **Woodley Station**. Return from **Broadbottom** to **Manchester Piccadilly**.

We leave **Woodley Station** (Wp.1 0M) on the uphill ramp and turn right (SSE) along **Station Road**. Turning left (ESE) at **Werneth Road** we walk through the leafy suburbs of **Woodley**. Carrying straight on at the mini roundabout we arrive at **Pennine Road** (Wp.2 9M). Crossing the road into **Hillside Road** we pass **St Mark's Cricket Club** and soon leave the suburbs behind as we continue up the private road. Rising up, we follow a finger post (Wp.3 16M) to **Back O'th Hill** and pass through a gateway marked **Hillside House** and **Wood Lane Farm**.

Hillside House

Still climbing, we pass **Hillside House** on the cobbled road and continue straight on at **Wood Lane Farm** over a step stile. Swinging left (NNW) to pass **Back O'th Hill Farm**, we drop down slightly to a finger-post (Wp.4 21M), **Jodrell Bank** visible (on a clear day) to our left, the **Manchester** metropolis ahead and **Winter Hill** beyond the city.

Turning right (NE) towards **Gee Cross** we stroll along the green lane enjoying panoramic views as we swing round towards **Hollingworthall Moor** ahead of us. Passing a gate, we come to a junction and two finger-posts, turning right (Wp.5 26M SE) to follow the **Broadbottom** sign, the second post confirming we are heading for **Werneth Low**.

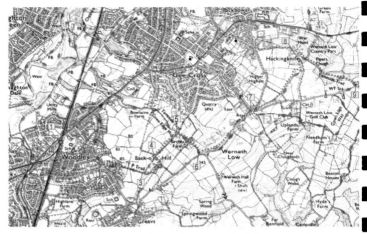

Crossing a stile we head up the (muddy) path towards buildings. Passing between the houses and stable we come to a broad concrete track and continue uphill to the next fingerpost where we turn left (Wp.6 31M ENE) towards **Werneth Low Country Park**. Heading towards the radio masts our path is separated from the road by a stone wall on our right. Stopping to look out across **Manchester**, we can pick out such land marks as the **Imperial War Museum** at **Salford**, the **CIS** building in the city centre, and the **Commonwealth Stadium**, now **Manchester City** football ground. The well-made path soon ends and we follow any one of several paths all heading the same way. Coming to a fence, we go through the gap stile back onto a well made path taking us towards **The Hare and Hounds**. The path leads us onto tarmac near the **Hyde Squash and Cricket Club** and we continue along the road until we come to a junction (Wp.7 42M).

**The Cenotaph**

At the junction we turn by the red phone box, into **Werneth Low Road** and soon reach **Quarry Car Park** where we swing left (NNE) across the road and follow the fingerpost to the **Cenotaph**. Passing through two gates and a picnic area we have the option to go to the **Visitor Centre**. (N.B. With limited opening times, it's a risky choice to go the quarter mile down hill only to find it closed, so check the opening times beforehand.)

Carrying on along the well-defined paths, we continue as the path twists and turns on its way to the monument (Wp.8 55M).

You'll want to spend some time here; maybe have lunch if it's not too windy; looking at the monument and the toposcope which details the hills, moors and other points of interest.

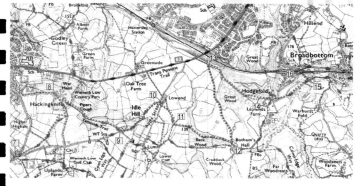

Taking account of the time spent enjoying the view, we retrace our steps to the point where the track splits. Taking the left hand fork we head east with **Kinder Scout** ahead of us. Passing through two gates we cross a track and continue easterly following the clear path as it twists and dips on the way out of the park. Coming out onto tarmac (Wp.9 66M) we follow a yellow waymarker on a metal post to go left (ENE) by a stone wall on our right. A short diversion across the car park takes us to a second, more detailed toposcope on **Idle Hill**; it's worth taking time to get to know these hills and moors. Returning to the wall we continue (ENE),following the path towards a bungalow.

From the back of the bungalow we follow the well defined path to drop down through heather. As we come to a wall we follow a 'Trans Pennine Trail' (TPT) marker through a gap stile heading south on an indistinct path across the field to the hedge line. Following the hedge down we have a very overgrown track down to our left. Passing giant holly bushes, we ignore the gap and after the second holly bush, turn left over a well hidden stile. Dropping down a few steps we join the track, which is now clear, and continue to the road (Wp.10 79M).

Turning right (SSE,) we go a short distance to a stile on the left and follow the TPT marker into the field. Heading for the wooden power line pole and then a stile we follow the TPT along a farm track.

At the next opening we turn left (Wp.11 84M ESE), following the TPT with a hedge to our right as we head downhill. A yellow marker leads us into **Back Woods** at the bottom of the field and across a stile to follow the path down towards a stream. Meandering through the woods, we cross several footbridges; with only the babbling stream for company, it's hard to believe just how close we are to housing estates and busy roads. After crossing a stile, our fifth footbridge and another stile lead us out of **Back Woods**; we see steps to our right, the route in from **Marple** via **Etherow**. At a finger post beyond a gate (Wp.12 96M) we turn left (N) to **Great Wood**.

Our itinerary takes us through **Great Wood Local Nature Reserve** which is the largest ancient woodland in **Tameside**, once part of the **Longdendale Forest**.

Crossing a cattle grid as we walk up the broad track, **Coombes Edge** is to our right and we enjoy views into **Longdendale**. Further along, the **Cenotaph** at **Werneth** is visible to the left as we continue to the next cattle grid and turn right (Wp.13 107M ESE) and cross a stile into **Great Wood** to follow a clear path. Depending on time of year you'll find campion, bluebells and wood sorrel as the path leads us down over a footbridge and eventually out of the woods at a gate (Wp.14 120M).

Continuing south-east, we follow the clear path until we reach cottages, then follow the fingerpost to **Hodge Lane Dye Vats**. We cross a stream on tarmac, and as the tarmac swings left we continue straight on (ESE) following a TPT marker.

Where the track forks we take the right hand, downhill track. The track climbs a little as we pass **Wier Lodge** and climb to the three-storey cottages at **Summerbottom** (Wp.15 128M). These weavers' cottages ( built in the 1780s) have a common top storey which housed wool weaving looms for the workers who lived below. We almost turn back on ourselves as we head up by the side of the first cottage. Turning left, following the yellow marker on the telegraph pole to head uphill and turn right just before the steps, bringing us onto **Broadbottom Station** (Wp.16 131M) for our return to **Piccadilly**.

Unfortunately the Station Bar is no longer open; there are refreshment opportunities in **Broadbottom** but all involve crossing the railway and leaving the station for a walk into the village. Leaving the car park to head downhill, **The Harewood Arms** is on the right and **The Cheshire Cheese** is beyond the railway bridge on the left. Their low refreshment rating is solely due to the fact that, as I've never found them open, I usually head back to one of the many city centre hostelries.

Purists may dismiss this walk with cries of, 'too many hard surfaced tracks', and for avoiding the path round the edge of **Coombes Rocks**. But for those who like quiet country lanes, gentle slopes and edges that won't put the wind up you; read on. Leaving **Marple** we make our way past **Bottom's Hall** (the hall and adjacent farm were built in 1800 by Samuel Oldknow). **Mellor Mill**, originally powered by water from **Roman Lakes**, was destroyed by fire in 1892. Clear tracks and a short road section take us to **Mellor Church**, then past **Mellor Hall** before heading to the legendary **Ludworth Moor**. In the 1st century AD the last great battle for the north was fought, when the Roman Army led by Julius Agricola annihilated the British warriors.

**Robin Hood's Picking Stones**

Perhaps less credible is the legend that recounts how, in order to free a maiden imprisoned by her guardian the Baron, Robin Hood fired an arrow and hit the upright druid stones from a great distance, the notches on the stones giving rise to the name **Robin Hood's Picking Stones**. Of course, the Baron reneged on the deal and demanded further improbable feats to be performed before releasing the maiden. Well, it's a good story and not a bad place to stop before making our way to the **Edge**.

Actually, two for the price of one as we take a safe path between **Cown Edge** on one side and **Coombes Edge** on the other. The final stage through **Tom Wood** was mainly impassable when I first surveyed the route.

Fortunately a friendly fellow walker told me about new bridges being airlifted into the area and clearance work on the paths. Though not complete when I re-surveyed the route I am sure you'll enjoy this re-opened route.

3 | 4H | 9.4 miles/15km | 441m / 410m | 1

**Access by train:** from **Manchester Piccadilly** to **Marple Station**. Return from **Broadbottom Station** to **Piccadilly**.

We leave **Marple Station** (Wp.1 0M), crossing the car park to our left. At **Station Road** we turn left (NE) and head downhill towards the traffic lights. Crossing the road at the lights we follow the sign to **Mellor** into **Town Street** heading SE. Taking the right hand pavement we stroll through **Marple Bridge** with the **Goyt** down to our right. Shortly after passing **The Royal Scot** we leave the pavement and continue up **Low Lea Road** (Wp.2 6M).

**Low Lea Road** takes us gently uphill past renovated cottages. Over to our left is **Mellor Church**, our first objective. The track starts descending, becoming **Bottoms Mill Road** before a junction where we turn left (Wp.3 18M SSE) following a sign to 'Roman Lakes'. At the next junction we carry straight on (SE) following a sign to 'Old Hall Farm'. Passing the entrance to **Bottoms Hall**, we take the left hand fork following a sign to 'Longhurst Lane'. Look out for the decorative stone arch over the mill *leat* on the left before heading uphill. As we reach the top of **Old Hall Lane** we turn right (ESE) towards the phone box and cross the road at the **Royal Oak** (Wp.4 29M).

We stroll along **Longhurst Lane** to **Knowle Road** where we turn left (NE) passing **Mellor Primary School** before leaving the tarmac to continue along the rough track. The track dips down before climbing again with **Knowle Wood** to our right. Passing the sign to 'Knowle Farm', we come into the farmyard (Wp.5 42M) to swing right through a gap stile, then across two more stiles as we make our way up to steps taking us into **Mellor Churchyard**.

**Mellor Hall Farm (Wp.6)**

I usually take a short break here to enjoy the views or to check on progress of the dig just outside the church grounds as we head east along the track. The track swings left at a gate with a sign, 'HGV access' to **Mellor Hall Farm**, then right and left again bringing us to the farm gates (Wp.6 54M).

We pass through the pedestrian gate, ignoring a footpath sign to the left, and pass between the 17th century buildings on stone flags.

Leaving the farm by another pedestrian gate, we follow a bridleway sign to continue straight ahead on a grassy track where the farm track drops away to the left (not shown on the OS Map). Going through a five bar gate, we pass **Horsepool Farm** on the rough track to a junction where we continue straight ahead (NE) on **Chatterton Lane**. Ignoring several footpath signs, we stroll on, passing **Chatterton End Farm**.

Our road dips down to a fork where we follow a sign 'BOAT 22 Marple' up the left hand fork (Wp.7 68M ENE). Our track swings sharp left and soon drops to another fork where we go right (NNE), ignoring a footpath sign as our track swings sharp left. Our rocky track brings us down to tarmac where we turn right (NNE). The single track road climbs gently up towards buildings and we turn right (ENE) over a stile (Wp.8 83M), following a damaged 'Cown Edge Way' sign.

So far our itinerary has followed clear tracks but we now need to pay more attention to navigation. We start on a clear path leading us behind buildings to a gate and continue to the confluence of two streams (87M) which we cross and turn left to follow the second stream (NNE). Climbing gently, we swing (N) to follow the line of gorse bushes on an unclear path to reach a stile hidden at the side of two large holly bushes (Wp.9 91M).

Over the stile, we turn right (NNE) to cross a field to a high stile over a stone wall next to another holly bush. Heading towards farm buildings, we follow the fence round to and through a gate on our left, then passing in front of the farm following the track until we reach tarmac. Turning right, we soon come to a gate on our right (Wp.10 98M) cross a stile and head (ENE) up a track ('Cown Edge Way' sign is missing at the stile). The OS Map can be a bit misleading, the path appears to head NE from the stile but has been re-routed. We follow the track for 100 yards, pass under power lines, before turning left (NNE) over a large stone that bridges a stream and follow the path between barbed wire fences.

Following clear paths again, we cross a wooden footbridge before climbing steadily to cross **Gun Road** (Wp.11 109M) and continue (ENE) on the broad track opposite. After 200 yards the track splits and we take the right hand fork heading east. Another 500 yards brings us to **Robin Hood's Picking Stones** (Wp.12 121M, see the photo on Page 77) on the border of the **Peak District National Park**, a place to stop for refreshment while contemplating the **Dark Peak** over to our right.

Continuing (E) along the track we pass a solitary building, ignoring a path to the right; we pass through a gate, our path now climbing between a fence and stone wall. A sharp left brings us to a stile which we ignore, as we turn right (E) through a gate for a short climb bringing us to a point where the path starts to drop (Wp.13 134M).

Looking across the valley, we can see **Chunal Moor**. Turning left (NE, and another missing 'Cown Edge Sign') we cross a stile to follow the well-trodden path above **Cown Edge Rocks** on our right to cross another stile and continue (NE) towards trees. Following the fence as the trees end (NNE), brings us above **Coombes Edge Rocks**, on our left. There are two stiles over to a path along the edge, which can be treacherous during winter months and is not for vertigo sufferers, so we keep the fence to our left and continue to a ladder stile which drops us into a lane, safe from the edge, leading us down to two metal gates (Wp.14 154M).

A path joins ours from **Monks Road** on our right as we continue with the fence to our right. Crossing two stiles by sheep pens and soon across a third, we swing left to a fourth by a cattle grid. Crossing the stile we continue (WNW) staying close to the edge to cross 4 more stiles. Below us are **Charlesworth Church** and the railway viaduct at **Broadbottom**; in the far distance **Winter Hill** is visible on a clear day.

Continuing downhill, we come towards a dry stone wall and see a stile ahead, but to get there we have to turn right, cross a stile, drop into the lane, and turn left back towards it (Wp.15 177M). Keeping the field boundary to our right, we skirt round the field and drop down to a stile taking us into a recreation area. Just to our left **Charlesworth and Chisworth Cricket Club** nestles below **Coombes Edge**. Swinging right (NNW), we head across the football pitch, provided there is no game in progress, to bring us down to **Marple Road** (Wp.16 183M).

Turning right (NNE) and crossing the road we pass **Tom Wood Rise** and turn left (WNW) between two houses. Crossing a stile we head across the field on a left hand diagonal (W), our path clearer for a short distance as we pass through bushes, then disappearing as buildings come in to sight. Maintaining our westerly course, we cross the field to a stile (Wp.17 191M).

Heading towards a solitary tree (NW) we continue on to cross the next stile to head down the field (NW), the boundary on our right swinging away. We join it towards the bottom of the field to cross another stile into **Tom Wood**.

After a short distance on a clear path we descend steep steps into the wood, more steps leading us to a footbridge with hand rails. We swing left across a stream and then a second railed footbridge, meandering in a northerly direction with more short sections of steps. (Don't take the steps going steeply out of the wood to the right.)

Footbridge, Tom Wood

Dropping down to a third railed bridge (Wp.18 206M) we leave the wood, the **River Etherow** down to our left. Following one of several well-trodden paths, we come down by the river and turn right (NNE) slightly uphill. Crossing a stile and an old wooden footbridge our path leads us to a gate into the grounds of the **Church of the Immaculate Conception**, through the grounds and out the gate at the front of the church.

Turning left on **Long Lane** (W) we follow the road to the railway viaduct and cross the **Etherow** on a metal footbridge. Climbing **Lower Market Street** we cross the road to head (S) downhill to **Lymefield Visitor Centre**. (See refreshment notes at the end of this description for an alternate route to the station.)

Passing the centre (Wp.19 221M) (toilet facilities), we turn right (SW) following the fingerpost to **Broad Mills**. We pass through the site, information boards detailing the workings of the mill, then leave the **Heritage Area** by a kissing-gate (Wp.20 227M) to continue straight on (N) following the sign to 'Hodgefold'. A short climb brings us by houses and we again follow a 'Hodgefold' sign left.

At the top of the climb we pass a gate and continue a short distance to a lamp post where we leave the track to turn right up the side of **Summerbottom Terrace** and turn left following a yellow waymarker on the telegraph pole for the final uphill stretch. Reaching tarmac, we turn sharp right and take a final few steps onto **Broadbottom Station** (Wp.21 235M)

An alternative route to the station carries on up **Lower Market Street** passing **The Cheshire Cheese** (a Thwaites house) on the right, passing under the railway onto **Market Street**. Crossing the road, we pass **The Harewood Arms** (a free house), and continue to the station. The low refreshment rating is due solely to the fact that I've never found either pub open.

For those who prefer a less demanding route linking **Broadbottom** and **Stalybridge** than Walk 1, this itinerary takes us through **The Mudd** to the **Church of St Michael and All Saints** in the village of **Mottram in Longdendale**. Explore the village **Market Place** with its pole and stocks in front of the **Old Court House** complete with blue plaques and water fountain, There's a statue of **LS Lowry** (1887-1976), and **The Elms**, his retirement home. Next on our itinerary is the deepest air shaft on the **Mottram Tunnel** (200ft) which carries water from the six mile chain of reservoirs in **Longdendale**. Built in the 1800s, they formed the largest water conservation project in Europe. Leaving **Mottram**, we make our way across fields ( muddy after heavy rain) to pass below **Harrop Edge** to **Matley**. There are great views along the way, the gentle climb up **Hough Hill** providing vistas of the **Tame Valley**. We end with a descent into **Stalybridge** and an abundance of refreshment opportunities, not least of which is the **Station Buffet Bar**.

3 | 2½ H | 5.6 miles/9km | 209m / 244m | 5

**Access by train:** from **Manchester Piccadilly** to **Broadbottom Station**. Return to **Manchester Piccadilly** or **Victoria** from **Stalybridge**.

We leave **Broadbottom Station** (Wp.1 0M) via the ticket office and climb the steps to **Market Street** where we turn left (E). Crossing the road at the zebra crossing, we head up steps to the right of the crossing and continue (N) up the sett-paved path. As the path becomes a wide track we watch out for the footpath sign on our right (Wp.2 7M) which we take between houses (NE). Entering a small estate our path continues slightly to the left between houses opposite. Coming to a stile, we continue on a clear path between trees and continue to a kissing-gate (Wp.3 12M).

Turning right (NNE), we stroll up the road towards a stone terrace soon reaching stone steps and a stile on our left which we cross, then passing behind the houses and turning right at the next stile to cross the road and yet another stile.

Crossing a field with **Harrop Edge** over to our left, we cross another stile and continue straight ahead, the field boundary to our right. Over another stile in the right hand boundary, we cross the field diagonally left (NE) to the final stile of this section and turn left on **Littlemoor Road** (Wp.4 19M NNE) to pass **The Mudd**.

**The Mudd**

**Hollingworthall Moor** is ahead of us and the **Dark Peak** to our right as we stroll to a junction and take the right hand fork into **Warhill**, continuing to **St Michael and All Angels Church** (Wp.5 26M). We turn left (NW) down the sett-paved path which brings us to **Church Brow**, where we turn right to head downhill. Watch out for the blue plaque high up to the right, which commemorates 'Sir Edmund Shaa Lord Mayor of London 1482'.

The statue of L S Lowry

Turning right at the **Market Place**, we pass **The White Hart** (Free House), cross the road and continue to the traffic lights (Wp.6 32M). Crossing the road, we pass the statue of **L S Lowry** and head up **Stalybridge Road**. Passing **Rushy Croft** we come to **The Elms**, Lowry's home from 1948 to 1976.

The first air shaft

Retracing our steps, we turn right into **Rushy Croft** to visit the air shaft. Again retracing our steps we return to the lights and turn right on **Hyde Road**. After 100 yards we take a path (Wp.7 38M) on our right to stroll between houses.

At the first junction we turn left between fences on a clear path bringing us to a stile. Following a yellow waymarker (NW) we follow the left hand fence to the next stile. Turning left through a metal gate, we turn right by the cattle grid following a yellow waymarker (NW).

Passing a second air shaft we cross another stile and take the best line we can towards the next stile and waymarker, **Werneth Low** to our left and **Coombes Edge** across the valley. From the stile we continue to the next which has a number of waymarkers, and head towards power lines. Keeping the fence on our right, we make our way up the field to a gate and cross another stile, turning left (SW), following the yellow waymarker.

Crossing another stile we reach a clear path as we walk between holly bushes. As the path surface changes to gravel we come to a junction (Wp.8 55M) and continue (SW) on the bridleway, swinging right (NW) between broken-down walls and ignoring a track off to our left. A gentle rise brings us to a Y-junction (Wp.9 59M) where we ignore the yellow waymarker and turn left (SW) on a broad track. As it is sheltered, the track makes an ideal place for a break, especially on a windy day. The view towards **Werneth** and **Stockport** to the right is only marred by the M67 below us, but far enough away not to bother us.

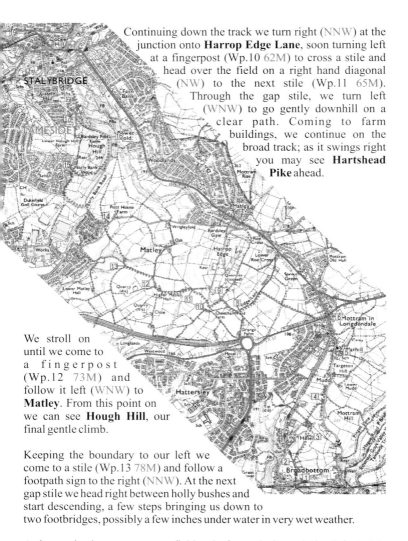

Continuing down the track we turn right (NNW) at the junction onto **Harrop Edge Lane**, soon turning left at a fingerpost (Wp.10 62M) to cross a stile and head over the field on a right hand diagonal (NW) to the next stile (Wp.11 65M). Through the gap stile, we turn left (WNW) to go gently downhill on a clear path. Coming to farm buildings, we continue on the broad track; as it swings right you may see **Hartshead Pike** ahead.

We stroll on until we come to a fingerpost (Wp.12 73M) and follow it left (WNW) to **Matley**. From this point on we can see **Hough Hill**, our final gentle climb.

Keeping the boundary to our left we come to a stile (Wp.13 78M) and follow a footpath sign to the right (NNW). At the next gap stile we head right between holly bushes and start descending, a few steps bringing us down to two footbridges, possibly a few inches under water in very wet weather.

A clear path takes us to an open field and a footpath sign pointing left. As it is slightly off line, we continue to the next fingerpost beside a tree which points us to a dip. We continue down the clear path to cross a footbridge and go straight on to the next fingerpost pointing towards power lines. With the fence to our left, we pass under the lines and come out on **Matley Lane** (Wp.14 87M) near **The Rising Moon** pub.

We cross the lane to continue (NW) up the track opposite, **Early Bank Road**, and pass **Matley Moor Manor**, converted for commercial use. Our track soon splits and we take the left hand fork. There is the option to take the right fork and meet our route at (Wp.16), saving a gentle climb, but it can be very muddy in wet weather. Our gentle climb brings us to a housing estate where we turn right to stay on the track which swings down to the left to a group of stables, where we take the track diagonally to the right.

A short distance brings us to a fingerpost (Wp.15 99M) where we turn right (WSW), cross a stile and follow the field boundary on our right. At the next stile we follow a yellow waymarker on a left hand diagonal over the hill, soon seeing and crossing the next stile and heading for the next one. At this stile we follow the yellow waymarker straight on, rather than the one down a very steep slope. The next waymarker points sharp right and downhill to follow the path marked on the OS Map, but we ignore this to follow a well-trodden path that gently descends the hill to rejoin **Early Bank Road** (Wp.16 123M).

Joining the old track we turn left (WNW), following the track as it skirts **Cheetham Park** to the urban edge of **Stalybridge**, with **Winter Hill** and the **West Pennines** in the far distance. Turning right into **Laurel Bank** (Wp.17 128M) we take the path at the side of Nº7 which brings us onto **Chapel Walk** again, by the side of the park.

The sett-paved path brings us down to steps and a slope into the **Labour Club** car park. After a left hand diagonal towards the road (Wp.18 136M), we turn left to traffic lights and cross the road, skirting Tesco's car park, heading towards the church to reach **Armentiers Square** by **The Millpond** pub (J W Lees). We continue to the canal and turn left, crossing the road near the first lock and taking the footbridge to **Melbourne Street** where we turn right.

Crossing the **Tame**, we turn left on **Market Street**, currently undergoing redevelopment. We pass several bars, the last being **Q Bar**, and go under the railway, turn left and enter **Stalybridge Station** (Wp.19 150M). The **Buffet Bar** is on the Leeds Platform.

A little more demanding than Walk 12 of similar title, we traverse the eastern flank of the **Tame Valley** on ancient tracks. Leaving **Stalybridge Station**, we join the canal for a short distance before climbing gently to the lower reaches of **Hollingworthall Moor**. Contouring around the moor, we drop down through **Cock Wood** to **Walkerwood** reservoir. A steady climb takes us via a chain of four reservoirs onto the moors, designated an Environmentally Sensitive Area (ESA) in which dogs are not permitted; dog walkers see Short Walk (a). Whilst this is Access Land, the words from the poem 'Harridge Pike' by Rita Eden are a reminder of our responsibility to wildlife, especially during the nesting season:-

> "Underfoot all in feather
> Are grouse, nestin in t'heather"

GPS users can take a small diversion from the clear path to grid reference SE00000000, one of only 20 sites on mainland Britain with all the zeros.

Leaving the moor, we descend to **Carrbrook** where new housing replaces the Buckton Vale Dye & Print Works, then climb gently onto **Moor Edge Road**, thought to have Roman origins, which later became a Turnpike route; the track remained an important supply route in medieval times. We pass below **Buckton Castle**; originally Roman, and a fine example of a Norman 'motte and bailey'. Although we don't include the steep climb on Access Land in this itinerary, you can take a virtual visit on the internet (see glossary for web address).

We then drop down **Shadworth Lane** and find a county boundary stone, sadly defaced. The **Royal George** garden provides a welcome refreshment stop, offering a good range of food and Lees beers. A final pleasant stroll through **Friezland** brings us back to **The Railway** (Free House) and our last refreshment opportunity opposite **Greenfield Station**.

**Access by Train:** from either **Piccadilly** or **Victoria Stations** to **Stalybridge**. Return from **Greenfield** to **Victoria** or change at **Stalybridge** for **Piccadilly**.

**Access by Car:** Limited car parking is available at **Stalybridge Station**, especially midweek. Return by train from **Greenfield**.

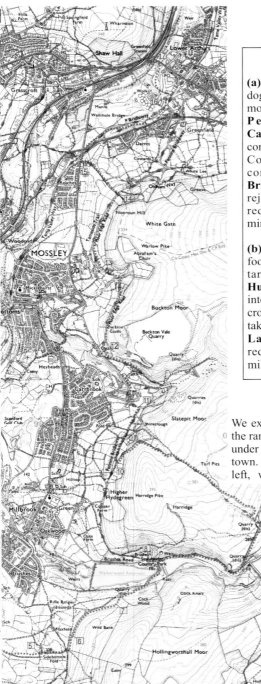

We exit the station (Wp.1 0M) via the ramp and turn right (SE) to pass under the railway and walk into town. Passing the bus station on the left, we continue to **Melbourne Street** and turn right (S). Crossing the **River Tame** and the canal, we turn left (E) on **Armentieres Way** (Wp.2 8M); over the footbridge, we join the towpath by the canal locks. Continuing past Tesco's, we pass under one bridge before taking the uphill ramp to **Mottram Road**, then turn right (SE) and cross the road at the pedestrian crossing.

Soon after **Staly Ward Working Men's Club**, a left turn takes us into **Stocks Lane** (Wp.3 16M). We follow the lane to a footpath sign (Wp.4 23M) where we turn left, heading for **Sidebottom Fold Farm**, with **Hollingworthall Moor** ahead. We ignore the waymarker pointing left at **Sidebottom Fold** (Wp.5 33M) and continue in front of the building to the white five-bar gate. A few more steps bring us to a stile and into open fields; heading east, we climb gently, passing two pylons before coming to a battered old stile.

Over the stile, we ignore the gate on the left, and follow the yellow waymarker left (NNE), still climbing gently. At the next waymarker (Wp.6 40M) we take the right hand fork, staying on the clear path to contour round the lower reaches of the moor. The derelict construction down to our left is a disused rifle range; then **Walkerwood** and **Bushes** reservoirs soon come into view. Approximately 600 metres after the last waymarker, we go left at a fork in the path (Wp.7 48M), our heather-lined path descending steadily down towards the reservoir to reach **Cock Wood**. Still on the path, we come to a fence which we follow right (E) for a short distance to and across a stile. We continue a gentle descent to the next stile where we swing left (N) between the two reservoirs. Crossing an overflow channel we rise gently up to a kissing-gate (Wp.8 59M). (N.B. See Short Walk Option (a).)

Turning right (NE), we follow a **Pennine Bridleway** (PBW) fingerpost towards **Tintwistle**. The steady slog up the tarmac access road takes us past **Brushes**, **Lower Swineshaw** and on to **Higher Swineshaw** reservoirs, passing a disused quarry along the way. The latter reservoir provides an opportunity for a refreshment stop before we follow the fingerpost (Wp.9 81M) left (WNW) on a public footpath. (N.B. Walkers extending Walk 1 join us here from Wp.19 of Walk 1.)

A few steps brings us to a gap stile as we enter an ESA with nesting and breeding birds on the managed moor and where dogs are prohibited. A little further on, by a concrete structure, we follow the **Tameside Trail** waymarker right (NNE) on the broad track. The OS map conflicts with the sign, showing the Trail going straight on. We continue to rise gently, on the broad track with **Harridge Pike** to our left and **Slatepit Moor** ahead. SE00000000 is just off the track to the right. We start descending on the thin peat, **Hartshead Pike** in the distance. The less attractive sight of **Buckton Vale Quarries** might give pause for thought. The steady descent brings us down to another broad track where we turn sharp right (Wp.10 117M N), (N.B. Short walk option (a) rejoins us here.)

We drop past a cottage as the track alternates between reclaimed stone and tarmac, finally coming down to a new development replacing a former mill (Wp.11 136M) where we turn left (W) to follow the wall around the estate. Passing **Calico Crescent**, we continue straight ahead (N) at the mini roundabout and swing left (NNE) after **Printer's Drive**, following the fingerpost to 'Greenfield'. Passing **Oak Villas** we turn right (NE) at the end of **Beaconsfield Terrace** and rise up **Spring Bank**

Coming to a **Tameside Trail** waymarker on a post, we turn sharp left (NW) behind the cottages, following a yellow waymarker on the other side of the post. A reasonably clear path brings us to a stile, and we cross into fields following the boundary on the right. Half way across, we spot and aim for a gate with a stile to the left. Over the stile, we turn right for a short distance, then cross the quarry access road to the broad track opposite. A little way up the track we follow a **PBW** waymarker (Wp.12 156M) up to the right (N).

We follow **Moor Edge Road** as it contours below **Buckton Castle**, then descend gently to the next **PBW** sign before swinging left over a stream and climbing again. Soon after the next **PBW** post we turn right (N) at a fingerpost to 'Greenfield' (Wp.13 185M). (N.B. Short walk (b) follows the footpath sign down to the left.)

Passing **Top O' Th' Green Farm** on the track, we soon have the obelisk at **Pots and Pans** in view.

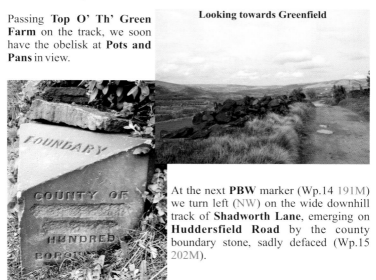

Looking towards Greenfield

At the next **PBW** marker (Wp.14 191M) we turn left (NW) on the wide downhill track of **Shadworth Lane**, emerging on **Huddersfield Road** by the county boundary stone, sadly defaced (Wp.15 202M).

The county boundary stone

Crossing the road we turn right (N), and at a finger post to 'Friezland' follow it right, crossing the road again; **The Royal George** is a few steps down from the fingerpost. A short path leads us into a lay-by and we cross **Manchester Road** to the 'Friezland' sign where we follow the path down and turn right (NE). The well-made path takes us past a fingerpost for 'Greenfield' before coming to a **PBW** fingerpost (Wp.16 222M) where we turn left (N) for **Greenfield**. The path meanders along and drops down to cross the **River Tame** on a wide wooden bridge.

We turn left (NW), following the 'Tame Valley Way' sign for a pleasant riverside stroll behind houses. Coming out onto **Chew Valley Road** we turn left (NW) and cross the **Tame** and the **Huddersfield Narrow Canal** before ascending and crossing the road, swinging right round the hairpin bend to **The Railway. Greenfield Station** (Wp.17 235M) is just opposite on the left.

The Railway

Our second circular route from **Greenfield Station** takes us into **Chew Valley** below **Alphin Pike** to **Dovestone Reservoir**. The area abounds with myth and mystery; the story goes that the huge boulders littering the valley below **Alphin Pike** were hurled by giants fighting for the attentions of the water nymph Rimmon. The unsolved murders of the landlord of Moorcock Inn (now demolished) and his son on 2 April 1832 are marked by **Bill o' Jacks** plantation above **Yeoman Hey** reservoir. Crossing the dam, we pass a stone laid by the King of Tonga in 1981, then head below **Alderman Hill** for the steady climb to **Pots & Pans** and the war memorial. Now designated Access Land, the hill is criss-crossed with clear paths, providing opportunities to vary the itinerary.

Our return route drops gently to **St. Chad's Church**, and the opportunity to sample the range of beers, many brewed on site, at **The Church Inn** which also has an extensive menu. Further down the valley we join the **Huddersfield Narrow Canal** for the walk back to **Greenfield** where **The Railway Free House** provides a last refreshment opportunity before our return to **Manchester**.

**Access by Train:** from **Manchester Victoria** to **Greenfield** or from **Piccadilly** changing at **Stalybridge**. Return from **Greenfield** to **Manchester Victoria** or change at **Stalybridge** for **Piccadilly**

**Access by Car:** Parking at the station is limited but on-road parking along **Shaw Hall Bank** is permitted.

We leave **Greenfield Station** (Wp.1 0M), cross the road to **The Railway** Free House, and turn right (SSW) and downhill.

Goblin Manor

Swinging sharp left round **Goblin Manor**, we continue downhill on **Chew Valley Road**, and cross with care. Over the canal and the **River Tame** we turn right (SSW), following a fingerpost to walk by the river. At the footbridge (Wp.2 9M) we follow the **Pennine Bridleway** (PBW) left (NE) passing **Tame Court** and swinging right (SE) past the entrance onto **Greenbridge Lane**. After passing **Primrose Bank** cottages we swing right over a bridge, then turn left (SE), following a footpath sign to walk by the **Tame** on a firm path. At a small estate our path continues (SE), climbing steps to **Manchester Road** (Wp.3 16M).

Over the road, we follow a footpath sign at the side of Nº47 and cross a stile at the rear of houses into a field. Climbing steadily on a left hand diagonal (SE), we cross a broken-down wall and follow the fence up to a gate. Turning left (ESE), we head towards a metal gate and over a stile (Wp.4 24M), following the fence uphill (SSE) for two thirds of the field's length. Following an **Oldham Way** (OW) marker left (ESE) we cross two stiles and head to and across a group of three stiles, continuing (ESE) to a gate where we swing right (SE) rising up between cottages. Another gate brings us onto **Intake Lane** (Wp.5 38M).

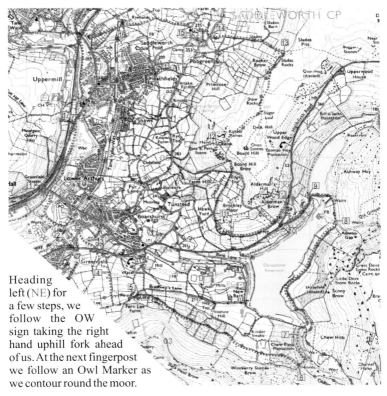

Heading left (NE) for a few steps, we follow the OW sign taking the right hand uphill fork ahead of us. At the next fingerpost we follow an Owl Marker as we contour round the moor.

The clear path takes us by a wood on our left to a gate, where we continue straight ahead (ESE) following an OW marker. At the next gate we continue (SE) as our fairly clear path meanders below **Wimberry Stones**, then at a broken gate we follow an OW marker cross a stream and continue along the bolder-strewn hillside towards trees.

We turn left (NE) after the next stile (Wp.6 71M) and start descending to the valley bottom, following the fence line downhill to its end where we swing left (N) towards **Alderman Hill**. At a fork by a tree (Wp.7 87M), we take the steep path right (NNE), towards the stream. Continuing along the path to **Dovestone Reservoir**, we swing right to and over a bridge along a tarmac track, then swinging left over a second bridge to follow the track around the reservoir.

Again following OW markers, we continue by the reservoir to the picnic area at **Ashway Gap** (Wp.8 110M), then on over the inlet channel and along the broad track to reach the dam at **Yeoman Hey Reservoir** where we turn left (E) over the dam. Looking out for the **Tonga Stone** (Wp.9 118M) on the far side, we turn left (S) following an OW marker. After passing through a kissing gate, we rise up the gentle hill to gates on either side of the track (Wp.10 123M) turning right (N) over a stile. A few more steps, and we cross a step and gap stile to continue up steps to **Binn Green** car park.

Following OW marker we exit the car park on **Holmfirth Road**, crossing the road to pass through a gate that's opposite and slightly to our left (126M), then follow **Long Lane** onto Access Land, rising gently (SW) and contouring **Alderman Hill**. Coming to a gate on the right (Wp.11 133M) we turn right (NNE) over a stile following an OW marker.

**Pots and Pans**

The reasonably clear path climbs steadily towards two dry stone walls where we continue on the clear path between them. Crossing a dry stone wall, we continue steadily uphill on the clear path to a disused quarry where we swing left and finish the climb to **Pots and Pans** and the war memorial (Wp.12 151M).

The Access Land on **Board Hill** has number of clear paths and you may want to explore **Alderman's Hill** to the SW or go via **Oven Stones** below **Dick Hill** to **Sugar Loaf**. Our itinerary takes us east from the obelisk towards a fence and a stone OW marker where we swing left NE below **Kinder Stones** towards **Sugar Loaf** where an OW marker takes us left (N) to pass by **Shaw Rocks**.

**St. Chad's Church**

We begin to drop steeply down on the clear path to a broken OW fingerpost (Wp.13 173M) where we turn left (W) and follow the broken-down wall steadily downhill towards **St. Chad's Church**. At a stile by a gate, we follow the OW Link marker straight ahead (WNW) to continue our descent between stone walls.

We head straight on as the wide track swings left, following the OW Link over a stile towards the church. Our descent ends at a stile (Wp.14 192M) which brings us onto tarmac on **Running Hill Gate**.

Heading between signs for 'Ivy Bank Farm' and 'Clerk's Cottage', we drop down north-west between the buildings towards the rear of the church. A small gate to our left takes us slightly downhill to come out at the church entrance by the stocks. **The Church Inn** and micro-brewery is just to our left and offers a range of fine ales and food. **The Cross Keys**, visited on walk 13 is just above us to our left.

Passing the front of the church, we swing right by the graveyard and then turn left (NW), following the Owl marker on the telegraph pole (Wp.15 199M). Our rough path descends to a stile, and staying by the fence, we cross a stream and continue through a gap stile. At the next gap stile we turn immediately left through another gap stile.

Keeping the boundary to our right, we continue to a metal gate and go through the kissing-gate onto tarmac. Passing **Ryefields**, we ignore the PBW sign and continue on the tarmac for a short distance. Just before two Private Road signs we follow a footpath fingerpost (Wp.16 213M) on a gentle uphill path behind houses.

We emerge on tarmac and go (SW) gently downhill, passing under the railway viaduct to reach **High Street**. Carefully crossing the busy road to the **Brownhill Visitor Centre**, we make our way to the canal and turn left (S) to pass under the viaduct by locks.

Following the towpath we continue to a bridge where we ascend to rejoin the towpath on the opposite side of the canal. Strolling along to lock Nº21 (Wp.17 230M), we again carefully cross **High Street**, following the fingerpost to **Greenfield**. Across the road we descend steps to rejoin the towpath for the gentle stroll to the next bridge where we leave the canal via steps up to **Chew Valley Road**. Turning right (W) we climb the hill to pass **Goblin Manor** and our final refreshment opportunity before crossing the road to **Greenfield Station** (Wp.1 242M).

Hadfield (or Hertfield) in the **Longdendale Valley** where our route starts, can be traced back to 650AD though man has settled in **Longdendale**, meaning long dale or valley, for over three millennia. It's unlikely that those early settlers would recognise the valley today, with its chain of reservoirs built along the **River Etherow**, the busy A628 **Woodhead Pass** and the line of pylons that march up the valley. The full circuit takes us to all five reservoirs, and despite the recorded ascent, the walking is easy and all the climbing gentle as we make our way up past **Crowden**, the first stop on the **Pennine Way** heading north. Our outward leg ends at **Woodhead Dam** on the site of the former **Crowden Station** on the old Manchester - Sheffield line.

We return along the **Longdendale Trail** which also forms part of the **Trans Pennine Trail** from **Liverpool** to **Hull** and Euro Route 8 from Holland to Turkey, obviously designed for those who think the **Pennine Way** is too easy! With plenty of seats on the outward journey, we can sit and enjoy the views whilst information boards along the return route educate us on wildlife, the former railway and other points of interest. Back at the station, **The Palatine** serves Robinson's Ales, and the station buildings have been transformed into **Edward's Wine Bar**.

**Short Walks**

(a) Follow the TPT fingerpost over **Rhodeswood Dam**. On the far side, follow the **Longdendale Trail** left (ENE), uphill towards the pylon. Soon after the pylon, turn right (SW) by a fingerpost and then sharp left (SE). Over a stile at the next fingerpost brings you to the **Longdendale Trail** to turn right (SW) joining the main walk at Wp15. (2 hours, 4.7 miles/7½km)

(b) Either follow the track down to **Torside Dam**, or follow the **Pennine Way** from the seat at Wp.8, down steps to the dam. Continue on the **Pennine Way** to meet the **Longdendale Trail** and head right (W), following the TPT west to **Hadfield**. (2½ hours, 6.6 miles/10.5km)

We leave **Hadfield Station** (Wp.1 0M), crossing the car park towards **The Palatine Hotel** (NW) and continuing down **Station Road**, then turning right (ENE) into **Lambgates** opposite **The Mason's Arms**. Walking between hedges, we maintain our course through a housing estate to a football field (Wp.2 9M) where we turn left (NNW). Coming to a road, we turn right (NE) heading towards **The Victoria Inn** and **Padfield Main Road**. Crossing the road, we head NNE on a public footpath. At the second gate we ignore the **Longdendale Trail**, maintaining our course as we gently descend towards **Bottoms Reservoir**. A few steps bring us down to cross a wall on stone steps to come down by the reservoir (Wp.3 16M).

Turning left (WNW), we follow a 'Trans Pennine Trail' (TPT) sign to the dam wall where we turn right and cross the dam.

Swinging right (ENE) as we leave the dam; a small TPT sign on the fence directs us up the access road to a gate. Just before the gate (Wp.4 27M) we turn right (ESE) following the **Bottoms Concessionary Path** sign. A few steps and a footbridge bring us to **Bottoms Wildlife Area** where we turn right to follow the path as it swings left around the wildlife area bringing us on to an ESE heading on a clear path. Several choices of path all bring us to a well-made track and a barn where a 'Bottoms Path' sign directs us right, keeping close to the reservoir.

Our path brings us out on tarmac where we ignore the TPT fingerpost heading over the dam, to go between the gate posts on the **Concessionary Horse Route and Footpath** (Wp.5 38M). Strolling along a dismantled railway line with **Valehouse Reservoir** to our right, we pass a cottage and have the choice of taking steps (Wp.6 51M) up to **Rhodeswood Dam**, or following the road as it hairpins gently up to the same point.

(N.B. Short Walk (a) leaves us to cross the dam at this point, rejoining us at Wp.15.)

We swing left to cross a channel and then right, we head north-east up a gently rising track on the concessionary footpath. At a Y-junction (Wp.7 62M) we take the right hand fork to stay near the reservoir. The undulating rough track takes us between the reservoir and the busy **Woodhead Pass**. Future generations will be able to enjoy the large number of native trees which have been planted on this section. Rising up to a gate, swing left (ESE) on the concessionary path.

(N.B. Those taking Short Walk Option (b) can either continue down the track to the dam, or join us as we make our way up to a point where the **Pennine Way** joins our route (Wp.8 73M); there's a well-placed seat here ideal for taking a break overlooking the reservoirs. From here the short walk option takes the steps down to the dam to rejoin us at Wp.14.)

We go left and climb a few steps after the seat, and then swing right (E) through the trees. Coming to a kissing-gate (Wp.9 80M) we leave the **Pennine Way** as is it heads up steps to **Crowden**, and continue on the **Torside Concessionary Path** through **Tinsel School Wood**.

The clear path crosses a footbridge and has the benefit of a number of seats overlooking **Torside Reservoir**. We cross a stile, descend some steps and cross a footbridge, leaving **Tinsel Wood** at a kissing-gate to continue ENE. Crossing **Crowden Brook** (Wp.10 97M), we have fine views up the valley at **Crowden** to our left before swinging left at the wildlife sanctuary.

A fingerpost directs us right (NE) to **Crowden Dam** via a kissing gate, and a second fingerpost confirms our route as we head for the dam. After climbing steps (Wp.11 109M), we cross the footbridge over the overflow channel (see the picture on the next page) and swing right (ESE) gently rising between trees.

**The footbridge over the overflow channel**

Coming to a kissing-gate, we cross a road, pass through another kissing-gate heading north-east.

The route rises up to the **Longdendale Trail**, then continues to **Woodhead Dam** (Wp.12 117M), where information boards and seating (our last opportunity for a seat before the walk ends) overlook **Woodhead Dam** and **St. James' Church** opposite.

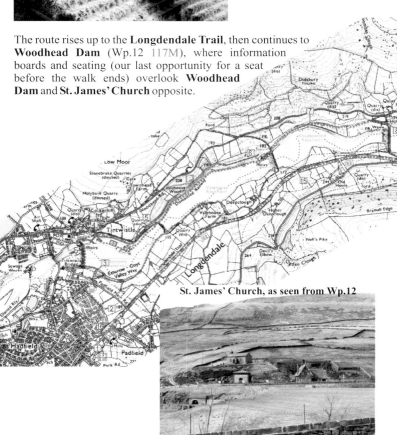

**St. James' Church, as seen from Wp.12**

Retracing our steps for a short distance, our return route along the **Longdendale Trail** (also marked as 'TPT West') takes us south-west along the other side of **Torside Reservoir** with **Bleaklow** high up to our left.

Ignoring signs to 'Crowden' and 'Wildboar Clough' along the way, we continue towards **Torside** car park entrance (Wp.13 136M).

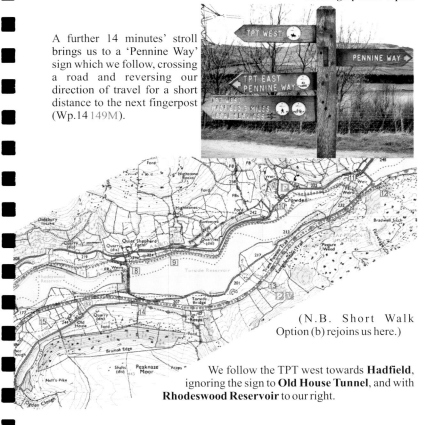

A further 14 minutes' stroll brings us to a 'Pennine Way' sign which we follow, crossing a road and reversing our direction of travel for a short distance to the next fingerpost (Wp.14 149M).

(N.B. Short Walk Option (b) rejoins us here.)

We follow the TPT west towards **Hadfield**, ignoring the sign to **Old House Tunnel**, and with **Rhodeswood Reservoir** to our right.

(N.B. Short Walk Option (a) rejoins us at the fingerpost for **Rhodeswood Dam** (Wp.15 164M.)

We continue on the Trail (SW), passing a sign to 'Deep Clough' and passing under an old bridge. Soon **St. Michael's Church** in **Mottram** comes into view, perched on a hill looking up the valley.

We pass a fingerpost confirming our route to **Hadfield**, and then an information board above **Bottoms Reservoir**, and ignoring a sign for 'Padfield', we continue to **Padfield Main Road** (Wp.16 208M) keeping straight on to **Hadfield Station** (Wp.1 212M). We pass public toilets on this last stretch. For well-earned refreshment there's a choice of **The Palatine Hotel** or **Edward's Wine Bar**.

Our itinerary takes us to **Hartshead Pike** (280 metres) which sits on a promontory, or tongue, separating the **Tame** and **Medlock** valleys. Looking at the statistics, it would be easy to underestimate this walk; but with four steady climbs and matching descents, your knees will be grateful for a rest at the end of the walk. The first climb takes us to **Luzley** where both the **Working Men's Institute** and Hall have been renovated for residential use, then we descend to the aptly named **Tongue Bottom Farm**, now **The Hartshead Inn**, before commencing the climb to **Hartshead Pike**.

From early times the hill was used for a signal beacon; the current tower was rebuilt to commemorate the wedding of the Prince of Wales to Princess Alexandra of Denmark. With a toposcope and benches, it offers us the chance of a break while we admire the view. Today, **Park Bridge** is hidden from view as we enjoy the silence, though it wasn't always the case; with mines and an iron works, the smoke and noise would have been all too evident. From our vantage point there's no faulting the surveyor's Euclidean eye for a straight line as **Lees Road** heads almost true north in the valley below.

On leaving the Pike, we head north along **Back Lane** before our next climb over **High Knowls**. Dropping down to another **Lees Road**, we head to our fourth and final climb to **Quickedge Road**. The track was an important trade route between **Stalybridge** and **Rochdale** well before the turnpike roads. From **Quickedge**, we make our way back down into the **Tame Valley** passing through **Quick** and **Grasscroft** to join the **Huddersfield Narrow Canal**, the short stroll along the canal makes a welcome change after our roller coaster walk. The short pull up **Chew Valley Road** can hardly be called a climb when relief is at hand at **The Railway**.

**Access by train:** from **Manchester Victoria** to **Mossley Station**, returning from **Greenfield** to **Manchester Victoria**. Car parking is available at **Mossley Station** (return to **Mossley** from **Greenfield** by train).

As we leave **Mossley Station** (Wp.1 0M) via the ticket office, we turn hard right (SW) to re-cross the railway on **Stamford Road**. Approaching the bank, we head up **Old Brow** (WSW) and swing left (SSW) onto **Park Street** after **Bramble Lodge**. At the end of the street we cross over on a left hand diagonal up a track between houses (Wp.2 5M). Following the rough track round, we come onto tarmac by new houses and follow the fingerpost left (SSE) towards 'Luzley' on a fairly steep track leading to a second fingerpost by a gate (Wp.3 9M), which we follow (S) on the steady climb towards **Luzley**.

Taking time to catch our breath and enjoy the view across the **Tame Valley** towards **Buckton Castle** and our route on Walk 21, we continue the steady climb. Coming to a gate at the side of a barn, we continue (WSW) to a stile bringing us out on **Luzley Road** by **Smithy Farm** (Wp.4 22M).

Turning right (NW) towards **The Hare and Hounds**, we continue (N) along **Luzley Road**, noticing the stone of **Luzley Working Men's Institute** as we continue along the road ignoring the first fingerpost to 'Hartshead Pike'. At the second fingerpost (Wp.5 27M) we turn left (WSW) down a broad track to descend gently to **Mossley Road** (Wp.6 37M).

**The Hartshead Inn**

Crossing the busy road, we follow the road opposite down to **The Hartshead Inn**. With no signs to guide us, we turn left down the steps towards the inn and cross the beer garden on a left hand diagonal to the south-west corner and cross a stile (Wp.7 40M).

Over the stile we turn right (WNW), follow the boundary for a short distance, and then maintain our course gently downhill, crossing a footbridge to an old footpath sign (Wp.8 43M). It's better to ignore the fingerpost to our left as we head up hill to the right (NW) keeping close to the shallow clough as there is no clear path. A waymarker guides us down to a stile where another waymarker leads us WNW steadily uphill until we meet the field boundary where we swing left (W) and follow the boundary to a fingerpost (Wp.9 53M).

The fingerpost directs us right (N) to **Hartshead Pike** as we follow the boundary on the left gently uphill. A waymarker on a telegraph pole guides us (N) between stone walls on a long abandoned lane. Another marker leads us on towards farm buildings (Wp.10 58M). Following an overhead cable we take the path between a fence and a wall behind the farm yard which leads us to a stile. Over the stile we can see **Oldham** to our left before we follow the fingerpost right (ENE) along **Lily Lane**. There's no mistaking our next left turn (N) as we head for the **Pike** by a 'Medlock Valley' sign (Wp.11 63M) on a clear path taking us past a toposcope and benches to the tower (Wp.12 67M).

**Hartshead Pike**

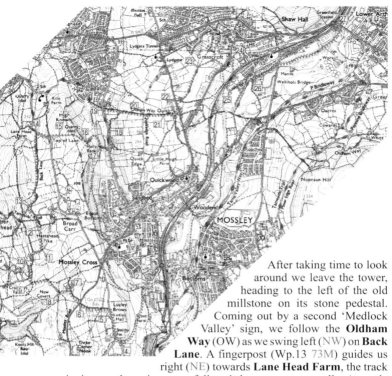

After taking time to look around we leave the tower, heading to the left of the old millstone on its stone pedestal. Coming out by a second 'Medlock Valley' sign, we follow the **Oldham Way** (OW) as we swing left (NW) on **Back Lane**. A fingerpost (Wp.13 73M) guides us right (NE) towards **Lane Head Farm**, the track soon swinging north again as we follow it between stone walls. A gentle descent brings us out by **Thimble Cottage** (Wp14 85M) where we turn right (E) to follow **Lane End Road** gently uphill.

As the road swings right by the last cottage on the left, we follow a fingerpost, tucked up to our left, over a stile. Following the field boundary on our right, we head east, uphill to a stile (Wp.15 91M). With no clear path to follow, we continue east to the brow of the hill. Changing course we head right (ESE) down the hill towards a fence line, above a disused quarry, looking out for a gap stile (Wp.16 97M). Following the **Tameside Trail** (TST) we turn left (NE) and head for the holly bushes below us, where the clear path swings right (SE) to continue the steady descent down **Holly Bank** to cross another stile (Wp.17 103M). A clear path leads us to a waymarker; turning left (E), we follow the track down to **Lees Road**, but not the one mentioned in the introduction. Following a TST marker we turn left (N) to walk along the road, then crossing over to continue past **Butt Lane** (Wp.18 108M).

The OS map shows a path going up the lane and joining our route on the OW. I've attempted this path and even with the guidance of a local resident found it impassable. But it is worth stopping here and looking back at our route. It's clear to see how **Holly Bank** came by the name, though I'm sure there would have been more bushes at one time.

We continue along the road to the **Saddleworth** border at **Grotton**. Just before the border we turn right (E) and climb steps at the gap in the wall

(Wp.19 111M) for a steady uphill climb following both TST and OW markers. Following the field boundary, on our left, to a stile, we continue to climb to the next stile where we can stop to catch our breath and admire the church at **Lydgate** and the mast at **Wharmton**. Cresting the hill we finish the climb and start the descent with views into **Chew Valley**. Coming down to a fingerpost on **Quickedge Road** (Wp.20 121M) we cross the track and continue (E) up a few steps and cross the field on a vague path. Dropping down to a gap stile (Wp.21 126M) we do a quick right and left, following the OW, keeping the field boundary to our left we continue down to the rear of buildings and follow an OW marker right (SE) on a clear path. We descend two sets of steps before coming out onto **Strawberry Lane** where we turn left (NNE) and continue to **Quick Road**. Turning left (NNW), we head gently uphill, crossing the road as we pass the **Old Pump House**, we continue to an OW fingerpost (Wp22 133M) where we turn right (ENE) towards farm buildings.

Passing through a gate by the farm an OW marker, further along the track, guides us on to the next gate. Following another OW marker (NE) we continue to a gap stile, keeping the boundary to our right. Through the next stile, we maintain course to a short section of stone flagging and another gap stile where an OW fingerpost (Wp.23 140M) swings us right (ENE) through a gap stile.

The vague path crosses the field on a left hand diagonal but we soon spot and then cross the next stile, then swing right (SE) at the next fingerpost through a gap stile. We cross a field towards houses, an OW sign directing us down a driveway to **Mossley Road**. Crossing the road, we turn left (NE) to follow the road for a short distance to a gap stile where an OW marker and footpath sign (Wp.24 148M) point us right (SE) on a vague field path.

After crossing the first of two stiles we follow an OW marker (SE) on a clear path taking us over the railway, then heading behind houses. We gently descend to a square brick chimney, an OW marker guiding us along. Keeping the barbed wire fence to our left, the next OW marker (Wp.25 154M) swings us left (NE) on a broad track.

Ignoring a footpath sign to the right, we continue along **Armit Road**, at the end of which a well hidden OW marker on the left, points us right (SSE) to **Lock N°19** (Wp.26 162M). Across the canal on a small footbridge, we turn left (NE) and follow the towpath, going under **Manns Wharf Bridge** (167M) to continue our canal side stroll. After going under one more bridge, we spot the rugby ground on the left, and at the next bridge climb steps to **Chew Valley Road**, turning left (NW) to head uphill.

Crossing the road, we swing right at the hairpin bend, and either stop for some well earned refreshment at **The Railway**, or cross the road to **Greenfield Station** (Wp.27 175M)

# 25 GREENFIELD TO NEWHEY VIA TAME VALLEY

The **River Tame** starts life in the hills surrounding **Denshaw** and flows south to meet the **River Goyt** near **Stockport**. In earlier walks we've explored the valley from **Stalybridge** to **Uppermill**, where the river swings west. On this itinerary we go on to explore the upper reaches of the river, almost to its source. Leaving **Greenfield**, we climb an old track to gain views across **Saddleworth**, then drop back down to the valley and follow the line of the **Delph Donkey**, reputed to have been horse drawn in its early days.

**The Longwood Thump**

It's an area of tradition and festivals, not least of which are the Brass band Contest and the Longwood Thump. The Thump, or Rushcart Festival, involves men hauling a rush-laden cart from village to village. Clogs, bells and flower-bedecked hats are de rigueur for the participants, or at least the ones not dressed as ladies. Brass bands lead the way; Morris Dancers entertain and the consumption of ale is almost obligatory.

Of course this doesn't happen every day; **Delph** is (normally) a peaceful, picturesque village. We continue along the valley bottom, the **Tame** meandering in the opposite direction, its true source lost in the reservoirs above **Denshaw**. We leave the river here; **Denshaw** is a small huddle of houses surrounding the meeting point of five roads. Just off our route, at the crossroads, **The Junction Pub** would have been a gold mine in its heyday and still enjoys a steady stream of visitors. Avoiding the road, we follow field paths before joining the original track at **La Pergola**, over to **Ogden**. The hotel offers en-suite accommodation, and the area obviously has high aspirations as further up the road **The Alpine Restaurant** plies its à la carte menu in the white building. Our steady climb levels out before descending to **Higher Ogden**, then into **Lane Bottom** where **The Bull's Head** offers our final refreshment opportunity en route to **Newhey Station**.

| 3 | 3½ H | 8.1 miles/13km | | 373m / 384m | | 3 |

**Access by train:** from **Manchester Victoria** to **Greenfield** or **Manchester Piccadilly** changing at **Stalybridge**. Return from **Newhey** to **Manchester Victoria**.

**Short Walk**

The walk described climbs over 90 metres in the first ½km and offers wonderful views, but for a less energetic option, follow Walk 13 to the railway viaduct at **Brownhills**. Turn left over the canal to follow 'Delph Donkey' signs. Continue along the disused line, rejoining the walk as we leave the donkey down steps (Wp.7) and cross the road.

Leaving **Greenfield Station** (Wp.1 0M) we turn left (NE) heading uphill to the busy road junction where we cross carefully to continue (NE) up **Ladcastle Road** for a short distance. Watching out for a grassy bank and two old gate posts on our left, we leave the road and cross a stile to start the steady northerly climb up **Colt Hill Lane**. We soon have splendid views of the **Tame Valley** with **Uppermill** ahead, and **Pots and Pans** over to the right. As we pass a gas pipeline marker we swing left (NW) to follow the fence to a stile (Wp.2 13M).

Keeping the fence to our right, we finish our first climb and swing right (N) round the upper edges of the disued **Moorgate Quarry**. Leaving the fence, a fairly clear path leads us across the field to the edge of **Saddleworth Golf Course** (Wp.3 19M); over a stone step stile, we walk through it (NW), taking the left hand fork to stay on the broad cinder track. Coming into an open area (Wp.4 28M), we swing right (NE) towards a pond, passing a waymarker as we head to, then follow the fence on our left, soon descending gently. Leaving the course by a stone gap stile (Wp.5 33M) we find a convenient bench from where we look towards the picturesque village of **Dobcross**, featured in films including 'Yanks'; though the rash of 60/70s houses do not fit in well with the surroundings.

From the bench, we follow a field path (WNW) and continue towards buildings and through a gap stile. Coming onto tarmac, pass the buildings and swing right by N°14, passing **Mount Lane** to gently descend the hill (NNE). Passing three-storey weavers' cottages, we swing left, as the road continues to the right, dropping down by the side of a cottage onto a sett-paved track before coming to **Delph New Road** (Wp.6 39M).

Turning left (NW) we follow the road for a short distance to a gap stile, on our left. A fingerpost points the way to 'Delph' (NW) on the **Delph Donkey**. The pleasant stroll takes us through rock cuttings and under a skew arch bridge as we follow the tree-lined route of the former railway. A new development at **Delph Station** halts our progress, so we leave the track down steps to our right (Wp.7 52M), cross the road and turn left (NE) following the **River Tame** to the incongruous buildings of **Gateshead Business Park** (Wp.8 55M).

Turning right (SE) we pass between building to a footbridge. Turning left (NE), follow the path round by the river. Ignoring the first path on the right, we continue along the river to climb steps up (NE) into **Gatehead Croft**. Turning left (NNW) at **Gatehead Road**, we take a few steps before crossing **Huddersfield Road** to pass through the gateway at the side of **The Bell Inn**.

Weaver's Cottage

Passing quickly through **Saddleworth Business Park** (Wp.9 67M) we ignore a fingerpost to our right, staying by the river on a broad track. At **Hindel Terrace** we cross the footbridge, turn right and resume our northerly course with the river on our right. (There's also the option of heading up to the Co-op building and turning right to walk through the village at this point.) Staying by the river we pass weavers' cottages and the old feeder streams

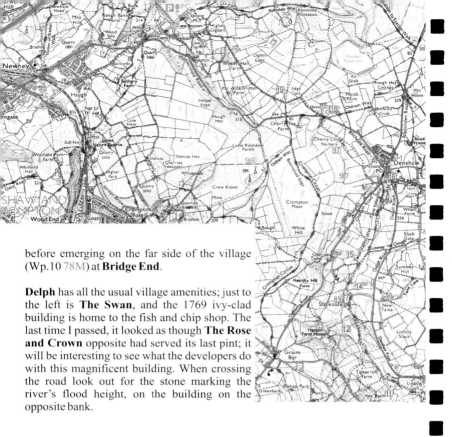

before emerging on the far side of the village (Wp.10 78M) at **Bridge End**.

**Delph** has all the usual village amenities; just to the left is **The Swan**, and the 1769 ivy-clad building is home to the fish and chip shop. The last time I passed, it looked as though **The Rose and Crown** opposite had served its last pint; it will be interesting to see what the developers do with this magnificent building. When crossing the road look out for the stone marking the river's flood height, on the building on the opposite bank.

Crossing the road, we swing right following the river, crossing it on a footbridge then swinging right (W) to follow the broad track. Passing through a gap stile by a gate, we continue on the track to and through the **Country Classics Mill** and shop complex (88M), emerging on a vague path (WNW) bringing us back to the **Tame**, on our right. Crossing the next footbridge, we swing left (NW), the path soon rising gently as the river meanders away from us.

Climbing up at the side of a cottage, we come to a broad track and cross a stile on our left (Wp.11 94M) to head downhill (WNW), soon rejoining the **Tame**. Ignoring the first footbridge, we cross a stile as we stroll along the valley bottom, the **Tame** rushing in the opposite direction, following the clear path over a stile and a footbridge. After another stile and footbridge in close proximity to each other, we swing right then left, back on a northerly course as the track opens out. The track gently rises and we come out at **New Barn** (Wp.12 107M) where the cluster of houses have their own tree-planted mini-roundabout.

Crossing the gravelled area we swing left (NNW) onto a concrete track which soon turns in behind buildings; we continue (NW) downhill on the broad grassy track. The track changes to gravel behind cottages at **Slackcote**, and we turn left (NW) down to an old mill (Wp.13 111M) where we turn right

(NE) and climb the gentle hill. Passing **Nature's Nursery**, we reach **Horest Lane**, turning left (NW) to follow the lane as it swings right and gently rises to a footpath sign (Wp.14 121M) where we leave the road, heading for **Ashley House** and passing in front of it, the **Tame** now no more than a stream as we continue towards a double garage and follow an 'Oldham Way' (OW) marker over a stile (NNE). We follow the track to a finger post on the right (Wp.15 125M) and a stile further to the right; crossing, we following an OW marker towards the next fingerpost, from which we head towards a small weir. Swinging slightly left to a stile, we follow an OW marker between fences towards **Denshaw Church** (the path can be muddy) across a stile and two footbridges.

Crossing fields with the church ahead, we reach a kissing gate and continue towards buildings. Heading towards a three storey building, we turn left between N°s14 and 16, turning right again behind a garage. Ignoring a path to our left, we climb gently, passing a mill pond and a gate before emerging opposite **The Black Horse** (Wp.16 141M); other refreshment opportunites are offered at **The Printer's Arms** within 100 metres to the left, and at a similar distance to the right, **The Junction** (Lees Beers).

Crossing the road, we follow a footpath sign by **Smithy Cottage** and climb a few steps. We swing left (SW) leaving the steps that continue to the cottage garden. Making our way through bushes, we come out on a track and turn right (NW) on the uphill track passing **Brownhill Naze Farm**. At the next farm building we turn (W) following a waymarker to a gate through which we turn right (NW).

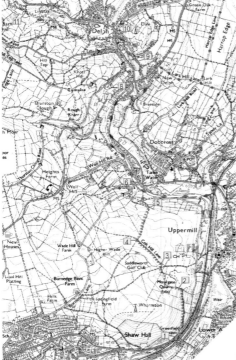

On reaching the next gate, we continue our course across a little-used field path towards the front of the next farm building, emerging on a track (Wp.17 152M) by **Boothstead Farm** (B&B accommodation) to continue across fields (NW), aiming for the next farm's barn which brings us to a stile.

A waymarker points the way towards two trees near the farm building, then a fingerpost by the trees points us to a gate and the farmyard where we turn right (NNE), following the farm track to **Rochdale Road** (Wp.18 158M) coming out opposite **La Pergola**.

Crossing the road, we turn left for a few steps then follow a footpath sign on an uphill track to the right (NW). Passing a house which appears to host a graveyard for mechanical diggers, we continue up the track. At the next farm, where they've made an attractive rock garden and water feature of the dry stone wall, we turn left (WSW) along a broad track.

At the next junction (Wp19 164M) we take the right hand fork (WNW) soon passing **Moorfield Boarding Kennels**. The track provides easy walking before starting a gentle descent as views of **Winter Hill**, **Holcombe** and **Watergrove Reservoir** start to open up; then **Ogden Reservoir** comes into view as we descend to a section of the original sett paving that would have surfaced the length of the track, finally bringing us to houses at **Higher Ogden** (Wp.20 189M).

**The Bull's Head**

Taking the right hand fork behind the houses, we pass **Oak Cottage** and the rear of **Manor House Farm** the sett paving giving way to tarmac. Continuing to descend, we pass the 18th century stable, barn and *shippon* of the farm as we continue to **The Bull's Head** at **Lane Bottom**.

Just after the graveyard, we turn left (SW) along **Ogden Road** bringing us to **Huddersfield Road** (Wp.21 203M). Turning right (W) we cross the road after 50 metres to follow a fingerpost (SW) up a rough track by cottages, our clear track taking us past houses to **Kiln Gardens**. Continuing to **The Wheatsheaf** (Wp.22 212M), we turn left (SW) following a 'Beal Way' marker into **Two Bridges Road**; crossing, we continue to a footpath sign and turn right (NNW) into **Railway Street**. Over a footbridge, we continue to meet **Huddersfield Road** again where we turn left (SW). **Newhey Station** (Wp.23 217M) is a few metres further along.

If you've resisted the numerous refreshment opportunities this far (which I usually do!) and now feel the need of liquid refreshment, cross over and carry on to **Newhey Road** and turn right to **The Waggon and Horses**, just round the corner.

This route takes us past **St. Thomas' Church** in its prominent position above the village onto an old, often deserted carthorse track that wends its way between hills to the moors, once the busy 'main' route echoing to the clatter of cartwheels and horses' hooves long before the existence of the M62, roaring below. As the track disappears we climb to the appropriately named **Windy Hill**; it's rare to find a truly calm day here when the wind isn't blowing.

When the **Pennine Way** first opened, the modern trade route of the M62 was in the planning stage, and two Transport Ministers (Ernest Marples and Barbara Castle, both keen walkers) planned the footbridge which now crosses it. I often wonder how many motorists must rush under this bridge, on the highest section of motorway (1121 feet) in England, without realising the **Pennine Way** is above them. We follow it to **Blackstone Edge**, described by Daniel Defoe as the "Andes of the North".

**The author en route**

Defoe describes a terrifying journey made through a snow storm (in August!) over **Blackstone Edge**. Maybe it's a sign of global warming, as I've never experienced snow here in August and I worked at the transmitter for a number of years. But don't underestimate the weather; it can change rapidly and visibility can be near zero at any time of year. I've done this walk in winter with snow drifts several feet deep on the way up, therefore changing the walk grade from 4 to 5.

Today the smoking mill chimneys have gone as we enjoy the view from the trig point on its gritstone pedestal before making our way to the **Aigin Stone**. On this itinerary we ignore the Roman Road (covered in Walk 4) and head for **The White House** and another old track, the turnpike we follow replaced by the A58 which we cross near **The Bar House**. Continuing round **Stormer Hill** to **Lydgate**, we arrive via **Owlet Hall** at **Littleborough**.

| 4/5 | 4H | 10 miles/16km | 437m / 456m | ⟷ | 4 |

**Access by train:** from **Manchester Victoria** to **Newhey**. Return to **Victoria** from **Littleborough**. Cars can be parked on **Railway Street** at **Newhey**. Return to **Newhey** by train from **Littleborough**, changing at **Rochdale**.

**Short Walk**

Our short walk option would be considered by many to be a walk in its own right. Follow the walk description to the fingerpost at Wp.7, then turn left to **Rakeswood**, to follow Walk 31 from Wp.15 to **Littleborough** (3 walker, 4.7 miles/7½km, 172 metres ascent, 191 metres descent).

Leaving **Newhey Station** (Wp.1 0M) by the uphill ramp, we cross **Huddersfield Road** and turn right (NE), taking a few steps to a footpath sign where we turn left (NNW) to climb stone steps. At the top we turn left (W) climbing gently on the sett-paved road. Passing **St. Thomas' Church**, now on tarmac, we turn right after **Bradstone House** (Wp.2 4M NNE) and follow the track towards and between farm buildings, swinging left (N) to pass behind the buildings to a gate and stile.

Over the stile, we continue up the track, looking for the waymarker post (Wp.3 12M) where we leave the track to follow a vague path by the boundary to a stile. (If you get as far as a gate, having missed the waymarker, the stile is downhill to your left.)

Continuing over the stile, we pass through the broken-down shell of buildings to a stile, continuing the gentle descent to and over another stile (Wp.4 15M). We turn right (NE), the path leading onto a sett-paved track.

This soon gives way to a rough track as we rise gently uphill to pass **New Field House**, ignoring a right hand fork (Wp.5 21M) and continuing up **Carr Lane** to **Carr Farm**.

We climb to a T-junction (Wp.6 30M) where we head right (ESE), continuing the ascent. Soon we have the mast at **Windy Hill** in sight. Coming to a gate, we follow the blue waymarker over a stile and continue on the track, catching glimpses of **Ogden Reservoir** to our right as we stroll on to the next junction. A fingerpost (Wp.7 41M) points our route towards **Piethorn Reservoir**

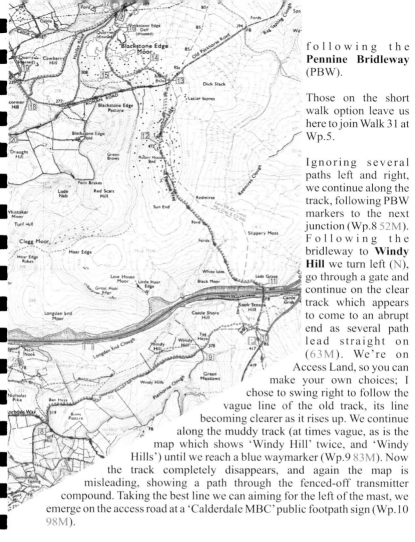

following the **Pennine Bridleway** (PBW).

Those on the short walk option leave us here to join Walk 31 at Wp.5.

Ignoring several paths left and right, we continue along the track, following PBW markers to the next junction (Wp.8 52M). Following the bridleway to **Windy Hill** we turn left (N), go through a gate and continue on the clear track which appears to come to an abrupt end as several path lead straight on (63M). We're on Access Land, so you can make your own choices; I chose to swing right to follow the vague line of the old track, its line becoming clearer as it rises up. We continue along the muddy track (at times vague, as is the map which shows 'Windy Hill' twice, and 'Windy Hills') until we reach a blue waymarker (Wp.9 83M). Now the track completely disappears, and again the map is misleading, showing a path through the fenced-off transmitter compound. Taking the best line we can aiming for the left of the mast, we emerge on the access road at a 'Calderdale MBC' public footpath sign (Wp.10 98M).

Turning left (N) on the **Pennine Way**, our path is clear and at times stone-paved as we head for the footbridge over the M62 motorway. Crossing the bridge to the roar of traffic below, we come to a 'Pennine Way' fingerpost (Wp.11 105M) where we swing left (NW) gently uphill.

It's easy walking, and we soon leave the roar of traffic behind, taking time to look back at the ant-like traffic as it makes is way across **Moss Moor**. The clear path comes to an abrupt end as we near **Blackstone Edge** but the trig point soon becomes visible (Wp.12 137M) as we make our way past **Robin Hood's Bed** on the rocky outcrop.

**At the trig point**

**At the Aigin Stone (Wp.13)**

Having enjoyed the views from the trig point we head north north-east, a few waymarkers and cairns guiding us across the moor, and boulder causeways helping us across some of the boggier sections. Finally coming to a gate, we reach the **Aigin Stone** (Wp.13 151M). From here, you can go left down the hill (WSW), following the **Roman Road** to the water channel and turning right to follow it round. I chose to head north-west to follow a path which at times shows evidence of having once been a track.

A cairn (Wp.14 156M) marks a rough and tricky route across to a disused quarry so we head west north-west following the path down to the water channel where we turn right (NW) to cross a footbridge (Wp.15 164M). Easy walking with the channel on our right allows time to enjoy the view as we make our way round to a broad crossing into the quarry (Wp.16 171M). From here we turn left downhill (SE), the path soon swinging round to bring us down to **Halifax Road** (Wp.17 175M).

Crossing, we turn right heading towards **The White House**; if not stopping for refreshment, turn left (SW) following the footpath sign. The clear track guides us down to cross **Halifax Road** (Wp.18 196M), near **The Bar House**, where we turn right (NW) to follow the road to the PBW (Wp.19 199M). Turning left (WNW) we follow the PBW, rising steadily towards **Hollingworth Lake**, following the track round to **Blackstone Edge Old Road** (Wp.20 209M). Turning right (SW) we follow the road passing **Lydgate Green House** to reach a stile on the left (Wp.21 214M). We follow the 'Pennine Chain' sign south, aiming for a wicket gate to the left of another gate. Through it, we follow the stone wall on our right (SW), our fairly clear path leading to a stile over a stream, and a second stile at **Owlet Hall** (Wp.22 223M).

Crossing behind the hall we pass through the right hand gate and follow the stream (WNW) to the rear of a golf course by a stone footbridge (Wp.23 228M), then descend gently to the stream and a footbridge. Over the bridge, we follow the path as it rises up behind buildings and then descends to a small gate. A yellow waymarker on a stump (Wp.24 234M) directs us right (NW) downhill, and ignoring waymarkers at a kissing gate, we descend steps to **Shore Road**. Following the lane and with the stream on our left, we pass cottages and continue behind a factory, turning right at its entrance (NW) to reach **Ealees Lane**.

For those who like to end a walk with a meal, turn right onto **Westview** passing modern houses and turn right at **Halifax Road**. **The Rake Inn** is on the right, a short distance ahead. Otherwise, continue to the end of **Ealess Lane** turning left at **Halifax Road** (Wp.25 243M). There's a last chance for refreshment at **The Red Lion** before we continue into **Canal Street** for the short walk to **Littleborough Station** on the right hand side of the road (Wp.26 246M).

Our second itinerary from **Hadfield**, though of a similar distance, is more demanding. The first part of the route through **Tintwistle** and **Arnfield** is little more than a stroll; then, still on clear tracks, we start the climb to **Ogden Clough**. A brief descent to **Ogden Brook** signals the start of a demanding 2½ mile section to **Chew Reservoir**. **Higher Bank** is the point of no return, so two short walk options are suggested for use if the weather is poor. Although we pick up a path along the edge of **Ogden Clough**, a compass at the very least, and preferably a GPS, will soon be essential. The footbridge over **Ogden Brook** provides a delightful resting place before we hone our pathfinding skills on the route over **Ormes Moor**. Picking our way over the rocky terrain we make our way to a point simply marked as 'Wilderness' on the map. After a brief section through peat *hags* and *groughs*, hard going after wet weather, we reach **Chew Reservoir**, in 1912, the highest man-made reservoir in England (488 metres). To ensure the dam wall was watertight, it was lined with over 30,000 cubic meters of clay, transported from **Mossley**.

We descend from the reservoir on clear tracks and paths, an information board along the way describing the transport of clay up to the dam by tram. Continuing down to **Dovestone Reservoir**, we reach **Bradbury Lane** to pass a row of cottages, then descend towards **Waterside Mill**. It must have been a hard slog back up this path for the mill workers after a long shift. The last section of the walk from **The Clarence Hotel**, (parties of walkers welcome), is just a pleasant stroll with only a short uphill pull to bring us to **The Railway** our last refreshment opportunity before the train home from the station opposite.

**Access by train:** from **Piccadilly** to **Hadfield Station**. Return to **Manchester Victoria** or change at **Stalybridge** for **Piccadilly**.

We leave **Hadfield Station** (Wp.1 0M) heading north-west across the car park towards **The Palatine Hotel** and continue down **Station Road**. Passing the surgery (Wp.2 3M) on the corner of **Lumbgates**, we turn right (NNE) onto a track behind buildings, soon swinging left (N) at a Y-junction to follow the broad track down towards a road. Crossing the road we continue (N) to and across the next road to follow a fingerpost (N) through a housing estate. Swinging left (W) at N°14 **Lodge Bank**, we come out of **The Croft**, cross the road and turn right (NNE) by a factory. Crossing the **River Etherow** on a footbridge, we continue on **New Lane** to N°40 (Wp.3 14M) where we turn left (W), following a footpath sign along a tarmac path which climbs gently towards houses. We take the right hand fork up to **West Drive**; crossing the road we continue the gentle climb (NNW), crossing over at **Manchester Road**, turning left (NNE) and continuing to **Crossgate Lane** (Wp.4 23M).

We turn right (NNE) up the lane, passing the entrance to **Arnfield Fly Fishery**. Just past the entrance, hidden by a bush on the left, we follow a footpath sign up steps to walk by the reservoir wall (NW), our clear path curling round to the right to bring us on a northerly course. Through a kissing-gate, we pass a nature reserve and continue between stone walls. Crossing a bridge we swing right (NNE) heading towards farm buildings and a fingerpost (Wp.5 37M). Following the **Pennine Bridleway** (PBW) to **Brushes Valley**, we start to climb steadily uphill (NNE).

**Heading to Ogden Clough on the clear track**

Crossing a stile by a gate, we continue climbing to the next stile and gate, where the sign informs us that we are in open country. We continue along the PBW taking a left hand fork on the clear track to the next PBW sign on our right (Wp.6 52M). It wouldn't matter if you missed this sign as the PBW continues on a longer but gentler route down

**Ogden Brook**

into **Ogden Clough**. Taking the shorter route, we follow a yellow waymarker (NNE) on the steep downhill path towards a bridge, to rejoin the PBW at a stile and gate. Here we turn left (NW) over the wooden footbridge. Again, it wouldn't matter if we followed the PBW. Over the bridge, waymarker posts guide us up the steep path to rejoin the PBW to continue uphill to the next PBW sign (Wp.7 63M).

You can confirm your position as we catch our breath, by looking for the 'Peak and Northern' sign down to the left by a stile. This is also the time to check the weather before deciding to continue over the open moor. See the short walk options in the box (right).

Leaving the track, we start by following a swathe of grass (NNE) towards the rougher ground. Checking GPS or compass, we make our way through heather towards the edge of **Ogden Clough**. This has long been a concessionary path and we come to a well-trodden route

### Short Walk 1

The weather can change rapidly in the Pennines; Wp.7 is the point of no return if you need to abandon the walk. The simplest option is to retrace your steps to **Hadfield Station** (5 miles/8km, ascents and descents of 169 metres).

### Short Walk 2

Our second option at Wp.7 can be used if either the weather is poor, or if you have any doubts about navigating across open moorland. From Wp.7, continue to climb following PBW markers; the track is clear and well marked. As you crest the moor, **Higher Swineshaw Reservoir** should come into view. Continue along the PBW to the far side of the dam wall; we are now at Wp.19 of Walk 1. Turn left and follow the instructions for the return to **Stalybridge Station** (7½ miles/12km, 322 metres ascent, 390 metres descent).

along the edge of the clough; it doesn't follow the line shown on the OS map but is by far the easiest route to the head of the *clough* where we find a substantial footbridge (Wp.8 74M), a delightful place on a sunny day to stop for refreshment, with only the sound of the stream and moorland birds for company.

We leave the bridge heading north, following a fairly well-trodden path that brings us to a stile (Wp.9 85M), somewhat off the line of the concessionary path shown on the OS Map. Taking a bearing north-east if using a compass rather than GPS, we identify a rock on the skyline (there are plenty to choose from, so pick one that you can identify easily) and watching our footing, continue the climb through the 'stones'. As we crest the hill, we come to a fence some 50 metres to the right of a stile which is bang on the path shown on the OS Map. This method of navigation is known as 'Aiming Off (course)'. Having reached the fence, the GPS confirms that the stile (Wp.10 103M) is to our left, and we make our way to it.

Over the stile, compass users again take a bearing north-east. If the day is clear enough, you should see the mast at **Holme Moss** on that bearing. The going gets tough on the peat-topped moor, especially after wet weather. Maintaining course is difficult as we negotiate our way, through peat *hags* and *groughs* to the upper edge of **Chew Valley**. Our path becomes clearer as we make our way to **Chew Reservoir** (Wp.11 134M).

Leaving the dam on the downhill tarmac track (NW) we start the steady descent. **Alderman Hill** and the obelisk come into view as the tarmac gives way to gravel (see photo on next page). Shortly before a gate (Wp.12 154M) we leave the track turning left (SW) the clear path swinging right (NW) as we

make our way down to a footbridge. An information board at the bridge gives details of the tramway. Our clear path guides us towards **Chew Piece Plantation**, and coming to a vague Y-junction (Wp.13 163M), we take the right hand fork down towards a stream in the valley bottom.

If you miss this rather vague junction, carry on to the plantation and turn right to follow the fence downhill. We continue downhill between **Chew Brook** and the plantation to reach a tarmac track where we turn left towards the sailing club (Wp.14 171M WNW).

Passing the clubhouse, we continue towards the car park, turning left into **Bradbury Lane** just before the toilets (Wp.15 178M). We pass a row of stone cottages and turn right (NNW), following the fingerpost at the far end of the row down a concrete path. As the path levels out and the wall ends we turn left (Wp.16 190M WNW) and follow a clear path with the stream to our right. The path brings us to a tarmac road which we follow (WNW) to the entrance of **Tanner Business Centre**. Following the road out we cross the brook, turn left and emerge near **The Clarence Hotel**, then head west along **Manchester Road** to the left of the hotel. Ignoring a footpath sign on the right, shortly after the large house on the opposite side, we continue to the next fingerpost (Wp.17 204M) and turn right through a gap in the wall.

A few steps lead us down into an estate where we cross the road and continue on the footpath by the brook. We pass a cricket ground on the opposite bank and come out by **Ladhill Bridge**; across it, we resume our course along **Greenbridge Lane** with the brook to our left. Passing **Primrose Bank**, we continue up the lane, turning left (SW) onto **Croft Edge** before **Boarshurst Band Club**. At **Water's Edge** we enter **Friezland** (Wp.18 211M) and turn right to follow the blue waymarker after the bridge, the brook to our left. We pass the confluence of **Chew Brook** and the **River Tame** as we follow the path round to **Chew Valley Road** (Wp.19 218M). Turning left (W) we cross the **Tame** and the canal, and climb towards the hairpin. After crossing the road we turn right by **Goblin Manor** bringing us to **The Railway**, our last refreshment opportunity. Crossing the road, we arrive at **Greenfield Station** (Wp.20 221M).

If, like me, you enjoy walking old paths and tracks, imagining what life was like in some bygone age, then this walk is for you. In his book 'A Passage Through Time', Bernard Barnes provides comprehensive details of the roads and tracks of **Saddleworth**, some of which we walk on this itinerary.

Leaving **Greenfield** we make our way to **Shaw Hall** and onto what appears to be no more than a rather overgrown path, though later it will become clear that we've been following a long-abandoned track, once a **Turnpike Road**. After a section on field paths and a long straight section, paralleling the ancient track of **Doctor Lane** (an ancient track which became a Turnpike Road), we skirt round **High Moor Quarries**. Quickly passing the 'Waste Management Facility' (rubbish tip), we descend into **Thurston Clough**, our onward route visible ahead, climbing out of the *clough* between stone walls. Exactly why this track was constructed from the bottom of the *clough* is no longer clear, though it does lead up to **Hill Top Lane**, one of several routes to **Rochdale** before the turnpike era. I like to stop part way up this rise to look over towards **Pots & Pans**. You may need to look hard for the obelisk to identify the hill, as it looks so different from this perspective.

After visiting **Bishop's Park**, our route takes us through **Grains** - or **Grains Bar** as it's been known since the days when tolls were collected here at the crossing of two Turnpike Roads. Its former importance also explains why there are two pubs at this out of the way crossroads.

The last part of our journey is mainly along field paths as we make our way down to **Shaw Station**. Don't be fooled by the poor orientation of the footpath sign soon after **The Bull's Head**. I've seen (and helped) a few walkers found puzzling over maps, or wandering around the field looking lost!

**Access by train:** from **Manchester Victoria** to **Greenfield Station**, or train from **Manchester Piccadilly**, changing at **Stalybridge**. Return to **Manchester Victoria** from **Shaw Station**.

We leave **Greenfield Station** (Wp.1 0M) and turn right (SW) heading downhill into **Shaw Hall Bank Road**. Turning right at a fingerpost (Wp.2 4M WNW), we follow the path uphill to and across a road. Continuing on a path to the next road, we cross over to a gap in the wall (Wp.3 7M). Climbing a few steps, we head west, pushing our way through vegetation. Watching out for a stile on the right, we cross it and continue north-west uphill on an easier path. Rising up, we find a stile to our left at the end of the overgrown path (Wp.4 19M); over it, we continue to and over the next stile, maintaining course to cross a third stile. Our route contours the hill with a wall to our right, and squeezing through the gap by a gate, we continue gently uphill between walls to and over another stile, turning right (NE) by **Burnedge House** to go a short distance up **Burnedge Lane** to a white lamppost on the left (Wp.5 34M).

There's no footpath sign to guide us, but we turn left (NNE) despite the feeling we're entering someone's garden, to head up the side of the cottage. Steps bring us to a broken down building, and we continue (NNE) to a broken stile, then follow the field path, a wall to our right, to and through a gap.

**The fallen gap stile (Wp.6)**

We take a left hand diagonal (NW) towards a church, and on reaching a wall we find a gap stile partially blocked by fallen stones (Wp.6 43M). Carefully climbing into the next field, we follow its boundary west to a gateway. Turning right (N), we follow the dead straight wall on our left that stretches on into the distance through several fields - we'll be following it for the next few minutes, as we cross two step stiles before coming to **Oldham Road**.

Across the road, we go through a small gate and continue by the wall, passing another step stile before arriving at **Thurston Clough Road** (Wp.7 62M).

Turning left (W) we follow the road, passing **The Old Original** pub and restaurant to a junction where we turn right (N) into **Back Lane**. Gently climbing, we follow the road round to the left and pass the entrance to **High Moor Quarry**, also home to a waste management facility. Continuing towards power lines, **Hartshead Pike** is visible to our left. Turning right at a fingerpost (Wp.8 71M N), we cross a stile to continue between fences, and soon come to another stile on the right, where we follow a yellow waymarker at the side of the high quarry fence to the next stile. Dropping steadily down into **Thurston Clough** we cross the brook and start climbing steadily between broken down walls. As we climb we can see the obelisk at **Pots & Pans** to our right. Crossing a stile, we're now on **Badger Edge Lane** which we follow to **Hill Top Lane** (Wp.9 96M).

**The trig point and monument**

Heading left (WNW) we follow the lane as it contours **Badger Edge** to reach a junction where we turn left (SW) into **High Lee Lane**. Coming to a stile on the right (Wp.10 104M), we cross into a field taking a left hand diagonal (W) to follow the edge of rough ground, then swing left (SW) above the rough ground to follow the fence on our right to a stile (Wp.11 108M).

Going right (N) we climb gently, swinging slightly left to the trig point and monument (Wp.12 111M) where an inscription tells of the donation by Ellen

Ludlum of fifty acres of land for the benefit of the people of Oldham. We also find a pedestal for a toposcope; unfortunately there's no plate to detail our surroundings.

We leave the hill from the monument, heading north-west towards a car park and golf course. A 'Medlock Valley Way' fingerpost directs us across the car park to and through a gap stile to follow a path to the left of the golf course.

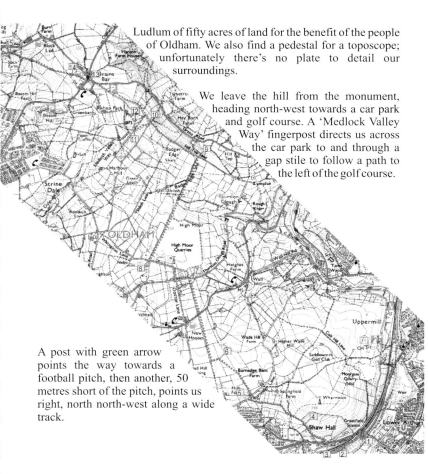

A post with green arrow points the way towards a football pitch, then another, 50 metres short of the pitch, points us right, north north-west along a wide track.

Following the track round to the club house, we turn right (NNE) following a small fingerpost with a wall to our left.

Emerging on **Grains Road**, we turn left (NW) and pass **The King's Arms** to the junction at **Grains Bar**, once a tollgate on the old turnpike road. Crossing the road to **The Bull's Head** (Wp.13 123M), we follow a footpath sign to the rear of the pub car park where we find a wooden fingerpost by a gap stile directing us west to the left of a gate and step stile across the field. Over the stile, we head for the next fingerpost and cross a stone step stile into the corner of a field.

Both the fingerpost (Wp.14 127M) and the 'Crompton Way' (CW) marker are most misleading; they point straight on in a north-west direction - which would bring us to the wrong corner of this field! Ignoring the sign we take a left hand diagonal (WNW) towards a stone wall. At the stone wall we swing right to follow the boundary gently down hill to and through a picket gate. Now we resume our course on the CW, following a stone wall now to our right.

Crossing a stile by a gate, we follow the CW on a clear track to pass through a farm, then follow the tarmac road, keeping our eyes open for a gap stile (Wp.15 138M) on the left.

Through the stile, we head west north-west, soon passing a bench and descending a few steps to another track. Across the track a CW marker, hidden under a holly bush, leads us over a stile for our continuation west and downhill. Passing through two more gap stile, CW markers leading the way, we come to an old track bounded by stone walls (Wp.16 142M) which we cross to a wide gap in the walls. It's worth taking the time here, to look at the next section of our route. Looking west, try to identify the bungalow almost hidden by trees and the well tended pitch of the **Shaw Cricket Club** beyond it.

Setting off downhill, we make our way towards the bungalow, soon coming to two gates (Wp.17 144M). Through the left hand gate, we step down into the field and follow the boundary on our right to and through a gap stile in the field corner. Maintaining our westerly course we head for the right hand corner of the bungalow. A gate leads us on to a rough track bringing us out by **Hillside Cottage** and **Shaw Cricket Club** (Wp.18 149M).

Swinging slightly right, we continue west on the broad, level track, soon coming onto tarmac through a housing estate. Emerging on a broad road, **Clough Cottage** on the left, we cross to find a fingerpost (Wp.19 154M) guiding us between metal railings to a zebra crossing. Turning right then left, we skirt the mill building round and cross the road. The **Manchester** Platform, at the **Shaw and Crompton Station** (Wp.20 157M), is just before the level crossing and footbridge.

Usually you'll find a pub close to most stations, but this is an exception. However, all's not lost, as **The Morning Star** can be found by turning right at the zebra crossing and heading up **Grains Road** for 300 metres. With its warm welcome, Lees Beer and a pleasant roadside beer garden, it comes well recommended.

**Shaw** and **Crompton** were once home to a number of 'Cotton Millionaires', though today most of the mills have been demolished. We soon leave the remaining ones behind to climb onto the moors where we join the **Crompton Circuit** and follow an old track above the **Tame Valley** as we make our way over to **Piethorne Reservoir**. Passing through bucolic scenery, the route also offers views of routes in this book that you might already have completed, and onwards to routes yet to be explored. At **Piethorne** we make our way through the wooded **Old House** grounds and pass the remains of a number of farms that were demolished to make way for the reservoirs. Only one working farm remains nestled in an idyllic spot between the reservoirs. After all the peace and quiet, the M62 provides a brief reminder that we're not far from civilisation before our final descent into **Newhey** passing the prominently placed **St. Thomas' Church** on the way to the station.

**Access by train:** from **Manchester Victoria** to **Shaw Station**. Return from **Newhey** to **Manchester Victoria**.

**By car:** parking is available **at Shaw Station**. Return by train from **Newhey**.

We leave the station (Wp.1 0M) via the car park, turn left (E), and cross the tracks using the pedestrian footbridge if the level crossing is closed. Crossing the road, we stroll by the mill and then turn right to cross a zebra crossing. Just to the right of the crossing, we follow a footpath between a fence and stream. Coming out by **Clough Cottage** we turn right (SE) for a gentle climb up **Clough Road**. A sign for 'Shaw Cricket Club' (Wp.2 6M) guides us along a rough track which swings right past the clubhouse where we continue the climb on a private road. Swinging left through the gate of **Cart Chief Nook Farm**, we continue to the farmyard (Wp.3 14M).

Crossing the yard (E) to its right hand corner, we climb 'giant steps' of reclaimed stone. Through a gate, we cross the field (E) to a gap where we turn left (N) through a kissing-gate, the broad track leading us between dry stone walls to a gate and ladder stile. Now heading west, the track brings us to a kissing-gate (Wp.4 18M) to turn right and leave the track through a gap in the wall, again turning right through a gap stile (ENE). Following the **Crompton Circuit** (CC) waymarker we cross a track and continue on the steady diagonal climb (ENE). Maintaining our course through a gap stile, we come to the next gap stile (Wp.5 23M) hidden by a holly bush.

After crossing a track we climb a few steps and continue following a CC marker to the next gap stile. Across another track, we pass through a further gap stile. Looking up ahead, we aim (NE) for a footpath sign beyond the larger road sign, a final gap stile bringing us onto **Buckstones Road** (Wp.6 27M) where we turn right (E) to follow the road for a short uphill tarmac stretch. Soon after the road swings right we cross over left (ENE), to a track (Wp.7 31M) at the side of **The Black Ladd** pub car park. With views of **Crompton Moor** to our left, we make the gentle climb between stone walls.

Staying on the track, we rejoin the **Crompton Circuit** as it swings left towards an isolated farm building.

**Tame Valley (near Wp.8)**

A CC marker before the farm guides us straight on to the left of the building (NNE), CC markers continuing to guide us towards and under power lines to reach a gate (Wp.8 49M). It's worth stopping here to admire the view. Below us are the upper reaches of the **Tame Valley**, while over to our right is a very different view of **Pots and Pans** - look for the obelisk - and you may also see the very top of **Holme Moss** transmitter peeking over the distant moors.

From the gate, we need to circumnavigate some rough ground before following the right hand boundary as we climb up **White Hill**. Continuing to follow CC markers, we keep the boundary to our right, pass through a gate and

try to avoid the boggy sections before **Rooden Reservoir** comes into view (59M). You'll soon notice a rough overgrown gully, which is the line of a long abandoned track. If ground conditions permit I like to walk along the gully, although there's a better track to its left. Coming to a small metal gate (Wp.9 68M) we continue to the tarmac track where a fingerpost with an 'Oldham Way' marker guides us right (N), gently downhill to the A640 (Wp.10 73M) on the **Saddleworth Denshaw** border.

We cross the road and follow the bridleway at the side of **Highland House**. At the junction we turn right (ENE), soon passing a building with a track-side rock garden, our rough but clear path leading us to a kissing-gate. A yellow waymarker guides us as **Piethorne Reservoir** comes into view. Look out for the **Norman Hill Reservoir** which is tucked into the hill above **Piethorne**, and beyond that we can see **Windy Hill Transmitter**.

At the next waymarker (Wp.11 86M) we ignore the path left and continue (NNW) gently downhill, our descent steepening a little as two more waymarkers guide us on towards the reservoir and a metal ladder stile (Wp.12 93M). Over the stile, we continue over the dam wall and the broad track brings us to a T-junction (Wp.13 98M) where we turn left downhill (NNW), towards the reservoir and waterfall on the **Norman Hill** overflow channel. Passing a building and the waterfall, we climb to a gap on the left before a gate (Wp.14 104M).

**The one remaining farm**

Turning left through a kissing-gate, we enter **Old House** grounds and head WNW through trees on a well-trodden path. We leave the grounds through a kissing-gate and continue (WNW) on a clear path which becomes a track with yellow waymarkers to guide us, passing the remains of more abandoned farms before coming onto a surfaced track (Wp.15 123M), taking a look back at the one remaining farm.

Turning right (W) we pass under power lines, noticing more ruins down to our left and a grass track (Wp.16 130M) dropping down left (SW) between the ruins and a wall. Following this path through **Rag Hole Farm**, we pass through a gap onto a path of reclaimed stone leading down into a *clough*. We cross a footbridge after some steps and follow a yellow waymarker left (SSW) to stroll along the track above **Ogden Reservoir**, going through a kissing gate and continuing to a step stile by a gate. At a junction leading down to the dye works we turn right (Wp.17 141M WNW), our track then turning back on itself (N) to pass through a scattered hamlet and a farm-yard.

The track surface changes to double stone, then to sett paving before reaching another junction where we turn left (Wp.18 154M SW), the M62 roaring away to our left. We pass the rebuilt **New Fold Head** and continue to a farm. By two oil storage tanks at the back of a barn (Wp.19 159M) we leave the track, turn left up a grassy bank (SW) and find a stile hidden behind bushes.

**St. Thomas' Church**

Over the stile, we follow the boundary on the right to the next stile, then pass through a ruined building, keeping to the boundary.

Our path becomes a track, the steeple of **St Thomas' Church** coming into view before the next stile which we cross, then pass behind the white farm building and swing right (SW) along the track with views over **Rochdale**, and **Winter Hill** visible on a clear day. Turning left (SE) by the large house to pass the church we come onto a sett-paved road. As the road swing left we look for a footpath sign on the right leading us down steps by a school.

Dropping down to **Huddersfield Road**, we cross it and take the few remaining steps to the station (Wp.20 176M), on our right.

For liquid refreshment before the train journey home, continue along **Huddersfield Road** turn right to find **The Waggon & Horses**, a Lees Pub.

This itinerary could be completed as a day walk, though it's designed as part of a two or three day break. Day one takes us from the **Tame Valley** and across the narrowest point in the Pennine Chain to **Marsden** in the **Colne Valley**. Starting from **Greenfield**, we make our way to **Pobgreen** following an old packhorse route, meandering past several farms as it makes it way to **Diggle**.

Joining the **Standedge Trail**, we start the climb over the Pennines, following the line of the **Standedge Tunnel**. Along the way we pass *air shafts* which were originally sunk as part of the construction process; full details of the construction technique are explained at **Uppermill Museum** using a model. Rising up to the A62 (one of two busy cross-Pennine routes prior to the M62's opening in the 1960s), we join the **Pennine Way** for a short distance, as we make the moorland crossing to **Mount Road**.

We continue on the packhorse route which was first replaced by **Old Mount Road** and then by **Mount Road** probably at the time that the mill, which dominates the town, was built. Entering the town which nestles amongst hills, it feels like a sleepy backwater today, but prior to the railway and the M62 this was a bustling crossroads on the route between the east and the west seaports. If you get a feeling of déjà vu, it's probably because scenes for the popular television series, 'Last of the Summer Wine' are filmed here.

For those making this a multi-day trip, there's the option of looking round the town and the tunnel **Visitors' Centre**, or of taking the short circular detailed in the next walk. I'm told there are eleven pubs within walking distance of the station, though I've yet to sample them all. The tourist information office can supply details of accommodation and restaurants in the area for those stopping over. The second day of the itinerary takes us to **Littleborough** where two circular routes allow you to tailor the perfect short break in the South Pennines.

| 3 | 3¼ H | 7.8 miles/12½km | 442m 421m | 4 |

**Access by train:** from **Manchester Victoria** to **Greenfield Station** or **Manchester Piccadilly** changing at **Stalybridge**. Return from **Marsden**, but note that the Rail Ranger ticket is not valid from **Marsden** and an additional fare is payable.

**Access by car:** parking is limited at **Greenfield Station** though on-road parking can be found at **Shaw Hall Bank Road**. Return from **Marsden** by train.

**Short Walk Option**

A short circular route returning to **Greenfield** can be completed by leaving the main route at the sign for 'Ivy Bank and Clerk's Cottage' to join Walk 22 at Wp.14 for the return to **Greenfield** (4.7 miles/7.5km, 235 metres ascents and descents).

We leave the station (Wp.1 0M), cross the road and turn right (SW), following the road downhill and turning left (SE) into **Chew Valley Road**. Continuing down the road past **The Wellington** pub, we look out for **Arthur's Lane** (Wp.2 6M) where we turn left (NE) and stroll on to **Higher Arthurs**.

Following the lane as it starts climbing gently, we ignore the PBW off to the right. Briefly walking through the leafy suburb, we watch out for **Lower Carr Lane** on the left and flagged steps on the right (Wp.3 13M) which we climb to a footpath sign.

**Uppermill, from Wp.4**

Following the sign (E) we cross an inclined footbridge, over a disused railway line, which brings us to a gap stile. Through the stile, we climb steadily (E), following the left hand field boundary. The view soon opens up with **Pots and Pans** ahead and **Uppermill** to the left below us. Towards the top of the field the well-trodden path veers to the right, bringing us to a stile (Wp.4 21M).

Over the stile, we follow the road towards a three-storey building where we turn left (N) following a fingerpost along a private road. Passing the pleasantly renovated **Dolefield Farm**, we continue to a Y-junction. Taking the right hand fork gently uphill, look out for a gap (Wp.5 29M) on the left a few metres before a gate, from where steps take us down to a field path leading to a gap stile.

Following a gully, we head uphill towards power lines and a stile bringing us onto a tarmac track. Following the track, look for the stile on the right (Wp.6 34M) which we cross into a field to climb gently, with the boundary to our left. A gate brings us between cottages to follow the tarmac track to **Knowl Top Lane** (Wp.7 40M).

Turning left (N), we follow the lane, the obelisk dominating the skyline. Passing **Pin Fold Farm Cottages** we stroll to **Knowl Farm** (Wp.8 44M), soon leaving the tarmac as we take the right hand fork (NE) on a rough track. Gently climbing, the surface becomes twin stone tracks which we leave by crossing a stile (Wp.9 49M) as it swings left into a farm. Following the field boundary (N) on the left, the farm appears to be the last resting place for old Land Rovers. Over a stile, we continue north with **St Chad's** coming into view. Over the next stile, the clear path has a wall to the right then another stile brings us to the top of a *clough*, dropping and rising around it, we contour **Primrose Hill** to reach houses at **Pobgreen**. A clearer track leads us to a farm

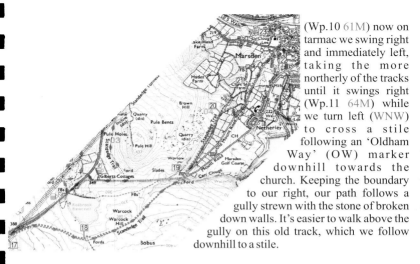

(Wp.10 61M) now on tarmac we swing right and immediately left, taking the more northerly of the tracks until it swings right (Wp.11 64M) while we turn left (WNW) to cross a stile following an 'Oldham Way' (OW) marker downhill towards the church. Keeping the boundary to our right, our path follows a gully strewn with the stone of broken down walls. It's easier to walk above the gully on this old track, which we follow downhill to a stile.

**Short Walk Option 1** leaves us here to join Walk 22 at Wp.14.

Over the stile, we cross tarmac and head (NNW) between the signs for 'Ivy Bank' and 'Clerk's Cottage'. A short downhill stretch brings us to a stile on the right (Wp.12 70M) before reaching the cottages. An OW marker guides us north across the stile where we walk between fences, cross the next stile and a footbridge where a post marks the clear path slightly to the left. Another OW marker leads us over a stile heading towards a garden wall, from where we head towards power lines where an OW marker on a stump swings us right as we drop into a *clough*. After crossing a stream we swing left, gently climbing as we resume our northerly course across a field. Beyond a smaller *clough*, we aim to the right of the buildings ahead, making our way across the field to a ladder stile (Wp.13 81M).

Dropping onto tarmac opposite **Running Hill Farm**, we follow a footpath sign to the right of the farm. A narrow path between hedges leads us to a stile and then a clear path brings us to a stone gap stile and wooden stile. Taking a slight left hand diagonal (N) we head towards a gate and finger-post. Through a kissing gate, we follow the right hand boundary (N) to a gateway where a yellow marker takes us into the next field to continue north with the boundary to our left. Passing a gate and stream, we continue to a stile by a gate.

A fingerpost guides us north to a gap in the wall to cross another field, pass through a gap and follow the well-worn path to a bridge made of railway sleepers. Our path swings right (NE) and takes us over a stone bridge (97M) as we follow drainage ditches on our right which made farming these fields possible. Dropping down to a track, we follow it to a stile and emerge by a damaged statue (Wp.14 103M). Turning left (NW) we cross a bridge and soon turn right (Wp.15 107M) following a sign to 'Diggle Shooting Range', we can ignore the warnings as we don't go near the range. As the track swings right, we continue straight on between stone walls, to a gate where we go left (NNW), following the left hand boundary to another gate and broken stile. Now between walls, we head for the buildings ahead, pass through the yard and come onto tarmac, heading for the fingerpost (Wp.16 121M).

We now follow the PBW, OW and for good measure the **Standedge Trail**, climbing steadily up a clear track (NNE) and soon following the line of the tunnels nearly 200 metres below us, passing outcrops of shale - spoil from the tunnel excavation. Various waymarkers guide us past a house in the process of renovation, and we can see one of the shafts used during the excavation. At the next fingerpost we leave the PBW as it heads to **Castleshaw**, staying with the OW and **Standedge Trail** to continue north to a gate, then on to the car park visible ahead (Wp.17 141M).

From the car park we follow the **Pennine Way** up steps, bringing us onto a wide track which we follow to a gate. Swinging right (E) we are now on **Marsden Moor Estate**. Following the track, we have **Redbrook Reservoir** to our left and can enjoy the view for a while. Leaving the **Pennine Way** on a path to the left (Wp.18 154M), clear but not waymarked and easy to miss.

**The road to Hades Farm (Wp.19)**

However, a stone stump marks the **Pennine Way** as it swings away right and the surface changes; this is just a few steps further on from the turning we want. The path leads us over the moor, finally dropping to a footbridge in **Carr Clough** before climbing out to **Mount Road** (Wp.19 171M) and crossing into **Old Mount Road**. We leave the road by a sign for 'Hades Farm', following the gently ascending **Standedge Trail** (NE), another opportunity to enjoy the views.

When we see an old barn down to our right we leave the track (Wp.20 181M) and head for it, leaving the **Marsden Moor Estate** heading for power lines.

**The mill dominates the town**

A waymarker on a pole well off to the left directs us right (SSE) through a gap in the stone wall (Wp.21 184M). Now following a wall on our left, we come down to **Old Mount Road** where we turn left (NE). With the mill dominating the town, we follow the road downhill to **Manchester Road** (Wp.22 199M). Crossing the road into **Towngate**, a sign directs us towards the station passing the front of **St Bartholomew's**, then left along **Station Road**.

**The Railway** is a smartly refurbished pub offering food, cask ale and a pleasant garden, just across the road from the station (Wp.23 194M). Other refreshment opportunities can be found by swinging right, following **Station Road** to **The Swan** (Thwaite's Ales), or by continuing into town and crossing the river to **The Riverhead Brewery Tap** which has a micro-brewery on the premises.

Designed as day two of a weekend break the itinerary offers a splendid day walk from **Marsden** to **Littleborough**. The route is marked on the OS Map as the 'Station to Station Walk' with alternative starts and finishes.

**Marsden** is a delightful village set amongst hills and is worth exploring in its own right. For those making a weekend of it, there's a short circular option that takes in the **Standedge Tunnel** entrance and Visitors' Centre, with the option of refreshment at **The Tunnel End Inn** free house (which describes itself as 'Flowers in Summer & Fires in Winter'), serving a selection of real ales and home-cooked food.

Our itinerary from **Marsden** takes us over **Close Gate Bridge** (known locally as **Eastergate**; see the plaque by the bridge for the full story). From the bridge we follow the old packhorse route to **Rochdale** known as **Rapes Highway**. The route over the moors is marked by stones inscribed 'PH Road' which were erected by the local council after a dispute with the landowner in 1908.

The route over the moor is well used and easy to follow taking us over to **Readycon Reservoir**, which together with three more reservoirs collect the water that becomes the **River Tame**. We pass the award winning **Ram's Head** (serving Timothy Taylor's ales and meat, game and seafood specialities) as we make our way to **Piethorne Reservoir** and **Rakewood**.

Originally called 'Rake Wood', the word *rake* describes the path descending the hill at an angle taking us under the M62 viaduct. The viaduct (800ft long and 130ft above the valley bottom) took 2 years to build in the 1960s which puts into perspective the achievement of the engineers who built the **Standedge Tunnel** in the 1800s. The gentle finish into **Littleborough** takes us past **Hollingworth Lake** and its Visitors' Centre. Our walk ends with the option of refreshment at **The Rake Inn** for locally produced food or **The Red Lion** for an extensive range of real ales.

This route is promoted by the 'Standing Conference of South Pennine Authorities' (SCOSPA) which publishes an informative leaflet; unfortunately the leaflet gives no route description and the route is not waymarked. If you do decide on following this route as a day walk, the cost of the fare to **Marsden**, which is one stop beyond the cheap Ranger Ticket, may come as a shock!

4 | 4H | 10.9 miles/17½km | 489m / 547m | 4

**Access by train:** from **Manchester Victoria** to **Marsden** or **Manchester Piccadilly** changing at **Stalybridge**. Return to **Manchester Victoria** from **Littleborough Station**.

We leave the station (Wp.1 0M) climbing steps to the road where we turn left (SSE) to cross the line, making our way down to the canal. A sign for the 'Visitors' Centre' at **Standedge Tunnel** guides us left (W) along the towpath, with the canal to our right.

The pleasant stroll brings us within 100 metres of the tunnel entrance (Wp.2 11M), turning right (N) to pass the Visitors' Centre as we make our way to **Reddisher Road** and **The Tunnel End Inn**.

Near the tunnel entrance

We have a choice of turning left (NW) for a gentle tarmac stroll (Short Start Option 2) along **Waters Road** where we meet the main walk at (Wp.5) **Eastergate Cottage**.

For a better view of **Marsden** we cross the road (NE) passing the main entrance of the pub to find a **Kirklees Way** marker on the right which we follow up the grassy bank. Crossing a track we head up steps by the side of a cottage; passing through the garden and play area, we make our way steadily uphill to a track. Turning left (W), we leave the KW, following the track through a cluster of cottages and continuing until it starts descending steeply. A yellow waymarker on a post directs us right (Wp.3 26M N) though we soon swing back to a westerly course.

**Short Walk Options**
**(1) Short circular** Follow the route description to Wp.5 (without taking the short start option) then return from **Eastergate Cottage** along **Waters Road** to **The Tunnel End Inn**. From the pub, reverse the route along the canal for the return to the station (approximately 3 miles/5km, 135 metres ascents & descents).

**(2) Short start** Follow the route description to **The Tunnel End Inn**, then turn left along **Waters Road** to **Eastergate Cottage** picking up the route description at Wp.5 (the main route is reduced by 0.6 mile/1km and 100 metres of ascent).

**(3) Newhey Finish** Follow the route description to Wp.13 and continue to the metal gate after the waterfall; from here follow Walk 29 from Wp.14 into **Newhey** (combined with Option 2, this reduces the walk to 8.75 miles/14km, 386 metres ascent and 419 metres descent).

Another yellow marker on a telegraph pole, directs us along a path behind a house; now bounded by walls we continue to a gap, then follow a well-trodden path as it leads us gently uphill. The next marker, near a Y-junction, is

a little vague; we take the right hand fork uphill, making our way to a gate and the mast beyond it. A sign on the gate tells us we're entering an Environmentally Sensitive Area; a clear path takes us to a footbridge. Over the bridge a marker swings us right (NNW). The vague path passes the remains of a building, becoming clearer as we drop into a clough, cross a stream and follow a yellow marker left (SSW). Keeping the boundary to our right we make the short steady climb towards a metal gate (Wp.4 40M).

Turning left (S), we make our way along the road with excellent views of **Marsden** nestling among the hills; ahead, the A62 was the main route to **Huddersfield** before the motorway was built. The road swings left as we drop down past houses to **Eastergate Cottage** (Wp.5 48M) and find a footpath sign on the right (see Short Option 1).

**Close Gate Bridge**

Turning sharp right (WSW), the path leads us through a gate following the **Standedge Trail**. With a stream down to our left, we continue to **Close Gate Bridge** (Wp.6 52M) where we take time to read the plaque before turning right (NW) on the broad track which soon swings left (W) as we climb **Willykay Clough**, heading away from the stream.

The well-used path over the moors known as **Rapes Highway** is easy to follow, and we're guided along by stones marked 'PH ROAD', the first of which we find at (Wp.7 69M). We pass two more markers before crossing a stream (Wp.8 85M). Taking time to look back (E) we can see the rocket-like **Emeley Moor** mast in the far distance; we then pass two more markers before meeting up with the **Pennine Way** as we ford a small stream (Wp.9 103M), following one of several paths that bring us to **Huddersfield Road**.

Turning left (WSW), we ignore the **Pennine Way** to follow the road for a short distance then turn right (NNW) at a gateway (Wp.10 109M) leading us onto a broad track. The hill to our right is **Rapes Hill** and the easy walking allows us to look around; to our left we can identify **Wharmton Hill** and **Crompton Moors** by their different styles of masts and the **Tame Valley** stretched out below them, and in the far distance the hills of the **Peak District**.

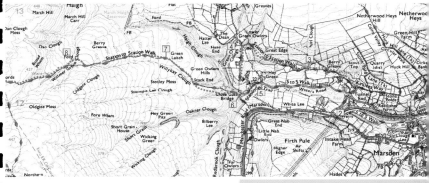

A fingerpost (Wp.11 118M) points the way to **Piethorn Reservoir** following the **Pennine Bridleway** (PBW) as we continue west, starting the descent to **Readycon Dean Reservoir**.

The reservoir

The track leads us by the side of the reservoir and swings right over the dam wall, then left below **Great Hill**. Looking down to our left we see **Crook Gate**, **Dowry** and **New Year's Bridge** reservoirs from which the **River Tame** flows. The track takes us onwards to **Ripponden Road** (Wp12 136M) where we turn left (SW) following the PBW track at the side of the road until it turns right (W), crossing the road by a sign for **The Ram's Head**. This award winning pub serves Timothy Taylor's, excellent food and is a popular venue for people travelling by car.

The waterfall

Our route bypasses the pub, bringing us to a track where we turn right (NW) with **Rochdale** and **Winter Hill** ahead of us and **Windy Hill** to our right. Ignoring a track off to the left we continue through a gate making our way to **Piethorn Reservoir**. A PBW marker (Wp.13 153M) guides us past another track to the left as we start descending to the reservoir and waterfall beyond it.

Crossing the dam, we pass a PBW fingerpost for **Hollingworth Lake** by a small building, pass the waterfall and continue through a metal gate, now climbing steadily. The next fingerpost (Wp.14 170M) takes us left (W) with the rumble of the M62 accompanying our descent along the broad track to the next fingerpost (Wp.15 181M) where we turn right (NNW); the Walk 26 short option joins us en route to **Littleborough**.

Looking out for steps on our left we follow the track for a short distance then turn left (NW) towards **Rakewood Viaduct** following the **Rochdale Way** (RW). Contouring the hills, we pass under the motorway, taking the right hand fork about 150 metres past the viaduct (Wp.16 196M), down towards a sports field. An RW marker points the way (NNE) towards buildings on the opposite side of the pitch. This direct route across the playing area isn't as shown on the OS map, but is the route most people use except on match days when a detour round the pitch is advisable. From the buildings (Wp.17 201M) we turn left cross the car park and exit via a small gate onto a concrete track. Swinging left by houses, we continue on the PBW towards **Hollingworth Lake**.

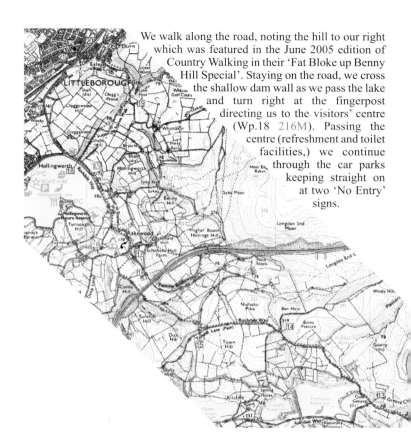

We walk along the road, noting the hill to our right which was featured in the June 2005 edition of Country Walking in their 'Fat Bloke up Benny Hill Special'. Staying on the road, we cross the shallow dam wall as we pass the lake and turn right at the fingerpost directing us to the visitors' centre (Wp.18 216M). Passing the centre (refreshment and toilet facilities,) we continue through the car parks keeping straight on at two 'No Entry' signs.

As the track swings right we continue straight ahead on a path through the picnic area. We then cross **Hollingworth Brook** on a footbridge, swing left through two gates and continue by the brook, then pass through two more gates. Over a stone footbridge (Wp.19 226M) we turn left following the sign to 'Littleborough' making our way past cottages and a factory.

After the factory entrance we have the choice of turning right, passing through the new housing estate along **West View** to **The Rake Inn** or carrying straight on down **Ealees** to **Halifax Road** (Wp.20 234M) where we turn left (WSW) past **The Red Lion**, keeping left into **Canal Street**. Crossing the street to our right when the sign for 'Littleborough Station' comes into sight, we take the last steps to the platform (Wp.21 238M).

## THE WAYFARER WALKS: AN INTRODUCTION

Our next three itineraries (Walks 33, 32A and 33) are designed to provide a weekend break using the Wayfarer Ticket; described as "the day ticket that lets you travel far and wide by bus, train and Metrolink tram". A weekend ticket is available that gives excellent value, offering travel from **Ashbourne** in the south to **Accrington** in the north; from **Owler Bar** in the east to **Earlestown** in the west.

The walks all end at **Whaley Bridge** which is situated in the **High Peak** (18 miles from **Manchester**, 7 miles from **Buxton** and 20 miles from **Sheffield**), an attractive small town built around the historic **Bugsworth Canal Basin**. The town offers accommodation, innumerable pubs, a good selection of restaurants and an alternative shopping experience making it an ideal weekend base.

Visitors from further afield may wish to take full advantage of the ticket, perhaps staying in or visiting **Manchester** and **Buxton**. **Manchester** offers all the usual culinary and cultural opportunities of a major city, whilst **Buxton** (the highest English town of its size at 300 metres above sea level) offers a more sedate alternative. With an annual Gilbert & Sullivan Festival at the Edwardian Opera House and a host of other events held around the town throughout the year, **Buxton** offers the chance to step back in time and enjoy the **Pavilion Gardens** and the chance to taste the world famous spa water, straight from **St. Anne's Well**.

## 32 DISLEY TO WHALEY BRIDGE

Our first itinerary follows part of the **Gritstone Trail**, the entire route comprising a challenging 35 mile/56 kilometre walk offering fine ridge-walking with stunning views over the **Cheshire Plain** as it makes its way to **Kidsgrove** (leaflets describing the walk are available form Cheshire County Council). We follow this well marked trail towards **Lyme Park** where an extension (Walk 32A) offers the opportunity of visiting the park on the way to the **Bowstones**. The main walk and the extension meet up at **Mudhurst Lane** at the access road to the 4-star **Hilton Moorside Grange Hotel**, set in rolling countryside, well placed for a luxury weekend break. From the hotel we make our way along a *rake* on the **Disley** to **Whaley Bridge** old road, passing below **Whaley Moor** where we have magnificent views over **Kettleshulme**, **Hoo Moor** towards the **Cat and Fiddle**, **Shining Tor** and - on a clear day - the tip of **Shuttlingsloe** which is just visible.

Our well-trodden path is not quite as shown on the OS Map, as we pass close by the **Dipping Stone**, visited on Walk 34. The final leg of our walk gently descends to **Yeardsley Hall**, finally passing **Ringstone Caravan Park** as we make our way into **Whaley Bridge** for some well-earned refreshment.

Ratings for the extension walk:
3 hours, 7.8 miles/12.5km, ascents 349 metres, descents 368 metres

**Access by train:** from **Manchester Piccadilly** to **Disley Station**. Return to **Piccadilly** from **Whaley Bridge**.

**Access by car:** parking is available at **Disley**; return by train from **Whaley Bridge**.

### Circular Walk Option

Make a circular walk from **Disley** via **Bowstones** by following the route to Wp.5, then follow the circular Walk 32A back to Wp.5, finally backtracking the outward route for the return to **Disley Station** (6¼ miles/10km, ascents & descents 288 metres).

At **Disley Station** (Wp.1 0M) we make our way towards the opposite platform, climbing the uphill ramp and turning right following the sign for the 'Manchester' platform. As we come down the ramp a large 'Gritstone Trail' (**GST**) notice board and fingerpost direct us south, climbing steps, then continuing uphill and turning left (E) by the sign to **St. Mary's Church** (Wp.2 4M). At the next **GST** fingerpost we swing right (SSE), still climbing gently along the tarmac road. **The Cage** at **Lyme Park** soon comes into view and we continue on the **GST**, ignoring a right turn towards 'The Cage'.

**A Gritstone Trail fingerpost**

Views open up as the track gets rougher and we soon pass **Stoneridge Cottage** (1786), on the left. Our well-signed track passes **Higher Stoneridge** (Wp.3 17M), then becomes a path as we continue (SE). Through a gate provide by Disley Parish Council, the path is a little vague but becomes clearer as we dip down to cross a stream. At the next gate we turn right (W) following the **GST** fingerpost (Wp.4 25M) gently downhill on a wide track.

**Looking back from Wp.5**

As we pass **Millennium Wood** on our left the track gets rougher before we cross a bridge and swing right, climbing gently. Pausing at the next **GST** fingerpost (Wp.5 36M), it's worth looking back at the views across **Manchester** to **Holcombe** and **Winter Hill** on clear day.

N.B. If taking the extension to **Bowstones** Walk 32A, ignore the sign and continue on the **GST** through the **East Gate** and into **Lyme Park**.

To continue to **Whaley Bridge**, we turn left (SE) and cross the stile, following the 'Bowstones' sign. The path is vague so we aim for the power-line pole and soon see a marker post; continuing south-east, the next marker swings us left soon followed by one turning us right, back onto a south-east course. Another marker points the way to a metal kissing-gate (Wp.6 41M), then a well-trodden path leads us through trees, the next marker swinging us left over a stream.

We follow the path to a stile; turning right over it (S), we make our way through rough grass, keeping as close as possible to the fence on the right. Gently climbing, we bypass a 'pointless' stile, aiming for buildings ahead, heading for a gate by the barn (Wp.7 49M) where a marker directs us through the farm yard. Swinging left (ESE), we follow the farm track to a road.

Ignoring the sign to 'Bowstones', we cross the road and head up the access road to **Moorside Grange Hotel**. As the road swings left we continue straight on (SE) along a rough track, crossing one cattle grid and continuing to a second. A 'PNFS' sign directs us left along the **Disley** to **Whaley** old road (Wp.8 58M E) . Keeping the boundary to our right we climb steadily to a ladder stile, enjoying fine views to our right, and follow the *rake* to a stone step stile in a blocked-up gateway (Wp.9 67M). At the end of the rise we start descending as the track swings left then right, leading us to a footbridge. A short climb to the right brings us to a stile (Wp.10 75M); the **Dipping Stone** is off to the right (SE), near the stone wall.

From the stile, we follow the broad grassy track (ENE) downhill to a stone step stile and **Whaley Lane**; turning left (N) we follow the right hand verge for a short distance, then leave the road as we turn right by a fingerpost (Wp.11 83M ENE), aiming for the far left hand corner of the field on a vague path which brings us to a stile. From here we can see the railway making its way to **Whaley Bridge** and to the left of the A6 we can just see **Bugsworth Basin** (Walk 33).

The vague path from the stile goes to the right of the wall as we make our way downhill towards the far left corner of the field. Passing through stone gateposts (Wp.12 91M), a clear track brings us to a metal gate by a farm; we continue straight ahead on the track, then turning right to follow a sign to 'Ringstone Caravan Park' (Wp.13 98M S). Gently climbing to a fingerpost, we pass to the left of the caravan park, then descend to a metal gate (Wp.14 106M).

Swinging left (SE), we climb gently to a stone step stile (Wp.15 110M). Following a fingerpost for a few steps, we swing right (SSE) gently downhill on tarmac. Following **Hockerly Lane**, we pass the entrance to a new estate and then **Hill Drive** before turning left (E) into **Jodrell Road**. Next we turn left onto **Whaley Lane** for the last steps to the **Manchester** platform at **Whaley Station** (Wp.16 121M). **Whaley Bridge** has many refreshment opportunities, **The Jodrell** and **The Railway** are both just a few steps away, on our next walk we'll pass five more pubs and **Teazel's Bistro**, 100 metres down **Canal Street**, offering afternoon teas.

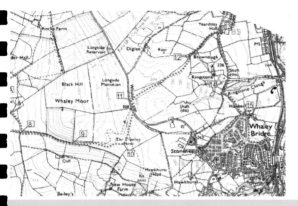

## 32A BOWSTONES EXTENSION

Our extension to the **Bowstones** is described as a circular route starting at Wp.5 on Walk 32. The description caters for people who are taking the short walk option from **Disley**; another alternative is to park at **Lyme Hall** and follow the route from Wp.2A.

On the main walk, we ignore the sign to 'Bowstones' (Wp.5) as we'll be following the trail in the opposite direction. The route takes us through the **East Gate** of **Lyme Park** soon passing a sign detailing the 'Lyme White Park Cattle', often seen grazing in the adjacent field. The gentle stroll towards the hall allows us to enjoy the view beyond **The Cage** over **Manchester**, with the **Welsh Hills** visible in the far distance on a clear day.

The park and hall are maintained by the National Trust; the BBC shot external scenes for Pride and Prejudice & Casanova on location at the hall. Leaving the hall, we pass the visitor centre before starting the steady climb to the **Bowstones**. Look out for the carved bench, pictured right, as we head towards **Knightslow Wood** on the way out of the park. The **Bowstones**, thought to be the remains of Anglo-Saxon crosses, provide the perfect reason to take a break.

The downhill route from the stones offers very different views to those on our outward journey, as we look across the **Peak District** and take the opportunity to enjoy the wayside flowers on our way down to **Mudhurst Lane**. At Wp.6A our route to **Whaley Bridge** turns right along the hotel access road; those returning to **Disley** or who have parked at **Lyme Park** follow the walk back to Wp.5 then either turn left for the park or right for the station.

| 4 | 1H | 3¾ miles/6km | 173m / 173m | ↔ ↻ | 3 |
|---|----|--------------|-------------|-----|---|

**Access by car:** for a short circular walk from **Lyme Park**, signposted off the A6. Parking is available on payment of the National Trust entrance fee to the park. Ample parking is provided at this popular tourist attraction; weekends, school and bank holidays can be very busy.

| Short Walk Option |
|---|
| Described in the overview above. |

We continue straight on from the fingerpost (Wp.5 0M SW), following the **Gritstone Trail** (**GST**) rather than the 'Bowstones' sign. The track soon leads us through the **East Gate** (Wp.1A 1M) **into Lyme Park**, the park track taking us past a sign for the 'Lyme White Park Cattle' as **The Cage** and views over **Manchester** open up. Ignoring roads off to the left, we continue along the track as it changes to tarmac, swinging right to descend to the hall (18M).

Turning right (W), we descend steps to the car park, go to its far right hand corner and rejoin the access road, continuing towards the cattle grid but turning left before it (Wp.2A 22M S). The track takes us to a large wooden gate, a **GST** fingerpost to the right confirming our route. Through the gate, a broad track heads gently uphill, passing a bench supported by carved sheep, pictured on the previous page.

**The Bowstones**

Crossing a ladder stile (Wp.3A 29M), we continue through **Knightslow Wood** to cross the next ladder stile (Wp.4A 35M). A fingerpost points the way to 'Bowstones' as we continue to climb, swinging onto an easterly course. The broad rough track is easy to follow as we ascend to the next ladder stile where we leave the park, perhaps taking a last look back at the

**Fine views from Wp.5A**

views across **Manchester**. The clear level path leads us to a stile where a fingerpost guides us left (NE) to 'East Gate'. The **Bowstones** (Wp.5A 49M) are on the left in a small enclosure.

A downhill stroll gives us time to enjoy views over **Whaley Bridge** towards **Chinley Churn** and the **Kinder** plateau beyond. Further downhill, **Moorside Grange Hotel** comes into view and we can see our route out to **Whaley Bridge** as it makes its way under **Whaley Moor**. Meeting **Mudhurst Lane** (Wp.6A 67M), our extension to Walk 32 ends and we turn right (E) along the hotel access road to make our way to Wp.8 on Walk 32.

For those returning to **Lyme Park** or **Disley Station**, turn left (NW) following the 'East Lodge' fingerpost along the farm access road.

Entering the farm yard we swing right (NW) by the first building, heading for a gate by the large barn, from where we head NNW towards a 'pointless' stile several metres away from the left hand wall. A marker guides us along a well-trodden path as we continue towards the left hand boundary, following it to a stile (Wp.7A 73M). Turning left (NW), we cross the stile and soon see the next marker post, veering right as we cross a stream to follow the path through trees to a metal kissing-gate.

From here the path is vague, but a marker post is visible ahead in a NNW direction. From this post (Wp.8A 78M) the path is barely visible but we head for a sycamore tree where a marker swings us left, soon followed by another guiding us to the right. We aim for the power-line pole and soon see the **GST** finger-post by our starting point (Wp.5 82M). Turning left (SW) takes us back to **Lyme Park**, or turn right (NE) to retrace our outward route to **Disley Station**.

You won't find **Bugsworth** on the map; the original name, recorded as 'Buggisworth' in 1275, originates from the Old English when a person's name (possibly 'Bucg' in this case) plus 'worth', meaning an enclosure, were used to name a place. Embarrassed by the name, the villagers held a referendum in the early 1900 and changed the name to **Buxworth**, prompting a lot of satirical comment. As recently as 1999 another referendum was held, the villagers voting to retain **Buxworth**; though you may well hear some of the older locals still refer to it as 'Bugsworth'.

The canal basin, built in the 1700s to transport limestone from local quarries, was Britain's largest inland port. It fell into disuse during the 1920s, was reopened on 3rd August 1999 and is now a scheduled Ancient Monument. The basin boasts a gruesome story; John Cotton, having been found guilty of murdering his wife on their boat, was the last man to be hung at Derby Jail in 1898. **The Navigation** inn (a Free House) also has its claim to fame, having once been owned by Pat Phoenix who played Elsie Tanner in Coronation Street. Open all day, it serves food and fine ales and offers accommodation.

Our short circular itinerary makes an ideal pre-prandial walk for those spending a weekend in **Whaley Bridge**. The route also passes seven of the many pubs in the town, starting with **The Jodrell Arms** at the station; we also pass a second hostelry named **The Navigation** as we make our way back into town down **Canal Street**.

Access by train: from **Manchester Piccadilly** to **Whaley Bridge Station**. Return to **Piccadilly** from **Whaley Bridge**

Car parking is limited at the station; the public car park off **Canal Street** is close by.

> **Extended Walk Option**
> Ignoring the footbridge at Wp.10, and continue along the towpath following Walk 34 from Wp.3.

Leaving **Whaley Bridge Station** (Wp.1 0M) we turn right (SSE) through the car park heading for **The Railway Hotel**, (Robinson's Ales). We cross the road at the pelican crossing and turn right (S) to walk along the main street. Passing **The White Hart**, we cross **Beech Road**, then make our way up **Old Road**, to the left of the main street. The road climbs past **The Shepherd's Arms** (Marston's Ales), then turns left into **Bings Road**. In fifty metres we follow a footpath sign on the right (Wp.2 5M) for a steady climb between stone walls.

Emerging on a lane, we turn left (ENE) to continue the climb, swinging right. The tarmac soon gives way to gravel, our broad track still climbing as we pass the new **Whaley Bridge Cricket Ground**. Ignoring paths off to either side we stay on the track and pass through a kissing-gate (Wp.3 12M). As the track levels out we pass the old cricket ground, keeping to the right hand fence which brings us to a stile (Wp.4 14M).

From the stile we keep the stone wall on our right and pass through a gate as we continue through a field. Passing through a wooden kissing-gate we continue by the wall, now gently downhill. A stone step stile by a small building (Wp.5 19M) brings us onto a lane where we turn left (NE). Strolling gently uphill on tarmac, views open out before we start to descend.

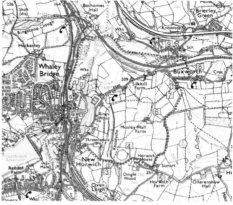

The track swings hard left while we carry straight on over a stile (Wp.6 26M NE) and follow the left hand wall. At the junction of two fields we again follow the wall to our left (NNE). After the wall ends we circle a deep depression, keeping it to our left; I don't recommend the path that follows the wall left as shown on the map. We follow the gorse bushes gently downhill to a gate (Wp7 31M NNW).

The downhill track, bounded by stone walls, leads us down to a road where we turn right (E) towards sports fields. A fingerpost guides us left (Wp.8 36M NNE), by the side of another cricket pitch. Through a gate, we cross the busy A6 on a footbridge then zigzag down steps into **Bugsworth Basin**.

**Bugsworth Basin**

Heading west, we make our way past **The Navigation** (Free House), cross a road (Wp.9 48M) and continue along a wide track with the canal to our left. The towpath leads us under the A6 before bringing us to a footbridge (Wp.10 56M). Climbing steps, we cross the bridge walking with the canal now on our right.

**The Goyt Inn**

Crossing a final footbridge over the canal overflow, we head for the Transhipment Shed and onto **Canal Street** (Wp.11 66M).Turning right, we follow the road as it swings left, first passing **Teazel's Bistro** and **The Navigation** on **Johnson Street**, then **The Goyt Inn**, to the left on **Bridge Street** as we make our way back to the Pelican Crossing and **Whaley Bridge Station** (Wp.1 69M). The **Manchester** platform is over the footbridge.

The final walk in our Wayfarer series goes in search of the **Dipping Stone**; its two carved holes once held the shafts of Saxon Crosses. In the 16th century it was also known as the 'Plague Stone'; money was left in the hollows, which were filled with vinegar for its disinfectant qualities, for plague victims who were kept in isolation.

Our itinerary starts in **Whaley Bridge** following the canal to **Furness Vale**, an alternative starting point.

A gentle climb takes us through **Diglee** and along **Whaley Lane** before the final steady climb to the stone. Those with GPS will find it accurately marked by a small dot under the name on the map. However, on leaving the stone the right of way (marked in green) is misleading, as we need to find the stile correctly located on the path (black dots) shown slightly to the east of the ROW. The rest of our route down from the stone follows vague paths; GPS users will again benefit from this navigational aid.

Once we meet the road, the route described to **Toddbrook Reservoir** and back to **Whaley Bridge** is easy to follow. But whilst researching this walk, I found a couple of other interesting paths; the footpath sign we ignore after Wp.14 leads down through a property; the owners were helpful but the path is very unclear - I'm sure there should be a path, as you'll discover after Wp.15 when we turn left at the next finger-post; another finger points right back to our missing path; quite how you are supposed to get through, round or over the wall is a bit of a mystery!

3 | 1¾ H | 4.7 miles/7½km | 221m 221m | 4

**Access by train:** from **Manchester Piccadilly** to **Whaley Bridge Station**. Return to **Piccadilly** from **Whaley Bridge**.

Car parking is limited at the station, though there is a public car park off **Canal Street**.

**Short Walk Option**

The canal section from **Whaley Bridge** to **Furness Vale** can be omitted by starting at **Furness Vale Station** and returning to **Manchester** from **Whaley Bridge**.

Leaving **Whaley Bridge Station** (Wp.1 0M), we turn right (SE) and head through the car park. Looking left we can see **Canal Street**, and make our way to it using the Pelican Crossing in front of **The Railway Hotel**. Heading north along **Canal Street**, we pass **The Navigation** inn & **Teazel's Bistro** which you may want to visit at the end of the walk. As the street swings right, we cross over to the transhipment shed (Wp.2 3M) heading north towards a footbridge over the canal overflow. Across it, we join the towpath and continue north, crossing the canal junction to **Bugsworth Basin** at the next footbridge (Wp3 11M), descending the steps and turning turn hard right to resume our northerly course, with the canal to our left.

Our pleasant canal-side stroll takes us under several bridges to bridge N°31 (Wp.4 28M) where we turn hard right to take the ramp up to **Station Road**. We turn left (SW) to cross the level crossing at **Furness Vale Station**, where the Short Walk Option joins us.

Passing **The Crossings** (Robinson's Ales), we continue to **Buxton Road**, cross over and head up **Yeardsley Road** opposite.

Swinging right (W) into **Diglee Road** (Wp.5 34M) we soon leave the houses behind as we continue the gentle climb into open countryside.

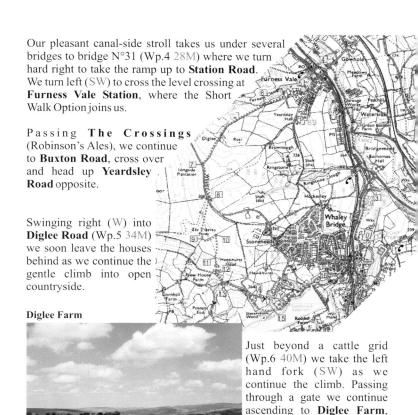

**Diglee Farm**

Just beyond a cattle grid (Wp.6 40M) we take the left hand fork (SW) as we continue the climb. Passing through a gate we continue ascending to **Diglee Farm**, sett paving leading us between the farm buildings. Taking time to look back, we continue to climb the rough track to **Whaley Lane** (Wp.7 56M).

Turning left (S), we stay on the left hand verge of the busy road as we make our way along, looking for the footpath over on the right. Crossing, we leave the road at a Peak & Northern sign for 'Bowstonegate & Lyme Park' (Wp.8 62M). This uphill track soon leads us to a fingerpost, and continuing (SSW), we follow the clear track as it climbs steadily through the fields.

As we reach the top of the rise, the path swings right to a stile, but we leave the path before the stile, turning left (SE) and aiming for the **Dipping Stone**, the large stone before the wall (Wp.9 71M).

**The Dipping Stone**

In summer the delicate harebell, (Campanula rotundifolia), is a delightful find as it dances in the grass nearby.

Leaving the stone, we make our way over to the stone wall and turn left to follow the wall down to cross a stile (Wp.10 74M). We're heading south on a very vague field path, and the field has large patches of rough grass making the next stile difficult to spot. Crossing the field as best we can, look out for the post that marks the stile, which is of unusual construction, having a piece of wood that passes through the wall to form one of the steps (Wp.11 77M).

**Harebells on the route**

Over this stile, the path is just as vague, but if we head slightly left (SE) towards the larger hawthorn bush a track becomes visible below, which we head for. We come down to a gate near a cattle grid and turn left (Wp.12 81M SE), following the track downhill and turning left when we meet a road (Wp.13 85M E).

Ignoring the first fingerpost, we continue on the road to the second fingerpost where we turn right (Wp.14 91M SSW). Our path takes us between a wall and a hedge to another fingerpost, where we turn left (SSE) on a well-trodden path through trees, perhaps checking for the missing path to the right before we set off. Gently descending through woodland, we emerge on a track and head left (Wp.15 99M E).

As we stroll along, we catch glimpses of **Toddbrook Reservoir** to our right; we pass a footbridge down to the reservoir, and continue past **Brookfield Pond** (Wp.16 108M). Following the road down, we swing left just before the railway bridge for the last few steps onto the **Manchester** platform at **Whaley Bridge Station**. There are a number of refreshment opportunities nearby, several of which we passed on the outward journey.

# 35 BROMLEY CROSS – A TASTE OF THE WEST

This flexible itinerary offers a taste of the West Pennines only seen from afar on some of our other walks; and you might well be walking in the footsteps of Mahatma Gandhi who visited this miniature lake district on his tour of Britain in 1931. Our route takes us through **Bradshaw Valley** which, with water and coal readily available, once supported a thriving textile industry.

Our route passes through **Ousel Meadows**, ('ousel' is Old English for blackbird), on our way to **Jumbles Reservoir** for a lakeside stroll. We join the **Witton Weavers Way**, passing the square **Old Russia Lodge Chimney** and the **Barlow Institute** (once a branch of the National Children's Homes) en route to **Turton** where **The Black Bull** offers a range of ales and a reasonably priced menu. Our second miniature lake, **Wayoh Reservoir**, is the ideal spot for a picnic whilst enjoying the view from its numerous benches.

Our second refreshment opportunity, **The Strawbury Duck**, is famous amongst walkers in the West Pennines. There's some debate about the name; some say the spelling is a sign-writer's mistake, but I prefer to believe the story told by John Speakman whose family ran the pub in the 80s and 90s. The **Edgworth** locals, referred to the pub as "The Strawberry" due to the glow of the south-facing gable at sunset. When Roger Duxbury (from the local town of **Bury**) converted the pub in the 70s, lowering the ceilings and adding false beams, he renamed it **The Strawbury Duck**, a play on his name; Dux – bury.

**Entwistle Station** provides one of our Short Walk Options, but make sure the driver can see you as this is a request stop. Another option is to include **Turton & Entwistle Reservoir** as a post-prandial stroll before returning from the station.

When first researching this route, several bridges and parts of the path round the reservoir had been washed away by flash floods; on my second visit restoration work was in hand, so you may find some new bridges not described in the walk.

Our route from **Entwistle** takes in **Cheetham Close** with its stone circle and enclosure, both of which are easily missed when the grass is overgrown. From the trig point there are stunning views over **Bolton**, a close up of **Winter Hill**; and - on a clear day - you may see the **Peel Tower** at **Holcombe**, **Windy Hill** transmitter and even **Pendle Hill** way off to the north. On the way downhill we cross a castellated railway bridge (built by textile magnate James Kay) before passing **Turton Tower**. Originally a 15th century Pele Tower, it was converted into a Tudor Hall before becoming a Victorian Country House. Set in 9 acres of land, it houses fine treasures and holds regular exhibitions as well as having a tea room. Our return via **Jumbles** to **Bromley Cross** is mainly downhill and **The Railway Hotel**, across the tracks, offers a final refreshment opportunity.

3 | 4½ H | 11.9 miles/19km | 412m / 412m | 4

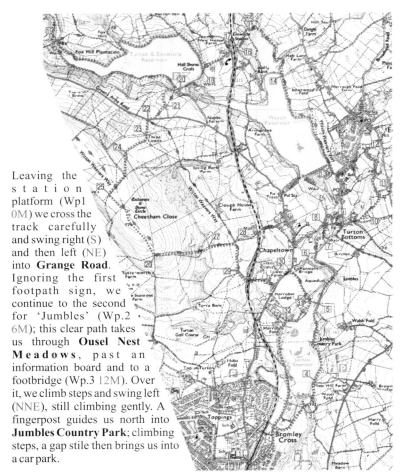

Leaving the station platform (Wp1 0M) we cross the track carefully and swing right (S) and then left (NE) into **Grange Road**. Ignoring the first footpath sign, we continue to the second for 'Jumbles' (Wp.2 6M); this clear path takes us through **Ousel Nest Meadows**, past an information board and to a footbridge (Wp.3 12M). Over it, we climb steps and swing left (NNE), still climbing gently. A fingerpost guides us north into **Jumbles Country Park**; climbing steps, a gap stile then brings us into a car park.

Still heading north, we pass toilets, then cross the access road to the information centre (Wp.4 18M), from where our broad, tree-lined track follows **Jumbles Reservoir**, supplied with plenty of seats for relaxing and enjoying the view. At the head of the reservoir (Wp.5 28M), we continue to **Jumbles Country Park Quarry**.

| **Short Walk Option 1** |
| --- |
| Leave the main walk at the head of **Jumbles Reservoir** (Wp.5), crossing the bridge to rejoin main walk at Wp.31 for the return to **Bromley Cross Station**. (1 hour, 2.5 miles/4km, ascents & descents 66 metres) |

The clear path leads us away from **Jumbles** with a stream down to our left. Crossing a footbridge, we follow the path, soon stone-paved, to a gate (Wp.6 37M) a footpath sign guiding us. The path brings us to a bridge where we turn left

(Wp.7 40M N), to follow the sett-paved road gently uphill. As the surface changes to tarmac (Wp.8 42M) a waymarker for 'Warpers Trail' guides us right (E) on a rough path; following it, we come to sett paving and turn right (SE), passing a row of cottages. Ignoring a track to the right, we carry straight on, following a **Witton Weavers Way** (**WWW**) marker as we pass a cattle grid.

Our path swings left then, as we join a tarmac road, a **WWW** marker (Wp.9 49M) guides us right (NE) to pass through an exclusive housing estate to a further **WWW** marker which takes us left (E) up a flight of stone steps, just before a gate. After the steps, we pass through a gate then head along a section of stone flags before turning left (NNE) through a second gate. Gently climbing, we maintain course past a square chimney, then go through another gate (Wp.10 55M). Following a well-trodden field path, a sign on the next gate asks us to keep dogs on leads as we continue on the **WWW**, heading gently downhill to pass through one more gate before crossing a stile and footbridge (Wp.11 62M).

Turning right (E), we pass through a kissing-gate near a weir and turn left (NNW), then ignore the 'Warpers Way' sign at a junction to turn left (W) and climb steps. At the next junction we again go left, staying on the high ground, our path leading to a gate (Wp.12 67M). Crossing a track, we go through a second gate and continue behind the **Edgworth Bowling Club** and past the **Barlow Institute** to **Bolton Road**. Turning left (SSW), we follow the road and cross over to **The Black Bull** where a footpath sign directs us through the car park and a couple of gates (NW).

The downhill path brings us to a fork (Wp13 75M) where a 'Warpers Trail' sign directs us (NNW) uphill on the path with a handrail. Steadily rising to an octagonal building, we pass through a gap stile and resume our course, strolling close to the water with splendid views over **Wayoh Reservoir** and ignoring any paths off right. At **Hob Lane** (Wp.14 91M) we cross the road, a **WWW** sign guiding us on by the pumping station.

**Wayoh Reservoir**

The path leads us over a stream, then swings left, gently climbing. After a long, gentle downhill section to a footbridge, we turn left (W) the **WWW** guiding us to the next footbridge (Wp.15 104M). Taking the right hand fork by a bench, we climb steadily to a stile, then follow the field boundary to a gate which brings us onto **Entwistle Hall Road** (Wp.16 111M).

| **Short Walk Option 2** |
| --- |
| End the walk at **The Strawbury Duck**, returning to **Manchester** from **Entwistle Station**. (2 hours, 5 miles/8km, ascents & descents 196 metres) |

Turning right (NNW) we follow the road, cross the railway and pass **Entwistle Station** before coming to **The Strawbury Duck** (Wp.17 115M), using the rear entrance if calling in for refreshments, where there's a handy boot rack for walkers' use.

If not stopping for refreshment, we turn left (SE)

on **Overshores Road** past the pub's main entrance. The broad track passes a row of terraced houses and the end of a row of bungalows. Taking the right hand fork at the next junction, we follow the downhill track passing **Entwistle Camping Barn**. Emerging on tarmac by **Entwistle Reservoir**, we turn right (Wp.18 121M N) to follow the broad track with **Turton & Entwistle Reservoir** down to our right.

| |
|---|
| **Short Walk Option 3** Omit the **Turton & Entwistle Reservoir** circuit, crossing the dam from Wp.18 to Wp.20, reducing the walk by approximately 50 minutes and 2.3 miles/3.75km. |

Staying close to the dam, we ignore all paths off to the right as the track narrows and we swing left around **Fox Hill Plantation**. The path takes us to the head of the reservoir to cross a footbridge (Wp.19 149M), then we turn left (S) for the return along the reservoir to the dam. At the dam we go right (171M) and pass a car park, looking out for steps on the right (Wp.20 173M) which take us to a second car park.

Following the access road, we pass through a gate on the right following the **WWW** sign (Wp.21 177M). The well-trodden field path leads us to a stile; turning right (SW), we follow the road for a short distance. A footpath sign (Wp.22 181M) directs us sharp left (SE) onto a broad track.

Leaving the track, we cross a stile on the right for a steady climb south, the boundary to our left. The clear path leads us to a stile (Wp.23 184M) then swings right (SW) as we pass the remains of a stone building.

| **Short Walk Option 4** |
|---|
| Omit the section over **Cheetham Close** to reduce the distance by 1km, the ascents/descents by 70 metres and the time by 30 minutes. |

Crossing three footbridges as the path meanders gently up to the next stile (Wp.24 191M), we continue our gentle climb, levelling out as **Winter Hill** comes into view. We turn left at a metal waterworks marker post (Wp.25 204M SE), following the path to a stile.

Continue along the track from Wp.22 and pass the red brick farm building with unfinished towers. Pass through a gate and rejoin the main walk at Wp.28, then continue to the kissing-gate by the larger gate at Wp.29.

From the stile our path heads past a stone circle on our left to a trig point, from where views over **Bolton** can be taken in. Leaving the trig point (SE), the path leads us gently downhill to cross a stile on the left (Wp.26 217M) and head east, following a yellow waymarker as we make our way steadily downhill to the next stile (222M).

Passing through trees, we cross another stile to continue on a stone paved path. Leaving Access Land at the next stile, we ignore the track and continue (ENE) towards the distant church spire. This vague path dips, becoming clearer as we head for a stile (Wp.27 228M). Still aiming for the spire, we head through the field to a broad track (Wp.28 232M) where we head right (SSE).

(Short Walk Option 4 rejoins us here.)

At a kissing-gate by a larger gate, we go left (Wp.29 236M SSE), following a **WWW** sign gently downhill, with a stream to our right.

**The castellated bridge**

Crossing the railway on a wonderful castellated bridge the track leads us past **Turton Tower**. Continuing down **Tower Drive** to **Chapeltown Road**, we turn left (NNE) following the road and noticing a WW2 pillbox on the right. Crossing the road, we follow the **WWW** sign (Wp.30 247M SE).

The track takes us gently uphill, narrowing to a path before descending to cross over a pipeline as we enter a wooded area. We descend steps before coming to the head of **Jumbles Reservoir** (Wp.31 254M).

**Turton Tower**

(Short Walk Option 1 joins us here.)

We swing right (SSW) with the reservoir to our left, passing through a gap stile with a small reservoir to our right. Joining a tarmac road, we swing right, following the road to a bridge (Wp.32 258M) just before the sett paving.

Turning left (SSW), we cross the bridge and pass through another gap stile to continue on the well-made path. After one more gap stile the path leads us between horse stables, at the far side of which a gate and a few steps bring us onto **Grange Road**. We're in familiar territory now as our uphill stroll takes us past **Ousel Nest Gate House** and cottage, then past the sign to 'Jumbles' (Wp.2 272M) as we make our way back along the road. Soon after passing a white bungalow we swing right and immediately left, bringing us back to **Bromley Cross Station** (Wp.1 277M). **The Railway Hotel**, across the track, offers a final refreshment opportunity before our return to **Manchester**.

# AN HISTORICAL STROLL: FLIXTON

Although this short half-hour stroll hardly qualifies as a 'walk' it's included here for its place in walking history. It takes us to the site of one of the early struggles to defend our freedom to roam. Most walkers will know the story of the Mass Trespass on Kinder which resulted in the formation of the Peak National Park. Although I was aware that nearly 50 years before Kinder, in 1896, some 10,000 people staged a demonstration on Winter Hill, Bolton, protesting a path closure, I was surprised to learn from David Bratt, Chairman of The Peak & Northern Footpath Society, of an even earlier struggle on my own doorstep.

The story starts in 1806 when a local magistrate, Ralph Wright, built **Flixton House** which would have had splendid views across fields to **St. Michael's Church**. A network of paths crossed the fields and locals used them on their way to church. Local accounts tell the story of a closure order being issued by two of Mr Wright's fellow magistrates in 1824 and the subsequent blocking of a path that ran in front of his house. Several appeals resulted in the formation of The Manchester Society for the Protection of Ancient Footpaths which raised funds to take the appeal to the King's Bench. On the 9th June 1826 the bench quashed the order to close the path. More closure orders were issued and challenged until finally on the 14th September 1827, when all but one of the orders for a short stretch of unused road were quashed, Ralph Wright finally conceded defeat. The cost of these challenges is recorded as being £750, an enormous amount of money at that time.

In 1894 The Peak District & Northern Counties Footpath Preservation Society was formed and funds from the earlier society were amalgamated into the fighting fund to defend a path from **Hayfield** to **The Snake Inn**. The name has since been shortened to The Peak & Northern Footpath Society and they proudly claim to be the oldest society still defending the rights of walkers.

**Flixton House** and grounds remained the home of Ralph's successors, the Worthington Wrights, until 1934. The following year, the local authority acquired the property, and the public can now enjoy a golf course, and attend concerts and other functions in the house.

You'll want to allow more than the 35 minutes walk time to look round the sites visited and maybe take a leisurely lunch. The short itinerary takes us along the disputed path, by the golf course, to the house with its beautifully maintained gardens. Next we retrace our steps to visit **St. Michael's Church**, which has Norman origins. At its gates, **The Church Inn** serves pub lunches and a range of cask ales, Next door on the edge of 'The Village' the recently refurbished **Greyhound Inn** offers regional cuisine and plans to offer cask ales. Finally we visit **Larkrise**, one of a handful of timber-framed buildings in England that carries an inscription - in this case '1672', before our return from **Flixton Station**.

This linear stroll takes only half an hour.

**Access by train:** from **Manchester Oxford Road** to **Chassen Road Station**. Return to **Manchester** from **Flixton Station**.

There is no station car park, but on-road parking is permitted nearby. Return to your car along the outward route.

Leaving the station on the uphill ramp (Wp.1 0M), we cross the road and head left (SSE), soon turning right (WSW) into **Balmoral Road**. Passing the entrance to **Townfields** and a few flats, we turn right by a sign (Wp.2 2M NNW), informing us that we are on a 'Dedicated Footpath'. A small wall guides us left (WSW), on a well trodden path with allotments on the right. Ignoring a path to the left, we continue ahead, emerging on a track and turning right (N). Just before the railway bridge a 'Footpath' sign guides us left (Wp.3 10M WSW), to walk between the railway and **William Wroe Golf Course**.

We continue on the well-trodden path until just beyond the golf course at a staggered metal barrier (Wp.4 16M) where we find a 'PNFS' sign on a metal post to the right. The path continues over a step stile, emerging by **Flixton Station** and continuing to **Flixton Road** (Wp.5 19M). Turning right (N), we cross the railway bridge and continue to **Flixton House** (Wp.6 21M) where an information board tells part of our story.

**Flixton House**

**St. Michael's Church**

Reversing our route, we head back to the station and turn left (ENE), retracing our steps. Just before the step stile we turn right between hedges, bringing us into a small housing estate. Continuing to the road, we cross and turn left, then turn right opposite a school by a small green. A path leads us north from the green to **Church Road** and across to **St. Michael's Church** (Wp.7 29M) where Ralph Wright is interred.

Turning right in front of the church. we pass **The Church Inn**, then soon after, **The Greyhound** which brings us to 'The Village' where we find **Larkrise.** Re-crossing **Church Road** to the right, we head for the petrol station and continue over the railway bridge to the **Manchester** platform (Wp.8 34M).

**Larkrise**

See the notes on GPS and using waypoints on page 17.

## 1 BROADBOTTOM TO STALYBRIDGE

| Wp | Zo | East | West |
|----|----|------|------|
| 1 | SJ | 99041 | 93793 |
| 2 | SJ | 99400 | 93793 |
| 3 | SK | 00027 | 94642 |
| 4 | SK | 00235 | 95055 |
| 5 | SK | 00213 | 95302 |
| 6 | SK | 00113 | 95951 |
| 7 | SJ | 99335 | 96409 |
| 8 | SJ | 99432 | 96680 |
| 9 | SJ | 99721 | 97175 |
| 10 | SJ | 99913 | 97460 |
| 11 | SJ | 99566 | 97547 |
| 12 | SJ | 98760 | 97611 |
| 13 | SJ | 98878 | 98007 |
| 14 | SJ | 99388 | 98089 |
| 15 | SJ | 99887 | 98428 |
| 16 | SK | 00277 | 98558 |
| 17 | SK | 00493 | 98780 |
| 18 | SK | 00777 | 99374 |
| 19 | SK | 00348 | 99563 |
| 20 | SJ | 99146 | 99189 |
| 21 | SJ | 98667 | 99823 |
| 22 | SJ | 98480 | 99845 |
| 23 | SJ | 97851 | 99786 |
| 24 | SJ | 96719 | 98594 |
| 25 | SJ | 95834 | 98597 |

## 2 SMITHY BRIDGE TO LITTLEBOROUGH

| Wp | Zo | East | West |
|----|----|------|------|
| 1 | SD | 92595 | 15195 |
| 2 | SD | 92278 | 14579 |
| 3 | SD | 92907 | 14191 |
| 4 | SD | 92971 | 14059 |
| 5 | SD | 93294 | 14092 |
| 6 | SD | 93325 | 14172 |
| 7 | SD | 93251 | 14483 |
| 8 | SD | 94241 | 14664 |
| 9 | SD | 93916 | 15196 |
| 10 | SD | 93998 | 15313 |
| 11 | SD | 94489 | 16019 |
| 12 | SD | 94050 | 16390 |
| 13 | SD | 93872 | 16242 |

## 3 RAKE INN CIRCULAR

| Wp | Zo | East | West |
|----|----|------|------|
| 1 | SD | 93834 | 16274 |
| 2 | SD | 94458 | 15939 |
| 3 | SD | 93924 | 15204 |
| 4 | SD | 94769 | 14928 |
| 5 | SD | 95137 | 14765 |
| 6 | SD | 95367 | 14965 |
| 7 | SD | 95438 | 15806 |
| 8 | SD | 95486 | 16450 |
| 9 | SD | 95206 | 16576 |
| 10 | SD | 95104 | 16955 |
| 11 | SD | 94806 | 16680 |
| 12 | SD | 94385 | 16586 |
| 13 | SD | 94169 | 16353 |

## 4 WHITE HOUSE CIRCULAR

| Wp | Zo | East | West |
|----|----|------|------|
| 1 | SD | 93811 | 16276 |
| 2 | SD | 94667 | 18095 |
| 3 | SD | 94226 | 18495 |
| 4 | SD | 94477 | 18997 |
| 5 | SD | 94096 | 20251 |
| 6 | SD | 94125 | 20716 |
| 7 | SD | 94567 | 20139 |
| 8 | SD | 95218 | 20307 |
| 9 | SD | 95807 | 20554 |
| 10 | SD | 96872 | 17893 |
| 11 | SD | 96751 | 17163 |
| 12 | SD | 97333 | 17071 |
| 13 | SD | 96239 | 16792 |
| 14 | SD | 95504 | 16457 |
| 15 | SD | 95474 | 16049 |
| 16 | SD | 94605 | 16022 |
| 17 | SD | 94042 | 16394 |

## 5 ROSE HILL TO ROMILEY

| Wp | Zo | East | West |
|----|----|------|------|
| 1 | SJ | 94984 | 88815 |
| 2 | SJ | 94869 | 87988 |
| 3 | SJ | 95628 | 87507 |
| 4 | SJ | 96020 | 88312 |
| 5 | SJ | 96195 | 89074 |
| 6 | SJ | 95566 | 90030 |
| 7 | SJ | 94735 | 90425 |
| 8 | SJ | 94606 | 90403 |
| 9 | SJ | 94167 | 90231 |
| 10 | SJ | 94085 | 90081 |
| 11 | SJ | 93975 | 90277 |
| 12 | SJ | 94143 | 90780 |

## 6 MIDDLEWOOD LYME PARK CIRCULAR

| Wp | Zo | East | West |
|----|----|------|------|
| 1 | SJ | 94536 | 84824 |
| 2 | SJ | 95103 | 84699 |
| 3 | SJ | 95148 | 84352 |
| 4 | SJ | 95231 | 84521 |
| 5 | SJ | 95526 | 84569 |
| 6 | SJ | 95807 | 84605 |
| 7 | SJ | 96189 | 84507 |
| 8 | SJ | 96506 | 83984 |
| 9 | SJ | 96635 | 83079 |
| 10 | SJ | 96437 | 82432 |
| 11 | SJ | 96043 | 82245 |
| 12 | SJ | 94403 | 83363 |

## 7 MIDDLEWOOD TO MARPLE VIA MARPLE BRIDGE

| Wp | Zo | East | West |
|----|----|------|------|
| 1 | SJ | 94495 | 84838 |
| 2 | SJ | 95095 | 84710 |
| 3 | SJ | 95314 | 85974 |
| 4 | SJ | 95518 | 85839 |
| 5 | SJ | 96109 | 86313 |
| 6 | SJ | 96440 | 86563 |
| 7 | SJ | 96510 | 86950 |
| 8 | SJ | 96166 | 88395 |
| 9 | SJ | 96327 | 89263 |

## 8 PIETHORNE VALLEY & CROMPTON MOOR

| Wp | Zo | East | West |
|----|----|------|------|
| 1 | SD | 93817 | 11620 |
| 2 | SD | 94296 | 11621 |
| 3 | SD | 94795 | 11922 |
| 4 | SD | 95209 | 12189 |
| 5 | SD | 95043 | 12771 |
| 6 | SD | 96186 | 12685 |
| 7 | SD | 96276 | 12355 |
| 8 | SD | 96420 | 11708 |
| 9 | SD | 96395 | 11177 |
| 10 | SD | 96062 | 10525 |
| 11 | SD | 95108 | 10033 |
| 12 | SD | 94620 | 10762 |

## 9 STRINES CIRCULAR

| Wp | Zo | East | West |
|----|----|------|------|
| 1 | SJ | 97849 | 86466 |
| 2 | SJ | 97357 | 86304 |
| 3 | SJ | 96990 | 86095 |
| 4 | SK | 00070 | 84550 |
| 5 | SK | 00264 | 85073 |
| 6 | SJ | 99967 | 85245 |
| 7 | SJ | 99450 | 85251 |
| 8 | SJ | 98656 | 85557 |
| 9 | SJ | 98622 | 86247 |
| 10 | SJ | 98568 | 86378 |
| 11 | SJ | 97852 | 86445 |

## 10 ROMILEY TO HYDE

| Wp | Zo | East | West |
|----|----|------|------|
| 1 | SJ | 94180 | 90806 |
| 2 | SJ | 93926 | 90359 |
| 3 | SJ | 93508 | 92006 |
| 4 | SJ | 93622 | 92371 |
| 5 | SJ | 93891 | 92508 |
| 6 | SJ | 94351 | 94690 |

7 SJ 94433 95051

**11**

## HYDE TO STALYBRIDGE VIA PORTLAND BASIN

| Wp | Zo | East | West |
|----|----|------|------|
| 1 | SJ | 94464 | 94901 |
| 2 | SJ | 94345 | 95100 |
| 3 | SJ | 93969 | 95888 |
| 4 | SJ | 93269 | 97437 |
| 5 | SJ | 93484 | 98401 |
| 6 | SJ | 93828 | 98419 |
| 7 | SJ | 94138 | 98664 |
| 8 | SJ | 95140 | 98492 |
| 9 | SJ | 96243 | 98417 |
| 10 | SJ | 95990 | 98638 |

**12**

## STALYBRIDGE TO GREENFIELD

| Wp | Zo | East | West |
|----|----|------|------|
| 1 | SJ | 95990 | 98638 |
| 2 | SJ | 96293 | 98409 |
| 3 | SJ | 96655 | 98541 |
| 4 | SJ | 97504 | 99922 |
| 5 | SD | 97320 | 00992 |
| 6 | SD | 97586 | 01959 |
| 7 | SD | 97366 | 02024 |
| 8 | SD | 97693 | 02553 |
| 9 | SD | 98109 | 03376 |
| 10 | SD | 98545 | 04230 |
| 11 | SD | 99185 | 04673 |

**13**

## GREENFIELD CIRCULAR VIA DIGGLE

| Wp | Zo | East | West |
|----|----|------|------|
| 1 | SD | 99185 | 04673 |
| 2 | SD | 99248 | 04666 |
| 3 | SD | 99518 | 05376 |
| 4 | SD | 99571 | 06246 |
| 5 | SD | 99641 | 06646 |
| 6 | SE | 00583 | 07920 |
| 7 | SE | 00612 | 07145 |
| 8 | SE | 00920 | 06401 |
| 9 | SE | 00747 | 06410 |
| 10 | SD | 99996 | 06427 |
| 11 | SD | 99667 | 04581 |

**14**

## MARPLE TO STRINES VIA ROMAN LAKES

| Wp | Zo | East | West |
|----|----|------|------|
| 1 | SJ | 96350 | 89296 |
| 2 | SJ | 96552 | 89264 |
| 3 | SJ | 96681 | 88463 |
| 4 | SJ | 96878 | 87886 |
| 5 | SJ | 96731 | 87375 |
| 6 | SJ | 97069 | 87310 |
| 7 | SJ | 97609 | 86842 |
| 8 | SJ | 97839 | 86469 |

**15**

## STRINES TO MARPLE VIA MELLOR

| Wp | Zo | East | West |
|----|----|------|------|
| 1 | SJ | 97850 | 86467 |
| 2 | SJ | 98568 | 86402 |
| 3 | SJ | 98620 | 86259 |
| 4 | SJ | 99444 | 86689 |
| 5 | SJ | 99307 | 87077 |
| 6 | SJ | 99341 | 87368 |
| 7 | SJ | 99033 | 87915 |
| 8 | SJ | 98722 | 88314 |
| 9 | SJ | 98658 | 88445 |
| 10 | SJ | 98647 | 88553 |
| 11 | SJ | 98199 | 88896 |
| 12 | SJ | 97877 | 88577 |
| 13 | SJ | 97912 | 88440 |
| 14 | SJ | 97732 | 88082 |
| 15 | SJ | 96856 | 88263 |
| 16 | SJ | 96312 | 89337 |

**16**

## MARPLE TO BROADBOTTOM VIA ETHEROW

| Wp | Zo | East | West |
|----|----|------|------|
| 1 | SJ | 96309 | 89305 |
| 2 | SJ | 96268 | 90206 |
| 3 | SJ | 96462 | 90529 |
| 4 | SJ | 96475 | 90852 |
| 5 | SJ | 97121 | 90914 |
| 6 | SJ | 97325 | 91272 |
| 7 | SJ | 97116 | 91593 |
| 8 | SJ | 96759 | 91895 |
| 9 | SJ | 96991 | 92182 |
| 10 | SJ | 97048 | 92770 |
| 11 | SJ | 97182 | 93013 |
| 12 | SJ | 97354 | 93044 |
| 13 | SJ | 97484 | 92978 |
| 14 | SJ | 97570 | 93018 |
| 15 | SJ | 97753 | 92948 |
| 16 | SJ | 98194 | 92998 |
| 17 | SJ | 98739 | 93468 |
| 18 | SJ | 98996 | 93765 |

**17**

## MILLS HILL TO NEWHEY VIA TANDLE HILL

| Wp | Zo | East | West |
|----|----|------|------|
| 1 | SD | 88735 | 06072 |
| 2 | SD | 89168 | 06366 |
| 3 | SD | 88469 | 08470 |
| 4 | SD | 89836 | 09127 |
| 5 | SD | 90081 | 08834 |
| 6 | SD | 90437 | 09194 |
| 7 | SD | 91129 | 09406 |
| 8 | SD | 91407 | 09704 |
| 9 | SD | 91988 | 10317 |
| 10 | SD | 92206 | 10185 |
| 11 | SD | 92815 | 10464 |
| 13 | SD | 93001 | 10592 |
| 12 | SD | 92931 | 10716 |
| 14 | SD | 92809 | 10876 |
| 15 | SD | 92688 | 11295 |
| 16 | SD | 93300 | 11620 |
| 17 | SD | 93802 | 11627 |

**18**

## WOODLEY TO BROADBOTTOM VIA WERNETH

| Wp | Zo | East | West |
|----|----|------|------|
| 1 | SJ | 93950 | 92566 |
| 2 | SJ | 94339 | 92216 |
| 3 | SJ | 94804 | 92168 |
| 4 | SJ | 94938 | 92349 |
| 5 | SJ | 95167 | 92599 |
| 6 | SJ | 95400 | 92375 |
| 7 | SJ | 95961 | 92836 |
| 8 | SJ | 96410 | 93512 |
| 9 | SJ | 97070 | 93117 |
| 10 | SJ | 97494 | 93449 |
| 11 | SJ | 97625 | 93185 |
| 12 | SJ | 98244 | 93022 |
| 13 | SJ | 98011 | 93828 |
| 14 | SJ | 98568 | 93504 |
| 15 | SJ | 99046 | 93678 |
| 16 | SJ | 98994 | 93765 |

**19**

## MARPLE TO BROADBOTTOM VIA COWN EDGE

| Wp | Zo | East | West |
|----|----|------|------|
| 1 | SJ | 96297 | 89331 |
| 2 | SJ | 96545 | 89259 |
| 3 | SJ | 96669 | 88452 |
| 4 | SJ | 97234 | 88582 |
| 5 | SJ | 97758 | 88748 |
| 6 | SJ | 98516 | 89243 |
| 7 | SJ | 99358 | 89634 |
| 8 | SJ | 99008 | 90185 |
| 9 | SJ | 99244 | 90483 |
| 10 | SJ | 99394 | 90737 |
| 11 | SJ | 99837 | 90921 |
| 12 | SK | 00607 | 90945 |
| 13 | SK | 01406 | 91038 |
| 14 | SK | 01892 | 92284 |
| 15 | SK | 00679 | 92639 |
| 16 | SK | 00372 | 92612 |
| 17 | SJ | 99979 | 92651 |
| 18 | SJ | 99866 | 93261 |
| 19 | SJ | 99603 | 93559 |
| 20 | SJ | 99317 | 93663 |
| 21 | SJ | 99006 | 93780 |

## 20
### BROADBOTTOM TO STALYBRIDGE VIA MOTTRAM

| Wp | Zo | East | West |
|----|----|------|------|
| 1 | SJ | 99020 | 93811 |
| 2 | SJ | 98941 | 94077 |
| 3 | SJ | 99085 | 94353 |
| 4 | SJ | 99272 | 94696 |
| 5 | SJ | 99417 | 95248 |
| 6 | SJ | 99302 | 95651 |
| 7 | SJ | 99176 | 95603 |
| 8 | SJ | 98379 | 95716 |
| 9 | SJ | 98178 | 95844 |
| 10 | SJ | 98045 | 95820 |
| 11 | SJ | 97874 | 95937 |
| 12 | SJ | 97461 | 96089 |
| 13 | SJ | 97179 | 96210 |
| 14 | SJ | 96954 | 96625 |
| 15 | SJ | 96616 | 97235 |
| 16 | SJ | 96995 | 97604 |
| 17 | SJ | 96631 | 97860 |
| 18 | SJ | 96535 | 98300 |
| 19 | SJ | 95975 | 98671 |

## 21
### ANOTHER VIEW OF STALYBRIDGE TO GREENFIELD

| Wp | Zo | East | North |
|----|----|------|-------|
| 1 | SJ | 95842 | 98619 |
| 2 | SJ | 96291 | 98402 |
| 3 | SJ | 96816 | 98409 |
| 4 | SJ | 97430 | 98225 |
| 5 | SJ | 97979 | 98149 |
| 6 | SJ | 98327 | 98351 |
| 7 | SJ | 98795 | 98690 |
| 8 | SJ | 99161 | 99155 |
| 9 | SK | 00345 | 99565 |
| 10 | SD | 98816 | 00236 |
| 11 | SD | 99062 | 00831 |
| 12 | SD | 98692 | 01447 |
| 13 | SD | 98668 | 02339 |
| 14 | SD | 98842 | 03184 |
| 15 | SD | 98475 | 03541 |
| 16 | SD | 99333 | 04115 |
| 17 | SD | 99187 | 04684 |

## 22
### GREENFIELD CIRCULAR VIA POTS & PANS

| Wp | Zo | East | North |
|----|----|------|-------|
| 1 | SD | 99182 | 04692 |
| 2 | SD | 99397 | 04271 |
| 3 | SD | 99726 | 04028 |
| 4 | SD | 99891 | 03766 |
| 5 | SE | 00117 | 03485 |
| 6 | SE | 01882 | 02738 |
| 7 | SE | 01869 | 02962 |
| 8 | SE | 02267 | 04294 |
| 9 | SE | 02001 | 04583 |
| 10 | SE | 01776 | 04297 |
| 11 | SE | 00983 | 04399 |
| 12 | SE | 01023 | 05122 |
| 13 | SE | 01731 | 06162 |
| 14 | SE | 00941 | 06338 |
| 15 | SE | 00749 | 06433 |
| 16 | SD | 99952 | 06437 |
| 17 | SD | 99530 | 05465 |

## 23
### HADFIELD CIRCULAR

| Wp | Zo | East | North |
|----|----|------|-------|
| 1 | SK | 02385 | 96029 |
| 2 | SK | 02530 | 96467 |
| 3 | SK | 02489 | 96882 |
| 4 | SK | 02464 | 97268 |
| 5 | SK | 03091 | 97363 |
| 6 | SK | 04207 | 98072 |
| 7 | SK | 04742 | 98488 |
| 8 | SK | 05553 | 98485 |
| 9 | SK | 06000 | 98586 |
| 10 | SK | 07248 | 99023 |
| 11 | SK | 07890 | 99328 |
| 12 | SK | 08188 | 99340 |
| 13 | SK | 07001 | 98307 |
| 14 | SK | 05783 | 98063 |
| 15 | SK | 04611 | 97946 |
| 16 | SK | 02514 | 96161 |

## 24
### MOSSLEY TO GREENFIELD VIA HARTSHEAD PIKE

| Wp | Zo | East | North |
|----|----|------|-------|
| 1 | SD | 97365 | 02035 |
| 2 | SD | 97208 | 01848 |
| 3 | SD | 97125 | 01698 |
| 4 | SD | 96887 | 01185 |
| 5 | SD | 96784 | 01550 |
| 6 | SD | 96473 | 01606 |
| 9 | SD | 95965 | 01842 |
| 7 | SD | 96348 | 01741 |
| 8 | SD | 96253 | 01743 |
| 10 | SD | 95981 | 02086 |
| 11 | SD | 96065 | 02196 |
| 12 | SD | 96055 | 02415 |
| 13 | SD | 95933 | 02672 |
| 14 | SD | 96018 | 03488 |
| 15 | SD | 96255 | 03449 |
| 16 | SD | 96548 | 03380 |
| 17 | SD | 96673 | 03371 |
| 18 | SD | 96779 | 03512 |
| 19 | SD | 96721 | 03755 |
| 20 | SD | 97141 | 03697 |
| 21 | SD | 97357 | 03695 |
| 22 | SD | 97498 | 03834 |
| 23 | SD | 97731 | 04212 |
| 24 | SD | 98074 | 04306 |
| 25 | SD | 98051 | 03952 |
| 26 | SD | 98321 | 04115 |
| 27 | SD | 99191 | 04686 |

## 25
### GREENFIELD TO NEWHEY VIA THE TAME VALLEY

| Wp | Zo | East | North |
|----|----|------|-------|
| 1 | SD | 99171 | 04688 |
| 2 | SD | 99184 | 05237 |
| 3 | SD | 99001 | 05508 |
| 4 | SD | 98761 | 05767 |
| 5 | SD | 98874 | 06112 |
| 6 | SD | 98752 | 06381 |
| 7 | SD | 98515 | 07253 |
| 8 | SD | 98661 | 07338 |
| 9 | SD | 98763 | 07712 |
| 10 | SD | 98532 | 07965 |
| 11 | SD | 97554 | 08267 |
| 12 | SD | 97144 | 08918 |
| 13 | SD | 97051 | 09132 |
| 14 | SD | 97029 | 09276 |
| 15 | SD | 97154 | 09567 |
| 16 | SD | 97408 | 10463 |
| 17 | SD | 96997 | 10914 |
| 18 | SD | 96791 | 11168 |
| 19 | SD | 96386 | 11324 |
| 20 | SD | 95593 | 12063 |
| 21 | SD | 94806 | 11943 |
| 22 | SD | 94229 | 11623 |
| 23 | SD | 93811 | 11623 |

## 26
### NEWHEY TO LITTLEBOROUGH VIA BLACKSTONE EDGE

| Wp | Zo | East | North |
|----|----|------|-------|
| 1 | SD | 93814 | 11605 |
| 2 | SD | 93682 | 11770 |
| 3 | SD | 93847 | 12150 |
| 4 | SD | 93894 | 12374 |
| 5 | SD | 94186 | 12587 |
| 6 | SD | 94658 | 12931 |
| 7 | SD | 95203 | 13313 |
| 8 | SD | 96061 | 13321 |
| 9 | SD | 97692 | 14130 |
| 10 | SD | 98274 | 14362 |
| 11 | SD | 98350 | 14820 |
| 12 | SD | 97217 | 16378 |
| 13 | SD | 97329 | 17073 |
| 14 | SD | 97087 | 17201 |
| 15 | SD | 96750 | 17155 |
| 16 | SD | 96805 | 17632 |
| 17 | SD | 96765 | 17795 |
| 18 | SD | 95844 | 16909 |
| 19 | SD | 95732 | 17074 |
| 20 | SD | 95578 | 16522 |
| 21 | SD | 95264 | 16526 |
| 22 | SD | 94917 | 16200 |

| 23 | SD | 94774 | 16093 |
| 24 | SD | 94521 | 15982 |
| 25 | SD | 94054 | 16385 |
| 26 | SD | 93839 | 16238 |
| 27 | | | |

### HADFIELD TO GREENFIELD VIA CHEW RESERVOIR

| Wp | Zo | East | North |
|----|----|------|-------|
| 1 | SK | 02378 | 96029 |
| 2 | SK | 02209 | 96278 |
| 3 | SK | 02010 | 97044 |
| 4 | SK | 01563 | 97240 |
| 5 | SK | 01645 | 98017 |
| 6 | SK | 01669 | 98734 |
| 7 | SK | 01479 | 99020 |
| 8 | SE | 01936 | 00223 |
| 9 | SE | 02250 | 00700 |
| 10 | SE | 02564 | 01297 |
| 11 | SE | 03556 | 01778 |
| 12 | SE | 02537 | 02389 |
| 13 | SE | 01958 | 02684 |
| 14 | SE | 01887 | 03160 |
| 15 | SE | 01311 | 03416 |
| 16 | SE | 00716 | 03731 |
| 17 | SD | 99750 | 04028 |
| 18 | SD | 99446 | 04286 |
| 19 | SD | 99293 | 04610 |
| 20 | SD | 99190 | 04688 |
| 28 | | | |

### GREENFIELD TO SHAW

| Wp | Zo | East | North |
|----|----|------|-------|
| 1 | SD | 99188 | 04692 |
| 2 | SD | 98973 | 04542 |
| 3 | SD | 98811 | 04571 |
| 4 | SD | 98572 | 04770 |
| 5 | SD | 98006 | 05074 |
| 6 | SD | 97673 | 05454 |
| 7 | SD | 97335 | 06348 |
| 8 | SD | 96919 | 06551 |
| 9 | SD | 97417 | 07683 |
| 10 | SD | 96900 | 08027 |
| 11 | SD | 96759 | 07971 |
| 12 | SD | 96759 | 08081 |
| 13 | SD | 96254 | 08522 |
| 14 | SD | 96100 | 08578 |
| 15 | SD | 95443 | 08822 |
| 16 | SD | 95229 | 08794 |
| 17 | SD | 95136 | 08818 |
| 18 | SD | 94838 | 08839 |
| 19 | SD | 94473 | 08850 |
| 20 | SD | 94181 | 08951 |
| 29 | | | |

### SHAW TO NEWHEY

| Wp | Zo | East | North |
|----|----|------|-------|
| 1 | SD | 94181 | 08919 |
| 2 | SD | 94665 | 08848 |
| 3 | SD | 95229 | 08701 |

| 4 | SD | 95214 | 08790 |
| 5 | SD | 95399 | 08816 |
| 6 | SD | 95560 | 08890 |
| 7 | SD | 95861 | 08962 |
| 8 | SD | 96537 | 09609 |
| 9 | SD | 96453 | 10840 |
| 10 | SD | 96391 | 11166 |
| 11 | SD | 96865 | 11961 |
| 12 | SD | 96819 | 12334 |
| 13 | SD | 97017 | 12558 |
| 14 | SD | 96798 | 12792 |
| 15 | SD | 95632 | 12797 |
| 16 | SD | 95157 | 12855 |
| 17 | SD | 94887 | 12262 |
| 18 | SD | 94187 | 12594 |
| 19 | SD | 93918 | 12395 |
| 20 | SD | 93798 | 11638 |
| 30 | | | |

### GREENFIELD TO MARSDEN

| Wp | Zo | East | North |
|----|----|------|-------|
| 1 | SD | 99185 | 04692 |
| 2 | SD | 99564 | 04441 |
| 3 | SD | 99729 | 04816 |
| 4 | SE | 00049 | 04736 |
| 5 | SE | 00214 | 05005 |
| 6 | SE | 00291 | 05213 |
| 7 | SE | 00537 | 05029 |
| 8 | SE | 00526 | 05304 |
| 9 | SE | 00731 | 05496 |
| 10 | SE | 01037 | 06164 |
| 11 | SE | 01104 | 06323 |
| 12 | SE | 00920 | 06394 |
| 13 | SE | 00983 | 06895 |
| 14 | SE | 01603 | 08031 |
| 15 | SE | 01469 | 08083 |
| 16 | SE | 01411 | 08615 |
| 17 | SE | 01862 | 09489 |
| 18 | SE | 02679 | 09449 |
| 19 | SE | 03745 | 10117 |
| 20 | SE | 04131 | 10820 |
| 21 | SE | 04443 | 11063 |
| 22 | SE | 04722 | 11534 |
| 23 | SE | 04714 | 11825 |
| 31 | | | |

### MARSDEN TO LITTLEBOROUGH

| Wp | Zo | East | North |
|----|----|------|-------|
| 1 | SE | 04671 | 11864 |
| 2 | SE | 04022 | 11966 |
| 3 | SE | 03585 | 12368 |
| 4 | SE | 02889 | 12625 |
| 5 | SE | 03029 | 12213 |
| 6 | SE | 02869 | 12100 |
| 7 | SE | 02079 | 12484 |
| 8 | SE | 01095 | 12465 |
| 9 | SE | 00251 | 12279 |
| 10 | SD | 99828 | 12138 |

| 11 | SD | 99203 | 12352 |
| 12 | SD | 97899 | 12211 |
| 13 | SD | 97022 | 12549 |
| 14 | SD | 96063 | 13316 |
| 15 | SD | 95209 | 13313 |
| 16 | SD | 94432 | 13907 |
| 17 | SD | 94445 | 14118 |
| 18 | SD | 93913 | 15196 |
| 19 | SD | 94452 | 15911 |
| 20 | SD | 94059 | 16407 |
| 21 | SD | 93850 | 16250 |
| 32 | | | |

### DISLEY TO WHALEY BRIDGE

| Wp | Zo | East | North |
|----|----|------|-------|
| 1 | SJ | 97236 | 84586 |
| 2 | SJ | 97300 | 84450 |
| 3 | SJ | 97870 | 83644 |
| 4 | SJ | 98092 | 83197 |
| 5 | SJ | 97658 | 83010 |
| 6 | SJ | 97902 | 82663 |
| 8 | SJ | 98425 | 81893 |
| 9 | SJ | 98976 | 81787 |
| 10 | SJ | 99510 | 81763 |
| 11 | SJ | 99577 | 82252 |
| 12 | SK | 00208 | 82709 |
| 13 | SK | 00506 | 82994 |
| 14 | SK | 00562 | 82356 |
| 15 | SK | 00764 | 08209 |
| 16 | SK | 01100 | 81477 |
| 32A | | | |

### BOWSTONES EXTENSION

| Wp | Zo | East | North |
|----|----|------|-------|
| 5 | SJ | 97656 | 83010 |
| 1A | SJ | 97549 | 82982 |
| 2A | SJ | 96203 | 82284 |
| 3A | SJ | 96264 | 81881 |
| 4A | SJ | 96570 | 81750 |
| 5A | SJ | 97392 | 81304 |
| 6A | SJ | 98145 | 82234 |
| 7A | SJ | 97974 | 82585 |
| 8A | SJ | 97871 | 82757 |
| 33 | | | |

### WHALEY BRIDGE CIRCULAR VIA BUGSWORTH BASIN

| Wp | Zo | East | North |
|----|----|------|-------|
| 1 | SK | 01132 | 81481 |
| 2 | SK | 01274 | 81159 |
| 3 | SK | 01644 | 80914 |
| 4 | SK | 01808 | 80944 |
| 5 | SK | 02046 | 80857 |
| 6 | SK | 02189 | 81404 |
| 7 | SK | 02331 | 81734 |
| 8 | SK | 02445 | 81839 |
| 9 | SK | 02228 | 82053 |
| 10 | SK | 01363 | 82282 |

| Wp | Zo | East | North |
|---|---|---|---|
| 11 | SK | 01190 | 81633 |
| 34 | | | |

**WHALEY BRIDGE CIRCULAR VIA THE DIPPING STONE**

| Wp | Zo | East | North |
|---|---|---|---|
| 1 | SK | 01132 | 81477 |
| 2 | SK | 01197 | 81592 |
| 3 | SK | 01331 | 82264 |
| 4 | SK | 00877 | 83595 |
| 5 | SK | 00661 | 83337 |
| 6 | SK | 00221 | 83191 |
| 7 | SJ | 99555 | 82521 |
| 8 | SJ | 99600 | 82163 |
| 9 | SJ | 99561 | 81717 |
| 10 | SJ | 99682 | 81744 |
| 11 | SJ | 99676 | 81518 |
| 12 | SJ | 99678 | 81342 |
| 13 | SJ | 99760 | 81229 |
| 14 | SK | 00067 | 81112 |
| 15 | SK | 00292 | 80936 |
| 16 | SK | 00774 | 81235 |

35

**BROMLEY CROSS - A TASTE OF THE WEST**

| Wp | Zo | East | North |
|---|---|---|---|
| 1 | SD | 72941 | 13151 |
| 2 | SD | 73203 | 13528 |
| 3 | SD | 73501 | 13726 |
| 4 | SD | 73622 | 14030 |
| 5 | SD | 73656 | 14831 |
| 6 | SD | 73640 | 15413 |
| 7 | SD | 73707 | 15589 |
| 8 | SD | 73735 | 15720 |
| 9 | SD | 73929 | 15749 |
| 10 | SD | 74184 | 15874 |
| 11 | SD | 74250 | 16265 |
| 12 | SD | 74182 | 16517 |
| 13 | SD | 73788 | 16345 |
| 14 | SD | 73292 | 17366 |
| 15 | SD | 72930 | 17869 |
| 16 | SD | 72812 | 17643 |
| 17 | SD | 72722 | 17679 |
| 18 | SD | 72437 | 17424 |
| 19 | SD | 70887 | 17749 |
| 20 | SD | 72183 | 17205 |
| 21 | SD | 72049 | 17037 |
| 22 | SD | 71858 | 16888 |
| 23 | SD | 71841 | 16723 |
| 24 | SD | 71620 | 16519 |
| 25 | SD | 71441 | 16073 |
| 26 | SD | 71923 | 15403 |
| 27 | SD | 72498 | 15494 |
| 28 | SD | 72774 | 15552 |
| 29 | SD | 72812 | 15234 |
| 30 | SD | 73359 | 15233 |
| 31 | SD | 73590 | 14900 |
| 32 | SD | 73333 | 14682 |

**AN HISTORICAL STROLL: FLIXTON**

| Wp | Zo | East | North |
|---|---|---|---|
| 1 | SJ | 75618 | 94418 |
| 2 | SJ | 75548 | 94303 |
| 3 | SJ | 75296 | 94327 |
| 4 | SJ | 74828 | 94198 |
| 5 | SJ | 74604 | 94158 |
| 6 | SJ | 74620 | 94366 |
| 7 | SJ | 74723 | 94005 |
| 8 | SJ | 74577 | 94192 |

## GLOSSARY

The following local dialect and rarely used specific words are marked in purple in the walk descriptions:-

| | |
|---|---|
| *clough* | a cleft in a hill; ranging from a steep sided ravine to a gently sloping gully |
| *groughs* | a channel cut into peat moorland by 'run off' water |
| *hags* | an isolated 'pedestal' of peat topped with grass |
| *leat* | a mill watercourse |
| *rake* | a track running at an angle across a hill |
| *shippon* | a cowhouse |
| *windinghole* | a wide area on a canal for turning narrow boats (pronounced as in the wind that blows) |

The following, used frequently, are included here for clarity of meaning:-

| | |
|---|---|
| *sett* | a cut stone block used for paving (as opposed to cobbles, which are rounded stones) |
| *turnpike* | an improved road administered by a trust, a toll is payable dependant on usage |

For those interested in the linguistic and cultural heritage of place names, I have included this small sample of places we visit with a brief explanation of common elements found throughout Britain (OE Old English):-

**Broadbottom**  broad valley bottom; from OE *brad + bothm*

**Delph**  a quarry; bakestones were quarried nearby

**Littleborough**  little fort or stronghold; OE *lytel + burh*, which means 'a fortified place'

**Lydgate**  OE hlid-geat; *geat* means gap, gate or path, in this case, to the moors We pass through a Lydgate near **Littleborough** and near another on the way back to **Greenfiled** from **Hartshead Pike**. We also come across **Bowstonesgate**, **Eastergate** and **Towngate** on the walks.

**Marple**  recorded as 'Merpille' in the 13th century; means pool or stream at the boundary; OE *pyll* means tidal creek, pool or stream.

| Mossley | woodland clearing by a swamp or bog; *leah* can mean wood, clearing or glade; later referred to a pasture or meadow |
| Rochdale | valley of the River Roch; *dale* refers to a valley |
| Saddleworth | enclosure on a saddle shaped ridge; *worth* denotes an enclosure or enclosed settlement |

## APPENDICES

### USEFUL TELEPHONE NUMBERS
GMPTE
Transport Helpline 01612 28 7811 Hollingworth Lake Visitor Centre 01706 373499
Hyde Bank Farm Tea Room
(closed Mon, except bank holidays)          01614 30 3582

**Local Authorities;-**

| | | | |
|---|---|---|---|
| Cheshire CC | 01244 602424 | Derbyshire CCl | 08456 058058 |
| Kirklees CCl | 01484 221000 | Lancashire CC | 08450 530000 |
| Macclesfield BC | 01625 500500 | Oldham MBC | 01619 113000 |
| Rochdale MBC | 01706 647474 | Stockport MBC | 01614 804949 |
| Tameside MBC | 01613 428355 | | |

### WEB LINKS
The Web is an enormous resource of useful information. The following is a selection of links I used whilst researching this book.

| | |
|---|---|
| Association of British Counties | www.abcounties.co.uk |
| Broadbottom History | www.longdendale.com/history_broadbottom.html |
| Buckton Castle | carrbrookvillage.users.btopenworld.com/buckton.htm |
| Bugsworth Basin | www.navigationinn.co.uk/history.htm |
| Chadderton Historical Society | www.chadderton-hs.freeuk.com |
| Chadkirk Chapel | www.marple-uk.com/chadkirkchapel.htm |
| Countryside Access | www.countrysideaccess.gov.uk |
| Friends of Real Lancashire | www.forl.co.uk/003/index.html |
| GMPTE and Journey Planner | www.gmpte.com |
| Hartshead Pike | www.ashton-under-lyne.com/hartshead.htm |
| History of Saddleworth Rushcarts | www.morrismen.saddleworth.org.uk/cart.html |
| Links to all breweries | www.beermad.org.uk |
| Longdendale Legends | www.longdendale.com/legends.html |
| Macclesfield Canal | www.macc-cs.org.uk/ |
| Marple Local History Society | www.marple-uk.com/lhs.htm |
| Marple Locks | www.marple-uk.com/locks/index.htm |
| Marsden General | www.bellastown.demon.co.uk |
| Marsden Pubs | www.marsdenhistory.co.uk/publichouses.html |
| Mellor Dig | www.art.man.ac.uk/FieldArchaeologyCentre/mellor.htm |
| New Mills Local History Soc. | homepages.tesco.net/~nmlhs/index.htm |
| Peak & Northern Footpath Soc. | www.peakandnorthern.org.uk/index.html |
| Pennine Waterways | www.penninewaterways.co.uk/index.htm |
| Roman Lakes | www.romanlakes.co.uk/index.htm |
| Saddleworth links | www.saddleworth.org.uk/index.asp |
| South Pennines Packhorse Trails Trust | www.rightsofway.org.uk/sppttfront.htm |
| Strines Area Residents' Ass. | www.strines.org.uk |
| The Mountain Rescue Council | www.mountain.rescue.org.uk/regions.html |

**Local Authority Links:-**

| | | | |
|---|---|---|---|
| Cheshire | www.cheshire.gov.uk | Derbyshire | www.derbyshire.gov.uk |
| Kirklees | www.kirkleesmc.gov.uk | Lancashire | www.lancashire.gov.uk |
| Macclesfield | www.macclesfield.gov.uk | Oldham | www.oldham.gov.uk |
| Rochdale | www.rochdale.gov.uk | Stockport | www.stockport.gov.uk |
| Tameside | www.tameside.gov.uk | | |

## BIBLIOGRAPHY
### Walking Guides
**One Hundred Walks around Manchester** David Firth (Mainstream Publishing **1-85158-717-9** £7.99)

**Walking in the South Pennines** Gladys Sellers (Cicerone **1-85284-041-2** £10.99)

**Bowland & the South Pennines** John Gillham (Grey Stone Books **0-9515996-0-7** £9.95)

**Pub Walks in the Pennines** Les Lumsden & Colin Speakman (Sigma Leisure **1-85058-261-0** £6.95)

**Rambles around Manchester** Mike Cresswell (Sigma Leisure **1-85058-233-5** £6.95)

**Manchester Moorland Hikes** Nick Burton (Sigma Leisure **1-85058-709-4** £6.95)

### Background Reading
**The Oxford Dictionary of British Place Names** A D Mills (Oxford University Press **0-19-852758-6** £8.99)

**Passage Through Time - Saddleworth Roads & Tracks** Bernard Barnes (Saddleworth Historical Society **0-904982-03-3** £5.95)

**The Wild Flowers of Oldham** Bruce Langridge (Oldham Education & Leisure **0902-809-377**)

**Viaducts and Vaults (3)** CAMRA Members (CAMRA **1-85249-188-4**)

**Good Beer Guide** CAMRA Members (CAMRA **1-85249-196-5** £13.99)

**A Tour Through England & Wales** (vol. 2) Daniel Defoe (Everyman's Library)

**A History of the Parish of Flixton** David Herbert Langton (Urmston Library)

**Millstone Grit; a Pennine Journey** Glynn Hughes (Pan Books **0-330-29718-X**)

**The Murder at Bill's O'Jack's** James Davenport (Neil Richardson **0-907511-71-6** £3)

**Rochdale Revisited A Town and its People** and **Rochdale Revisited: A Town and its People** (vol. 2)John Cole (Kelsall **0-946571-14-7, 0-946571-15-5,** both £4.95)

**Chadderton Chapters** Michael Lawson (Oldham Education & Leisure **0-9502475-0-2**)

**Tradition in Action** N J Frangopulo (EP **0-715-81203-3**)

**The Buildings of England: Derbyshire,** **The Buildings of England: Cheshire, The Buildings of England: North Lancashire, The Buildings of England: West Riding of Yorkshire** all by Nikolaus Pevsner (Yale University Press **0-300-09591-0, 0-300-09588-0, 0-300-09617-8, 0-300-09662-3,** all £19.95)

**A History of Chadderton's Pubs** and **Inns and Alehouses of Oldham** Rob Magee (Neil Richardson **0-907511-85-6, 1-85216-073-X**)

**Curiosities of Greater Manchester** Robert Nicholls (Sutton Publishing **0-7509-3661-4** £12.99)

**Saddleworth Villages** The Saddleworth Historical Society (Saddleworth Historical Society **0-904-982-08-4**)

**Seen on the Packhorse Tracks** Titus Thornber (South Pennine Packhorse Trail Trust **0-953-0573-3-X**)

**The Making of the English Landscape** W G Hoskins (Penguin **0-14-015410-8** £10.99)

## PEAK & NORTHERN FOOTPATH SOCIETY

The Peak and Northern Footpaths Society aims to preserve and defend the rich tapestry of public footpaths to be found in the Peak District and the eight counties of Cheshire, Derbyshire, Greater Manchester, Lancashire, Merseyside, South Yorkshire, Staffordshire and West Yorkshire. With roots dating back to The Manchester Association for the Preservation of Ancient Public Footpaths of 1826, it is the oldest outdoor amenities organisation in the country. In a typical year the Society will:-

> **Taylor House**
> **23 Turncroft Lane**
> **Offerton**
> **STOCKPORT SK1 4AB**
> Tel: 01614 803565
> Fax: 01614 297279
> www.peakandnorthern.org.uk

- investigate over 1000 proposals to divert or extinguish rights of way
- make numerous representations at public inquiries and magistrates courts
- write over 1000 letters to local authorities regarding obstructed rights of way
- hold some 50 liaison meetings or joint inspections of footpaths with local authorities and other responsible bodies
- continue to add to the Society's 250+ signposts and carry out the necessary maintenance

# PUBS AND INNS FOUND ON THE ROUTES

| PUB/INN | TEL | WALK | PUB/INN | TEL | WALK |
|---------|-----|------|---------|-----|------|
| Black Bull, Turton | 01204 852811 | 35 | Old Bell Inn, Delph | 01457 870130 | 25 |
| Black Horse, Denshaw | 01457 874375 | 25 | Old Original, Scouthead | 01457 874412 | 28 |
| Black Ladd Inn, Shaw | 01706 84755 | 29 | Palatine, Hadfield | 01457 852459 | 23, 27 |
| Boar's Head, | | | Pleasant Inn, Royton | 01616 24 0131 | 17 |
| Higher Poynton | 01625 876676 | 6 | Printer's Arms, Denshaw | 01457 874248 | 25 |
| Bull's Head Inn, | | | Q Bar, Stalybridge | 01613 03 9157 | 1, 11, 20 |
| Grains Bar | 01616 24 1759 | 28 | Railway, Bromley Cross | Not available | 35 |
| Bull's Head Inn, Lane | | | Railway, Romiley | 01614 94 1138 | 5 |
| Bottom | 01706 847992 | 8, 25 | Railway, Marsden | 01484 841541 | 30 |
| Cheshire Cheese Inn, | | | Railway, Whaley Bridge | 01663 732245 | 32, 33, |
| Broadbottom | 01457 762339 | 18, 19 | | | 34 |
| Cheshire Ring, Hyde | 01613 68 1826 | 10, 11 | Railway Hotel, Greenfield | 01457 872307 | 12, 13, |
| Church Inn, Flixton | 01617 48 2158 | 36 | | | 21, 22, |
| Church Inn, Uppermill | 01457 820902 | 13, 22 | | | 24, 27 |
| Clarence Hotel, | | | Rake Inn, Littleborough | 01706 379689 | 3, 4, 26, |
| Greenfield | 01457 872319 | 27 | | | 31 |
| Collier's Return, Shaw | 01706 841393 | 17 | Ram's Head, Denshaw | 01457 874802 | 31 |
| Cross Keys, Uppermill | 01457 874626 | 13, 22 | Red Lion, Littleborough | 01706 378195 | 2, 3, 4, |
| Crossings, Furness Vale | 01663 741657 | 34 | | | 26, 31 |
| Devonshire Arms, Mellor | 01614 27 2563 | 15 | Rising Moon, Matley | 0161 338 3014 | 20 |
| Diggle Hotel, Diggle | 01457 872741 | 13 | Riverhead Brewery Tap, | | |
| Edward's Wine Bar, | | | Marsden | 01484 841270 | 30 |
| Hadfield | 01457 868919 | 23 | Roaches Lock Inn, | | |
| Fox Inn, Brookbottom | 01614 27 1634 | 9 | Mossley | 01457 834288 | 12 |
| Free Trade Tavern, | | | Romper, Marple | 0161 427 135 | 7 |
| Milnrow | 01706 847056 | 17 | Rose of Lancaster, | | |
| George Hotel, | | | Chadderton | 0161 624 3031 | 17 |
| Marple Bridge | 01614 27 1299 | 16 | Royal Oak, Mellor | 0161 427 165 | 19 |
| Goyt Inn, Whaley Bridge | 01663 732840 | 33 | Royal Scot, | | |
| Greyhound Inn, Flixton | 01617 48 2063 | 36 | Marple Bridge | 0161 427 314 | 14, 15, |
| Hare and Hounds, Hyde | 01613 66 5526 | 18 | | | 19 |
| Harewood Arms, | | | Shepherd's Arms, | | |
| Broadbottom | 01457 763383 | 18, 19 | Whaley Bridge | 01663 732384 | 33 |
| Hartshead Inn, | | | Ship Inn, Slattocks | 0161 643 5871 | 17 |
| Ashton-U-Lyne | 01457 835753 | 24 | Strawbury Duck, | | |
| Jodrell Arms, | | | Entwistle | 01204 852013 | 35 |
| Whaley Bridge | 01663 734774 | 32, 33 | Swan, Delph | 0145 878658 | 25 |
| Junction Inn, Denshaw | 01457 874265 | 25 | Swan, Marsden | 01484 844308 | 30 |
| King's Arms, Grains Bar | 01616 24 7727 | 28 | Tandle Hill Tavern, | | |
| Mason's Arms, Hadfield | 01457 852510 | 23 | Slattocks | 01706 345297 | 17 |
| Midland Hotel, | | | Tollemache Arms, | | |
| Marple Bridge | 01614 27 237 | 15 | Mossley | 01457 832354 | 12 |
| Millpond, Stalybridge | 01613 384499 | 20 | Tunnel End Inn, Marsden | 01484 844636 | 31 |
| Morning Star, Shaw | 01706 845347 | 28 | Victoria Inn, Hadfield | 01457 855107 | 23 |
| Navigation Hotel, Marple | 01614 27 2270 | 5, 6 | Waggon and Horses, | | |
| Navigation Hotel, | | | Newhey | 01706 844248 | 8, 17, 25, |
| Woodley | 01614 30 2196 | 10 | | | 29 |
| Navigation Hotel, | | | White Hart, | | |
| Buxsworth | 01663 732072 | 33 | Whaley Bridge | 01663 732215 | 33 |
| Navigation Inn, | | | White Hart, Mottram | 01457 764307 | 20 |
| Whaley Bridge | 01663 732308 | 33, 34 | White House, Stalybridge | 0161 303 2288 | 11, 12 |
| Norfolk Arms, | | | White House Inn, | | |
| Marple Bridge | 01614 49 814 | 15 | Littleborough | 01706 378456 | 4, 26 |

Walk! Wire-O Spiral Bound Guidebooks are designed to be used with:

- DWG's plastic slipcover (PSC), which prevents the binding from catching on pockets and increases durability -
- - and our clear plastic All Weather Book Bag (AWBB) with grip-top seal which allows the book to be folded back displaying 2 pages, then sealed, impervious to weather conditions.

To obtain your PSC and AWBB for this book, send a C5 (9 x 7 inch) SAE with 47p stamp, to:

(Code 9781904946135)
Discovery Walking Guides
10 Tennyson Close
Northampton NN5 7HJ

# INDEX OF PLACE NAMES

**A**

Aigin Stone — 31, 107, 110
Alderman Hill — 90-92, 113, 114
Alphin Pike — 90
Armentieres Square — 24, 55, 87
Ash Tree Farm — 22
Ashley House — 105
Audenshaw Reservoirs — 23

**B**

Back O'th Hill — 73
Back Woods — 75
Bar House — 107
Barlow Institute — 143, 145
Beacom Houses — 67
Beaconsfield Terrace — 88
Bear Hill — 28
Benny Hill — 29, 131
Bishop's Park — 115
Blackstone Edge — 25, 27-29, 31, 33, 71, 107-110
Bleaklow — 96
Board Hill — 92
Boothstead Farm — 105
Bottom's Hall — 78
Bottoms Reservoir — 94
Bowstones — 132-136
Brabyns Park — 65
Bradshaw Valley — 143
Bradstone House — 108
Bramble Lodge — 98
Briggs House — 60
Broad Mills — 80
Broadbottom — 66, 68, 73, 76, 77, 81, 82
Bromley Cross — 144, 147
Brook Bottom — 48, 50, 63
Brookfield Pond — 142
Brownhill Naze Farm — 105
Brownhills Centre — 58, 59, 93, 102
Brushes Clough Quarry — 47
Brushes Valley — 24
Buckton Castle — 86, 89, 98
Buckton Vale Quarries — 88
Bugsworth Basin — 132, 134, 138-140
Burnedge House — 115
Bury — 143
Bushes Res. — 88

Buxton — 38, 41, 132
Buxworth — 138

**C**

Cage — 38-40, 50, 63, 133-136
Calderbrook — 31, 32
Calf Lee House — 32
Captain Clarke's Bridge — 51, 52
Carr Clough — 126
Carr Farm — 108
Carrbrook — 24, 86, 87
Cart Chief Nook Farm — 119
Cat and Fiddle — 132
Cawkwell Fields — 41
Central Hall — 54
Chadkirk Chapel — 55
Charlesworth — 79
Chassen Road — 148
Chatterton End Farm — 78
Cheetham Close — 143, 146
Cheetham Park — 85
Cheshire Ring — 35
Chew Brook — 114
Chew Reservoir — 111
Chinley Churn — 137
Christie's Coffee Shop & Tea Room — 65
Chunal Moor — 79
Clatterways Cottage — 22
Clegg Hall — 25
Clegg Moor — 26
Cleggswood Hill — 27
Cliff Farm Cottage — 63
Close Gate Bridge — 127, 129
Clough Cottage — 118, 119
Coal Clough — 32
Cock Brow — 67
Cock Wood — 86, 88
Colne Valley — 123
Coombes Edge — 76, 77, 79, 83
Cooper's Ride — 54
Cotton Tree Corner — 72
Cown Edge — 67, 77-79
Crompton - Circuit — 119, 120
Moor — 44, 46, 119, 129
Crook Gate Res. — 130
Crow Knowl — 46
Crowden — 94-96

**D**

Delph Donkey — 102, 103
Denshaw — 46, 102, 105, 121
Diggle — 55, 58, 59, 123,

125
Diggle Portal — 59
Diglee — 140, 141
Dipping Stone — 132, 134, 140, 141
Disley Station — 132, 133, 135-137
Dobcross — 59, 103
Dolefield Farm — 124
Dovestones Reservoir — 90, 111, 114
Dowry Res. — 130
Dukinfield Bridge — 54

**E**

Ealees Brook — 27, 28, 30, 34, 110, 131
Eastergate Cottage — 127-129
Edgworth — 143, 145
Ellenroad — 72
Emeley Moor — 129
Entwistle — 143-146
Erncroft Wood — 67
Etherow — 21, 66, 67, 68, 75, 80, 94, 111, 152
Etherow Valley — 21, 66-68, 75, 80, 94, 111

**F**

Fiddler's Ferry — 50
Flixton House — 148, 149
Fothergill's Mill — 27, 28, 34
Furness Vale Station — 140, 141

**G**

Gallows Clough — 23
Garden House — 47
Gatehead Croft — 103
Gee Cross — 73
Goblin Manor — 90, 93, 114
Gorsey Brow — 21
Goyt — 35, 37, 43, 48-50, 61-63, 66-67, 77, 102, 139
Goyt Way — 43, 48, 49, 62, 66
Grains Bar — 115
Grasscroft — 98
Great Bride Stones — 32
Great Hill — 130
Great Wood — 76
Greater Manchester — 23, 63, 72
Greehalgh's Die & Bleach Works — 45
Greencloug Farm — 62
Greenfield — 55-58, 86-89, 90, 93, 98, 101-103, 111-115, 123
Gritstone Trail — 132, 133, 136
Grotton — 100
Guide Bridge —

Junction 53

**H**
Hackingknife 73
Hadfield 94, 97, 111, 112, 153, 154
Hague 48, 50
Hague Square 47
Hague Terrace 45
Hard Times Farm 22
Harestead Farm 40
Harridge Pike 86, 88
Harrop Edge 82, 84
Hartshead Pike 24, 84, 88, 98, 99, 116
Haughton Dale 51, 52
Hayfield 148
High Knowls 98
High Moor Quarries 115
High Peak 40, 132
Higher Birchenough Farm 64
Higher Landslow Green Farm 22
Higher Poynton 38, 40
Higher Swineshaw Reservoir 21, 24, 88, 112
Highland House 121
Hillside Cottage 118
Hillside House 73
Hilton Moorside Grange Hotel 132
Hindel Terrace 103
Hobson Moor 22, 23
Hodge Fold 66, 68, 76, 80
Holcombe Moor 70, 72, 106, 133, 143
Hollin Hey Terr. 22
Hollingsworthall Moor 21, 73, 83, 86, 88
Hollingworth -
  Brook 27, 131
  Hall Farm 22
  Heights 26
  Lake 25, 26, 28, 32, 34, 110 130
Holly Bank 100
Holme Moss 113, 120
Horsepool Farm 78
Hough Hill 82, 84
Huddersfield Narrow Canal 21, 24, 53, 54, 55, 58, 89, 90, 98
Hyde Bank Farm 37
Hyde Central Station 52, 53
Hydebank Tunnel 37

**I**
Idle Hill 75
Imperial War Museum 74
Irk 69

Ivy Bank 60, 93, 123, 125
Ivy Dean Cottage 22

**J**
Jet Amber Fields 53
Jodrell Bank 23, 32, 73
Jumbles Reservoir 143, 144, 147

**K**
Kiln Gardens 45, 106
Kiln Green 59
Kinder Scout 72, 75, 137, 148
Kirk Wood 35, 37
Kirklees Way 128
Kirkwood House 37
Knightslow Wood 135, 136
Knowl Farm 124

**L**
Ladhill Bridge 114
Lambgates 94
Lancashire 31, 32, 40, 44, 54, 69, 72
Lane Bottom 102, 106
Lane Head Farm 100
Lantern Pike 63
Larkrise 148, 149
Leyland Farm 68
Light Hazzles Reservoir 32
Linnet Clough 63, 65
Littleborough 27, 28, 31, 34, 110, 127, 131
Longdendale 22, 67, 73, 76, 82, 94, 96
Longwood Thump 102
Lower -
  Birchenough Farm 64
  Hague Fold Farm 50
  Hyde Green Farm 24
  Swineshaw Reservoir 24
LS Lowry 82, 83
Lumb Farm 22
Lumber Hey Farm 41
Luzley 98, 99
Lydgate 29, 34, 101, 107
Lydgate Green House 110
Lyme Park 38-40, 50, 61, 63, 132-137, 141
Lymefield Visitor Centre 80

**M**
Macclesfield Canal 35, 38, 40, 41, 43
Manns Wharf Bridge 57, 101
Manor House Farm 106
Marple 35-37, 41, 43, 48, 61, 63, 65, 66, 75, 77, 78

Marsden 123, 126-129
Matley 68, 82, 84
Mawrode Farm 31
Medlock 98-100, 117
Mellor 61-64, 77, 78
Middlewood 35, 38, 40, 41
Midshires Way 37, 50
Millennium Walkway 48, 50, 133
Millward Memorial Bridge 49
Milnrow 46
Moorcock Inn 58, 90
Moorgate Quarry 103
Moss Moor 109
Mossley 24, 55-57, 87, 98, 99, 101, 111
Mount Vernon 40

**N**
Nettle Hall Farm 22
New -
  Barn 104
  Field House 108
  Fold Head 121
  Mills 48, 63
  Year's Bridge Reservoir 130
Newhey 44, 45, 47, 69, 72, 102, 106-108, 119, 128
Norman Hill Reservoir 121

**O**
Oak Cottage 106
Oak Villas 88
Ogden 44, 45, 47, 102, 106, 108, 111, 112, 121
Old -
  Brow 98
  Court House 82
  Hall Farm 62, 65, 78
  House Tunnel 97
  Mill Leat 49
  Pump House 101
  Russia Lodge Chimney 143
Oldham Way 46, 47, 60, 71, 72, 91, 121
Oozewood Clough 71
Ormes Moor 111
Ousel Meadows 143
Owl Hill 25
Owlet Hall 34, 107, 110

**P**
Park Bridge 98
Pavilion Café 26
Pavilion Gardens 132
Peak District Nat. Park 21, 23, 72, 79, 129, 136, 148
Peak Forest Canal 35, 41-43, 48, 51, 53, 54

Peanock Farm 26
Pear Tree
  Farm 21
Peel Tower 143
Pendle Hill 33, 143
Pennine
  Bridleway 24, 26, 28, 87,
    88, 90, 109, 112,
    130
Pennine
  Horsehoe 21, 23, 69, 72
Pennine Way 32, 34, 94, 97,
    109, 129
Piethorn
  Reservoir 44-46, 108, 119,
    121, 127, 130
Pin Fold Farm
  Cottages 124
Pingot Quarry 47
Pobgreen 123, 124
Portland Basin 53, 54
Pots and Pans 57, 58, 60, 89,
    90, 92, 103, 115,
    116, 120, 124
Primrose Bank 90, 114
Primrose Hill 124
Q
Queen's
  Cottage 26
Quick 98, 101
Quickedge 98, 101
R
Raghole Farm 45
Rakewood
  Viaduct 26, 127, 130
Rapes
  Highway 127, 129
Readycon Res. 127, 130
Redbrook Res. 126
Reddyshore
  Scout 32
Rhodeswood 94, 95, 97
Richmond Farm 62
Ringstone
  Caravan Park 132, 134
Robin Hood's
  Bed 109
Robin Hood's
  Picking Stones 77, 79
Roch 31
Rochdale 25, 27-29, 31, 32,
    34, 69-71, 98,
    105, 107, 115
Rochdale 122, 127, 130
Roman Lakes 61, 62, 65, 77, 78
Romiley 35, 37, 41, 51
Rose & Crown 104
Rose Hill
  Station 35, 41
Rossendale
  Moor 29
Running Hill 59, 92, 125
Rushy Croft 83
Ryefields 58, 60, 93
S
Saddleworth 46, 58, 60, 72,
    100, 102, 103,
    115, 121
SCOPSA 127
Scout Tunnel 55, 57
Shaw Hall 90, 115, 123

Shaw Moor 22, 23
Shaw Moss
  Farm 26
Shaw Station 115, 119
Sheep Bank
  Farms 29
Shining Tor 132
Shore Lane
  Brook 34
Shuttlingsloe 132
Sidebottom
  Fold Farm 88
Slattocks Top
  Lock 70
Smithy Bridge 25, 27
Smithy Farm 98
Spring Bank 51
Springfield
  Copse 48
St. Chad's Ch. 37, 51, 58, 59,
    60, 90, 92, 124
St. James' Ch. 24, 96
St. Martin's Ch. 65
St. Mary's Ch 133
St. Michael's Ch. 22, 82, 83, 97,
    148, 149
St. Thomas' Ch. 47, 58, 64, 107,
    108, 119, 122
St. Anne's Well 132
Staly Cricket
  Club 24
Staly Way 24, 56
Stalybridge 21-24, 51-58, 82-
    86, 90, 98, 102,
    111-115, 123
Standedge 58, 59, 123, 126,
    127, 129
Stansfield Hall 31
Station Buffet
  Bar 21, 24, 53, 54, 82,
    85
Steanor Bottom
  Toll House 32
Stoneridge 133
Stonypiece
  Farm 63
Stormer Hill 29, 107
Strines 48, 61-65
Sugar Loaf 92
Summer
  Cottage 68
Summerbottom 73, 76, 81
Summit 29, 31
Swineshaw 21, 24, 102, 103,
    123, 124
Syke Farm 28
T
Tame 21, 24, 51-60, 82,
    85-90, 98, 102-
    105, 114, 119,
    120, 123, 127,
    129, 130
Tameside 24, 76, 88, 100
Tandle Hill 69, 71
The Elms 82, 83
The Mudd 82
The Snake Inn 148
Thimble
  Cottage 100
Thurston
  Clough 115, 116

Tinsel Wood 95
Tintwistle 88, 111
Toddbrook Res. 140, 142
Todmorden 31, 32
Tom Wood 79, 80
Tonga Stone 90, 92
Tongue Bottom
  Farm 98
Top O' Th'
  Green Farm 89
Torrs Riverside
  Park 49
Townfields 149
TS Palatine 26
Turton 143, 146, 147
U
Upper Hague
  Fold Farm 50
Uppermill 58, 59, 102, 103,
    123, 124
V
Valehouse Res. 95
Victoria Bridge 24
Walkerwood
  Reservoir 24, 86, 88
Warland 31, 32
Warren Lodge 66
Wayoh Res. 143, 145
Welsh
  Mountains 32, 40, 73, 83
Werneth Low 67, 73, 74, 76, 83
West Pennines 40, 50, 85, 143
West Riding of
  Yorkshire 32
Whaley Bridge
  Station 132-140
Whaley Moor 132, 137
Wharmton Hill 57, 101, 129
White Hill 120
Whitecroft Farm 48
Whitelands
  Tunnel 54
Whittaker Moor 29
William Wroe
  Golf Course 149
Willow Bank
  Farm 21
Willykay Clough 129
Wimberry
  Stones 91
Windy Hill 23, 45, 72, 107-
    109, 121, 130, 143
Winter Hill 23, 32, 50, 70, 79,
    85, 106, 122, 130,
    143, 146
Witton Weavers
  Way 143, 145
Wood Lane
  Farm 73
Woodhead 94-96
Woodley 51, 52, 73
Woodside
  Cottage 40
Y
Yeoman Hey 92

# Walk!

# The South Pennines

*with*

*Clarke Rogerson*

## DISCOVERY WALKING GUIDES LTD

**Walk! The South Pennines**
**First Edition** - January 2006
**Copyright** © 2006

**Published by**
**Discovery Walking Guides Ltd**
10 Tennyson Close, Northampton NN5 7HJ,
England

Mapping supplied by **Global Mapping Limited**
(www.globalmapping.com)

Mapping sourced from | Ordnance Survey® This product includes mapping data licensed from **Ordnance Survey®** with the permission of the Controller of Her Majesty's Stationery Office. © Crown Copyright 2005. All rights reserved.
**Licence Number 40044851**

**Photographs**
All photographs in this book are the property of the author, Clarke Rogerson
**Front Cover Photographs**

**White Hill, from Piethorne (Walk 8)**      **Tame Valley (from Walk 31)**

**Brownhills Viaduct (Walk 13)**      **Mellor Church (Walk 13)**

ISBN 1-904946-13-5

Text and photographs* © Clarke Rogerson